EXPLORATIONS IN LOCAL AND REGIONAL HISTORY

Centre for Regional and Local History, University of Hertfordshire
and
Centre for English Local History, University of Leicester

SERIES EDITORS: NIGEL GOOSE AND CHRISTOPHER DYER

Previous titles in this series

Volume 1: *Landscapes Decoded: the origins and development of Cambridgeshire's medieval fields*
by SUSAN OOSTHUIZEN
(ISBN 978-1-902806-58-7)

Volume 2: *The Self-Contained Village? the social history of rural communities, 1250–1900*
edited by CHRISTOPHER DYER
(ISBN 978-1-902806-59-4)

DESERTED VILLAGES
REVISITED

EDITED BY CHRISTOPHER DYER
AND RICHARD JONES

UNIVERSITY OF HERTFORDSHIRE PRESS

Explorations in Local and Regional History

Volume 3

First published in Great Britain in 2010 by
University of Hertfordshire Press
College Lane
Hatfield
Hertfordshire
AL10 9AB

British Library Cataloguing in Publication Data
A catalogue record for this book is available from the British Library

ISBN 978-1-905313-79-2

Design by Geoff Green Book Design, CB4 5RA
Printed in Great Britain by Henry Ling Ltd, Dorchester, DT1 1HD

Contents

      in western Britain   140
      ROBERT SILVESTER

10   'At Pleasure's Lordly Call': the archaeology of emparked settlements   162
      TOM WILLIAMSON

11   Deserted villages revisited: in the past, the present and the future   182
      RICHARD JONES AND CHRISTOPHER DYER

      Bibliography   184
      Index   201

Figures

Tables

Tables

Contributors

JOHN BROAD teaches at London Metropolitan University and researches on English rural history mainly in the period 1600–1850. His edition of the Bishop Wake's Visitation Returns for Lincoln diocese c. 1710 will be published by the British Academy, and he is preparing a regional history of the south Midlands and a book on rural housing in Britain since the late medieval period.

GRAHAM BROWN is an archaeological field investigator with English Heritage who has undertaken a large number of analytical earthwork surveys of a wide range of sites including medieval settlements, monastic sites and castles, but also of landscapes such as Salisbury Plain, the Malvern Hills and Mendip Hills.

CHRISTOPHER DYER is director of the Centre for English Local History at the University of Leicester. His work on late medieval economy and society, based on both documentary and material evidence, is represented by his *Age of Transition?*, published in 2005 by Oxford University Press.

PAUL EVERSON has retired from a career in public sector archaeology with the Royal Commission on the Historical Monuments of England and English Heritage, specialising in non-excavational field investigation. His current research includes a contribution to the final, synoptic volume on Wharram Percy and a study of the landscape associated with Barlings Abbey near Lincoln.

DAVID A. HINTON is the author of *Gold and gilt, pots and pins. Possessions and people in medieval Britain* published by Oxford University Press in 2005, and has worked on artefacts since his career began at the Ashmolean Museum, Oxford. He is now an Emeritus Professor of the University of Southampton, and is currently co-editing *A handbook of Anglo-Saxon archaeology* for Oxford University Press.

RICHARD JONES is lecturer in Landscape History in the Centre for English Local History at the University of Leicester. His current studies of the medieval English landscape include a survey of *Thorps* and an exploration of Anglo-Saxon sense of place. He is a co-author of *Medieval villages in an English landscape: beginnings and ends*, published by Windgather Press in 2006.

CHRISTOPHER TAYLOR worked for the former Royal Commission on the Historical Monuments of England for over thirty years. As a result his interests include anything to do with landscape, although he has concentrated on the origins of rural settlement and the history of gardens.

ROBERT SILVESTER has been deputy director of the Clwyd-Powys Archaeological Trust since moving to Wales in 1989. His current interests focus on medieval and post-medieval rural settlement in Wales and the borders, and the use of historic cartography in understanding the landscape.

SALLY V. SMITH is a post-doctoral fellow in the School of Archaeology, University College Dublin. Her research interests lie in the archaeology of the late medieval English and Irish peasantry, particularly with respect to issues of power, resistance and the materiality of community.

TOM WILLIAMSON works in the School of History at the University of East Anglia. He has written widely on landscape archaeology, agricultural history, and the history of landscape design.

STUART WRATHMELL is manager of the West Yorkshire Archive, Archaeology and Ecology Services, and is also director of the English Heritage-funded Wharram Post-excavation and Publication Project. He has researched and published on various aspects of rural settlement at national, regional and local levels.

Abbreviations

BL	British Library
CBA	Council for British Archaeology
DMVS	M.W. Beresford and J.G. Hurst (eds), *Deserted medieval villages: studies* (London, 1971).
EPNS	English Place-Name Society
LRO	Leicestershire Record Office
LVE	M.W. Beresford, *The lost villages of England* (London, 1954).
Med. Arch.	*Medieval Archaeology*
MSRGAR	*Medieval Settlement Research Group Annual Report*
NMR	National Monuments Record
NYRO	North Yorkshire Record Office
Post-Med. Arch.	*Post-Medieval Archaeology*
RCHME	Royal Commission on the Historical Monuments of England
RUL	Reading University Library
SMAMS	Society for Medieval Archaeology Monograph Series
VCH	*Victoria histories of the counties of England*
WRO	Warwickshire Record Office

Series Editors' Preface

The series of *Explorations in Local and Regional History* is a continuation and development of the 'Occasional Papers' of the University of Leicester's Department of English Local History, a series started by Herbert Finberg in 1952. This succeeding series is published by the University of Hertfordshire Press, which has a strong profile in English local and regional history. The idea for the new series came from Harold Fox, who, with Nigel Goose, served as series editor in its first two years.

Explorations in Local and Regional History has three distinctive characteristics. First, the series is prepared to publish work on novel themes, to tackle fresh subjects – perhaps even unusual ones. We hope that it serves to open up new approaches, prompt the analysis of new sources or types of source, and foster new methodologies. This is not to suggest that more traditional scholarship in local and regional history are unrepresented, for it may well be distinctive in terms of its quality, and we also seek to offer an outlet for work of distinction that might be difficult to place elsewhere.

This brings us to the second feature of the series, which is the intention to publish mid-length studies, generally within the range of 40,000 to 60,000 words. Such studies are hard to place with existing publishers, for while there are current series that cater for mid-length overviews of particular historiographical topics or themes, there is none of which we are aware that offers similar outlets for original research. *Explorations*, therefore, intends to fill the publishing vacuum between research articles and full-length books (the latter, incidentally, might well be eligible for inclusion in the existing University of Hertfordshire Press series, *Studies in Regional and Local History*).

Third, while we expect this series to be required reading for both academics and students, it is also our intention to ensure that it is of interest and relevance to local historians operating outside an institutional framework. To this end we ensure that each volume is set at a price that individuals, and not only university libraries, can generally afford. Local and regional history is a subject taught at many levels, from schools to universities. Books, magazines, television and radio all testify to the vitality of research and writing outside universities, as well as to the sustained growth of popular interest. It is hoped that *Explorations in Local and Regional History* will make a contribution to the continued flourishing of our subject. We will ensure that books in the series are accessible to a wide readership, that they avoid technical language and jargon, and that they will usually be illustrated.

This preface, finally, serves as a call for proposals, and authors who are studying local themes in relation to particular places (rural or urban), regions, counties or provinces, whether their subject matter comprises social groups (or other groups), landscapes, interactions and movements between places, micro-history or total history should consider publication with this series. The editors can be consulted informally at the addresses given below, while a formal proposal form is available from the University of Hertfordshire Press at uhpress@herts.ac.uk.

Nigel Goose
Centre for Regional and Local History
Department of Humanities
University of Hertfordshire
College Lane
Hatfield AL10 9AB
N.Goose@herts.ac.uk

Christopher Dyer
Centre for English Local History
Marc Fitch Historical Institute
5 Salisbury Road
Leicester LE1 7QR
cd50@le.ac.uk

Preface

This book began its life in 2006 when one of us (RJ) noticed that June 2008 would see the sixtieth anniversary of the visit by a group of scholars to Leicestershire villages which has come to be viewed by many as a landmark in the study of village desertion and the 'genesis' of medieval archaeology in Britain. Marking this occasion offered a good opportunity to 'revisit' the subject ourselves in a short conference.

The 1948 field trip, which included visits to the earthwork remains at Knaptoft and Hamilton, outside Leicester, took place on either Friday 18 or Saturday 19 June 1948: key participants' recollections differ. It was occasioned by a seminar convened by M.M. Postan at Cambridge that aimed to explore the role archaeology might play in understanding village growth and decline. To that end, W.G. Hoskins, who had already published on the subject of deserted villages and was already engaged in 'excavation' (Hoskins' own inverted commas) at Hamilton was invited to give a paper. So too was Maurice Beresford, who was already undertaking fieldwork on sites in Warwickshire. The meeting was also attended by Axel Steensberg, a Danish archaeologist whose innovative excavation practices would later be adopted at Wharram Percy, Grahame Clark, whose *Archaeology and Society* had appeared in 1939, and two young and rising stars of social and economic history, Rodney Hilton, who had just published on Leicestershire estates in the later Middle Ages, and Edward Miller, who was preparing his work on the estates of the abbey and bishopric of Ely. With such a cast assembled it is perhaps no surprise that the outcome of this seminar and field visit would prove to be so influential. Although, as Hoskins would later recollect of the event itself, 'Postan's brilliant driving at times might have ended the subject for ever by extinguishing all the scholars interested in the subject.'

We were very conscious that to revisit the research questions of 1948 – essentially when, how and why were villages deserted? – was deeply old fashioned. Since the 1970s the subject had moved on to other issues and themes. Archaeologists and geographers had developed an interest in village origins, village planning and the smaller settlements that were especially common in the west and south-east of England, and dominant in other parts of Britain. Settlements, as they were now called, were studied in the context of the whole landscape. Mick Aston summed up in 1985 the new approach to Deserted Medieval Villages, or 'DMVs' (the term which had become by this stage universally adopted), in his book on landscapes, in which he pointed out that few settlements were deserted totally, but had shrunk in varying degrees, that their decline and abandonment often belonged to the post-medieval period, and that many settlements were not villages. The 'D', the 'M' and the 'V' were all misconceptions. Historians, meanwhile, were exploring the inner life of peasant society, and were preoccupied with families, inheritance, the land market, farming methods, lord–tenant relations and communities.

The original research agenda has not gone away, however, although few recent publications have addressed the subject directly, suggesting that village desertion no longer occupies the place it once did on the academic agenda. The same does not hold true in the public arena, where deserted villages still prompt the same excitement and speculation that made books such as Beresford's *The lost villages of England* such runaway successes. Nor has the question of desertion been solved. Whenever one gives a talk about medieval landscapes or settlements, whether to undergraduates or to the interested public, the question of the causes of desertion is always raised. The questioners have often gleaned from historical folklore a simple explanation, such as 'the Black Death' (of 1348–9), even though most villages that were eventually deserted had plenty of taxpayers in the poll taxes of 1377–81. The Wars of the Roses or the English Civil War are thought to have been responsible, although again the evidence is against that view. Better-informed students blame poor soils or climatic deterioration, and historians have written about the 'retreat from marginal land', but many villages occupied clay lands on low-lying sites in the midlands, which were scarcely inhospitable or teetering on the edge of sustainability. Villages that were later deserted lay on land cultivated since prehistoric or Roman times, so it was not a case of the failure of recently founded villages. In 1948 both Hoskins and Beresford were linking desertions with enclosure and the switch to sheep farming, and that line of explanation still has some validity.

Historical causation cannot be reduced to a single phrase or a simple process. When the lecturer has pointed out the flaws in the usual explanations for desertion, the listeners quite reasonably ask 'what is your explanation then?' and are frustrated by a long and inconclusive answer. The complexities of village origins provide a similar dilemma, but the fragmentary evidence in the eighth to eleventh centuries creates a formidable obstacle, whereas in the period 1300–1700 we are overwhelmed by a mass of information and still cannot make up our minds.

One problem is that the diversity of English regions prevents us from identifying a single universal cause.

In devising the programme for the conference, and therefore the layout of this book, we wanted to reflect the new thinking about desertion, because in spite of its venerable origin we knew that scholars had been quietly considering the question. While only a sample of this work can be offered here, we hope that its contents are representative of the diverse range of approaches that are being taken to this subject. Reflecting the meeting of 1948, historians and archaeologists have once again been brought together. All offer something new here. The historical contributions reveal how alternative stories of desertion can be coaxed from previously unexploited documentary sources. Many of the conclusions drawn from the re-evaluation of village plans and material culture as presented here result directly from new theoretical positions adopted by archaeologists. Where textual and physical evidence for desertion has been brought together, it has proved possible to undermine many of the accepted truths that have developed around the subject – in other words, to sow doubt where once there was only certainty. We are even asked to question whether the earthwork remains of villages are village remains at all! Individual contributors to this book have approached their subject at a number of scales, from national overviews to detailed regional and local case studies. As importantly, they lead us from the traditional desertion grounds of the English lowlands to the upland regions of north and west England, Wales and Scotland, and from villages to a consideration of hamlet desertion.

Together the contributors have been able to show why village desertion should remain an important part of our historical enquiry. For they demonstrate that as we seek to understand why some places failed, so many other aspects of rural life in the past are illuminated.

Christopher Dyer and Richard Jones

Acknowledgements

We are grateful to those who contributed to the conference on 21–22 June 2008, both the speakers and those who listened, questioned and discussed. Chris Lewis and Paul Stamper acted as chairs. The Medieval Settlement Research Group supported the event. The organisation depended on Lucy Byrne, Julie Deeming and Matt Tompkins. We are grateful to the staff of the University of Hertfordshire Press and especially Sarah Elvins. Jenny Dyer and Malcolm Noble prepared the index. Individual contributors have thanked those who helped them, including the landowners who made it possible for us to 'revisit' the deserted village sites.

1

The origins and development of deserted village studies

CHRISTOPHER TAYLOR

No academic study springs fully formed from a single event. Thus the meeting in 1948 when a group of distinguished scholars were guided around deserted villages in Leicestershire was far from the beginning of the understanding of such villages. They had been discovered, recorded, excavated – and misunderstood – for over a century and their former presence had been known for much longer. The Leicestershire meeting was indeed momentous, however, marking as it did the date at which the social, economic, geographical and historical links between individual deserted villages began to be drawn together. And, with the aid of new ideas and techniques, the study passed from the 'stamp-collecting' stage to become a proper, scholarly subject.

Nonetheless, the meeting did not ensure immediate success. There had long been scepticism among professional historians as to the significance, or even the existence, of deserted villages. In 1912 Tawney, while accepting that some desertions took place, called them 'isolated examples'.[1] Even after W.G. Hoskins had published his first seminal work on Leicestershire deserted villages in 1946 some scholars continued to question their existence, and as late as 1954 others remained doubtful as to whether any conclusions could be drawn from them.[2] Yet deserted villages had been known since the 1490s, when Rous listed fifty-eight 'depopulated places' in Warwickshire soon after their desertion had occurred. By the seventeenth century their sites were regarded as antiquities that could be mapped, as in Dugdale's *Warwickshire*. By the early eighteenth century deserted villages in Northamptonshire were being described. The phenomenon even entered literature, with Goldsmith's poem 'The Deserted Village' of 1770.[3]

1. R.H. Tawney, *The agrarian problem in the sixteenth century* (London, 1912), p. 261.
2. W.G. Hoskins, 'The deserted villages of Leicestershire', *Transactions of the Leicestershire Archaeological Society*, 22 (1946), pp. 241–64; E. Lipson, *The economic history of England*, 1 (London, 1947), p. 80; J.H. Clapham, *The concise economic history of Great Britain* (Cambridge, 1949), p. 197; DMVS, p. 3.
3. LVE, pp. 81–2; W. Dugdale, *Antiquities of Warwickshire* (London, 1656); J. Bridges, *History and antiquities of Northamptonshire* (London, 1791), p. 296; M. Batey, 'Nuneham Courtenay: an Oxfordshire 18th-century deserted village', *Oxoniensia*, 33 (1968), pp. 108–24.

The growth of antiquarianism in the nineteenth century led to the discovery of many more deserted villages; they were even dug into by local historians. The earliest known excavation was in the 1840s at Woodperry (Oxon.; see Figure 6.1, below pp. 85–6, 95, 106), and Saxon 'sunken huts' were uncovered on the Thames gravels at about the same time.[4] Yet the historical significance of this early work was not appreciated and its results remained largely unknown to the wider academic world.

Another potential source of information that was also ignored was the work of the Ordnance Survey. From its eighteenth-century beginnings the OS had always recorded antiquities on its maps, and the specific instructions issued in 1818 that 'all remains of ancient fortifications, Druidical Monuments ... shall be noticed on the plans' resulted in many more archaeological sites, including deserted villages, being placed on the Old Series 1-inch maps. The decision in the 1840s to produce 6-inch plans meant that individual surveyors, if so inclined, could include hitherto unrecorded antiquities, and the first plans of East Yorkshire of 1841–54 thus featured a number of deserted villages. One such plan was the 'Site of Village of Wharram Percy', which showed some of the crofts and even individual house sites.

Despite the increasing number of professional historians and archaeologists and the growth of local history studies in the twentieth century, the lack of information about and understanding of deserted villages continued. Even the work of economic historians, some of whom had begun to study the events that allegedly led to desertion, failed to have an impact. The only archaeologist to realise the potential of these sites was Hadrian Allcroft. In his ground-breaking work of 1908 on the earthwork remains of archaeological sites he published a plan of the former village of Bingham (Notts.), pointed to examples elsewhere and noted that 'there are indeed few counties which cannot show some such vestiges'. He even suggested that plague and sheep farming were possible reasons for desertion.[5]

Allcroft also commented on the difficulties of excavating such sites. He pointed out that because most of the buildings there had been insubstantial little but pottery could be found. This problem bedevilled the archaeological study of deserted villages until the 1950s. A number of excavations were carried out between 1900 and 1950 but, as John Hurst wrote, 'the subject might have died ... due to the unsatisfactory nature of the results of these'.[6] An example of such an excavation was that by Tebbutt in 1928 at the former village of Winteringham

---

4.   J. Wilson, 'Antiquities found at Woodperry', *Archaeological Journal*, 3 (1846), pp. 116–28; S. Stone, 'Antiquities discovered at Standlake', *Proceedings of the Society of Antiquaries*, 1st series, 4 (1857), pp. 70–1, 92–100.

5.   H. Allcroft, *Earthwork of England* (London, 1908), pp. 550–3.

6.   DMVS, pp. 82–4.

(Cambs., formerly Hunts.). Despite digging on what he (rightly) assumed to be the site of the medieval manor house, the only remains he found were seventeenth-century wall foundations and a handful of medieval pottery sherds.[7]

A larger number of excavations of Saxon 'sunken huts', as they were known, were carried out, particularly in Cambridgeshire and Oxfordshire. Yet, important as these were for the future, no real attempt was made to question why they were there at all if, as was assumed, the original Saxon villages still existed elsewhere. Indeed, because of the scattered nature of the excavated huts and the limited extent of the areas usually dug, the sites were not regarded as being deserted villages at all.[8]

By the later 1930s excavations by professional archaeologists on abandoned medieval settlement sites began in earnest, but these were almost entirely restricted to former farmsteads and hamlets mostly in the Highland Zone where the stone structures were more easily visible and understood.[9] It was not until Steensberg's method of open-area excavation was taken up by medieval archaeologists after the Second World War that any clear understanding of the overall structure and layout of most deserted villages became possible. Even the rapidly developing use of aerial photography was slow to be applied to deserted villages. However, Crawford was predictably quick to grasp its potential, and as early as 1925 he identified the former village of Gainsthorpe, Lincolnshire, on an aerial photograph and even found a document that established that desertion had taken place before 1697.[10]

It might be thought that the setting-up of the Royal Commission on the Historical Monuments of England in 1908 would have given an impetus to the study of deserted villages, but it did not. In its early years the Commission was not noted for its academic advances and in any case it was largely orientated towards architecture. As a result only major prehistoric and Roman archaeological sites were recorded in detail. In the first counties in which the English Commission worked moated sites were usually recognised but, although many were noted, few were planned or described and any associated earthworks were ignored. For example, in 1912 the huge double deserted village of Quarrendon in Buckinghamshire was apparently not even noticed, let alone recorded. However,

7. C.F. Tebbutt, 'Excavations at Winteringham', *Transactions of the Cambridgeshire and Huntingdonshire Archaeological Society*, 5 (1937), p. 103.
8. For example, T.C. Lethbridge and C.F. Tebbutt, 'Huts of the Anglo-Saxon period', *Proceedings of the Cambridge Antiquarian Society*, 33 (1933), pp. 133–51.
9. For example, A. Fox, 'Early Welsh homesteads on Gelligaer Common', *Archaeologica Cambrensis*, 94 (1939), pp. 220–3; E.M. Jope and R.I. Threfall, 'Excavations at Beere, North Tawton', *Med. Arch.*, 2 (1958), pp. 112–40.
10. O.G.S. Crawford, 'Air photograph of Gainsthorpe, Lincolnshire', *Antiquaries Journal*, 5 (1925), pp. 432–3.

possibly for the first time, shrunken settlements were recognised. And the Commission did improve: in 1926 a shrunken village was illustrated and deserted villages were listed in Huntingdonshire.[11]

Local historians continued to find and record deserted villages; most notably Canon Foster, who in 1924 published a list of over 150 'extinct places' in Lincolnshire. He summarised the documentary evidence for their existence, suggested reasons for the abandonment of some of them and even checked the sites of many on the ground. Almost at the same time the great Cambridgeshire local historian Palmer not only discovered the site of the deserted village of Clopton, but dug into it, albeit without much success. He then published its whole history, including the correct reasons for its late-fifteenth-century desertion.[12]

Perhaps the only person who grasped the historical significance of deserted villages before the Second World War was Hoskins, although his research was based largely on Leicestershire. Drawing on the work of earlier historians of the county, but firmly reliant on his own research on both documents and in the field, he came to realise that deserted villages were common and that they could and should be integrated into the account of wider social and economic events of the later Middle Ages. The war and Hoskins' time in London, during which he carried out more valuable documentary research, delayed the publication of his work on deserted villages, but even then his ground-breaking 1946 paper on Leicestershire villages, with its account of all he had discovered and, more importantly, his attempt to put the villages into their perceived historical setting, was not widely read.[13] Nor did Maurice Beresford's study of Warwickshire deserted villages, carried out during the war, advance matters. He did not publish the results until 1950, partly because it was not until he went to Yorkshire in 1947 that he realised that he was dealing with a phenomenon not confined to Midland England.[14]

Thus, although much work had been carried out on deserted villages by 1948, most of it had been uncoordinated and was not fully understood or published, or indeed easily available. So the momentous meeting took place. One of its great values perhaps was that it finally brought deserted villages to the notice of scholars who were astute enough to realise their historical significance. Those present on that occasion were also of sufficient academic stature to be believed by most of the

11. RCHME, *Buckinghamshire*, 1 (London, 1913), Cublington (2), Haggerston (2); RCHME, *Huntingdonshire* (London, 1926), Leighton Bromswold (2), Spaldwick (3), Washingley (2).
12. C.W. Foster and T. Longley, *Lincolnshire Domesday*, Lincolnshire Record Society, 19 (1924), pp. xlvii–xc; W.M. Palmer, 'A history of Clopton', *Proceedings of the Cambridge Antiquarian Society*, 33 (1933), pp. 3–60.
13. Hoskins, 'Deserted villages'.
14. M.W. Beresford, 'The deserted villages of Warwickshire', *Transactions of the Birmingham and Midland Archaeological Society*, 66 (1950), pp. 49–106; DMVS, p. 3.

doubters and, in particular, by a new generation of young professional historians, geographers and archaeologists.

The post-1948 development of deserted village studies is better known and perhaps does not require as much analysis as the earlier period.[15] But some points are worth making. Like many other subjects after the war, that of deserted villages suddenly took off. The reasons for this are complex. A general one was the optimistic outlook of many of those who had lived and fought through the war and who now had a thirst for knowledge at all levels and in all subjects. This soon produced new ideas, new scholars and new universities, the Workers' Educational Association and an explosion in Adult Education classes. Another contributing factor was the idea of studying something apparently as exciting and as unusual as 'lost villages'. More specific was the existence of a group of people whose interests and abilities were to transform an antiquarian sideline into a proper academic study, including Hoskins himself, Beresford, Hurst and J.K. St Joseph among many others, all of whom brought different ideas and expertise.

Hoskins, a poor fieldworker perhaps, but a great communicator, popularised the subject.[16] Beresford, whose *The lost villages of England*, when it finally appeared, was probably more influential than any other early work on deserted villages, perhaps had even more impact on the developing subject.[17] He also began and supported the most important archaeological excavation of any period since 1945, that of Wharram Percy (Yorks.). And he was helped here by Hurst, who, more than anyone else, saved the sites of so many deserted villages. As an Inspector of Ancient Monuments he travelled across England finding, checking, listing and describing hundreds of former village sites and ensuring that the best were protected. He also contributed greatly to the development of medieval pottery studies on which so much of the subsequent archaeological work came to depend. St Joseph, although concerned with much more than deserted villages, used his skill in aerial photography to enhance the understanding of their form and setting. All of these people and many other scholars were aided by new ideas and techniques from other subjects. In particular, improved open-area excavation methods were adopted, research into economic and social history was expanded and landscape history arrived. The setting-up of the Deserted Medieval Village

---

15. C. Gerrard, *Medieval archaeology. Understanding traditions and contemporary approaches* (London, 2003), pp. 138–42; C. Gerrard, 'The study of the deserted medieval village: Caldecote in context', in G. Beresford (ed.), *Caldecote. The development and desertion of a Hertfordshire village*, SMAMS, 28 (2009), pp. 1–19.
16. C. Taylor, 'W.G. Hoskins and *The making of the English landscape*', *The Local Historian*, 35.2 (2005), pp. 74–81.
17. LVE.

Research Group in 1952, together with its *Annual Report*, also did much to foster the growing interest in the subject.

Yet, in those early days, it remained a curiously restricted study. Almost all of the research carried out was concerned with how and when villages were abandoned and concluded that most desertion had taken place in late medieval times as a result of enclosure by lords and largely for sheep. Questions regarding the origins and development of these villages were not asked. Nor was the way of life of the people who had lived in them regarded as something on which light could be shed. The popular name given to these places, 'Deserted *Medieval* Villages', said it all.

From the early 1960s, however, deserted village studies became more complex and diverse. Archaeologists, historians and geographers, as well as others in the applied sciences, began to see deserted villages as tools that could be used to look beyond the process of abandonment and become part of the study of the whole history of rural settlement. One of the great advances was the realisation that there had been a pre-village pattern of dispersed settlement, particularly over much of central England, in early Saxon times.[18] Excavations indicated that nucleation occurred at a relatively late date. They also revealed complex sequences in the development of both individual structures and whole settlements.[19]

Aerial photography and field survey too showed that regular village plans were very common in both deserted and surviving villages, thus suggesting their perhaps deliberately planned beginnings.[20] This in turn led to the still current research into the instigators of such planned settlements and their motives.[21] Survey also showed that villages expanded, contracted, moved about and completely altered their layouts.[22] Most important perhaps was the discovery that villages were abandoned for a variety of reasons and at all periods from late Saxon times to the mid twentieth century and, of course, settlements were deserted before 850 AD.[23] The term 'Deserted *Medieval* Village' was thus completely wrong: the phenomenon was a normal component of all settlement history. More recently,

18. For example, D.N. Hall and P. Martin, 'Brixworth, Northamptonshire: an intensive field survey', *Journal of the British Archaeological Association*, 132 (1979), pp. 1–6.
19. For example, F.H. Thompson, 'The deserted village of Riseholme', *Med. Arch.*, 4 (1960), pp. 95–108; J.G. Hurst and D.G. Hurst, 'Excavations at Hangleton', *Sussex Archaeological Collections*, 102 (1964), pp. 94–142; H.C. Jones, 'Wawne, East Yorkshire', *Med. Arch.*, 6–7 (1963), pp. 343–5.
20. For example, P.A. Rahtz, 'Holworth medieval village', *Proceedings of the Dorset Natural History and Archaeological Society*, 81 (1959), pp. 127–47.
21. For example, P.D.A. Harvey, 'Initiative and authority in settlement change', in M. Aston, D. Austin and C. Dyer (eds), *The rural settlements of medieval England* (Oxford, 1989), pp. 31–43.
22. For example, RCHME, *Dorset*, 3, part 2 (London, 1970), Puddletown (2).
23. For example, M.W. Smith, 'Snap, a modern example of depopulation', *Wiltshire Archaeological Magazine*, 57 (1960), pp. 386–90.

with the development of new archaeological, geographical and scientific methods and in particular of much more historical research, great advances have occurred in other aspects of rural settlement.

The sixty years since 1948 have thus seen the development of a study that began as an investigation into one specific type of late medieval archaeological site, abandoned villages, and has evolved into an examination of all rural settlements, their people and their environment. In doing so it has helped settlement historians to appreciate that they are involved in trying to understand not a static dead world, as it was perceived in the 1940s, but a dynamic one that may not yet be fully understood, but is a much more exciting place in which to work.

Finally, and as exemplified by the papers in this volume, the academic wheel has turned full circle, with a reappraisal of the causes and chronology of desertion, while sixty years of detailed scholarship is shedding yet more light on the history of all types of rural settlement at all periods.

2

Contrasting patterns of village and hamlet desertion in England

RICHARD JONES

The last sixty years has witnessed a considerable shift in the approaches taken by landscape historians and archaeologists to the study of medieval settlements. Early interest in village desertions has been broadened to encompass the issue of village origins, a trend encapsulated in the changing emphasis of questions addressed on sites such as Wharram Percy (Yorks.). In fact, one of the most welcome outcomes of the development of field techniques designed specifically to elucidate the chronology of, and processes behind, village nucleation (one thinks in particular of fieldwalking) has been the identification of elements of an earlier abandoned dispersed settlement pattern.[1] We might view this as an important new dimension to the study of medieval settlement desertion, for it reminds us that the phenomenon was not an exclusively late or post-medieval affair. We have also seen, running parallel to this, the move away from the narrow and restricted study of nucleated villages towards the wider exploration of the full range of medieval rural settlement types.[2] Nucleated villages are now studied alongside both hamlets and individual farmsteads.[3] In addition, the last two decades have witnessed a retreat away from investigations that have tended to target only failed places, to the

---

1. For example, G. Foard, 'Systematic fieldwalking and the investigation of Saxon settlement in Northamptonshire', *World Archaeology*, 9 (1978), pp. 357–74; D. Hall and P. Martin, 'Brixworth, Northamptonshire: an intensive field survey', *Journal of the British Archaeological Association*, 132 (1979), pp. 1–6; R. Jones and M. Page, *Medieval villages in an English landscape: beginnings and ends* (Macclesfield, 2006), pp. 84–92; S. Parry, *Raunds area survey: an archaeological study of the landscape of Raunds, Northamptonshire* (Oxford, 2006).

2. C. Dyer, 'Dispersed settlements in medieval England: a case study of Pendock, Worcestershire', in idem, *Everyday life in medieval England* (London, 1994), pp. 47–76; C. Taylor, 'Dispersed settlement in nucleated areas', *Landscape History*, 17 (1995), pp. 27–34; S. Rippon, *Beyond the medieval village. The diversification of landscape character in southern Britain* (Oxford, 2008).

3. Jones and Page, *Medieval villages, passim*; S. Rippon, R. Fyfe and A. Brown, 'Beyond villages and open fields: the origins and development of a historical landscape characterised by dispersed settlement in south-west England', *Med. Arch.*, 50 (2006), pp. 31–70; C. Dyer, 'Villages and non-villages in the medieval Cotswolds', *Transactions of the Bristol and Gloucestershire Archaeological Society*, 120 (2002), pp. 11–35.

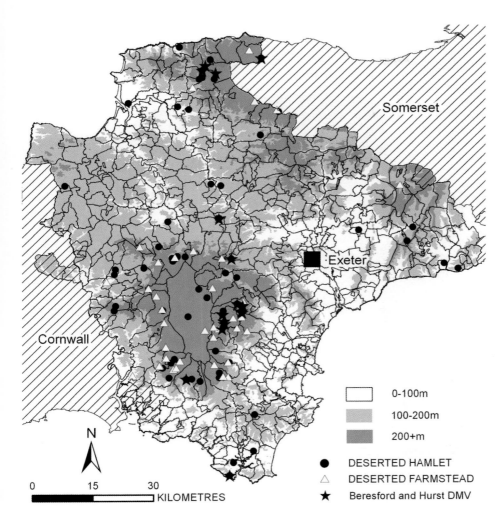

Figure 2.1 Changing patterns of desertion in Devon as known in 1968 and 2009 (sources: DMVS and Devon County Council SMR). The two maps show how the apparent association of deserted sites with upland areas has weakened over time as more abandoned sites have been identified beyond the edges of Dartmoor and Exmoor.

extent that living places now receive equal if not more attention.[4] Despite their focus on survival, these projects too have helped to provide new perspectives on desertion. For as we learn more about why some places endured and in what numbers, we can begin for the first time to evaluate the real scale of desertion, and

4. For example, C. Gerrard with M. Aston, *The Shapwick project, Somerset. A rural landscape explored*, SMAMS, 25 (2007); C. Lewis, 'New avenues for the investigation of currently occupied medieval rural settlements: preliminary observations from the Higher Education Field Academy', *Med. Arch.*, 51 (2007), pp. 133–64.

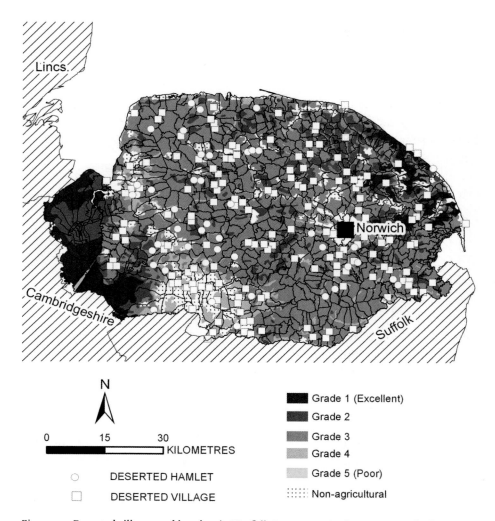

Figure 2.2 Deserted villages and hamlets in Norfolk (source: A. Davison, 'Deserted villages and rural depopulation', in J. Everett (ed.), *An historical atlas of Norfolk* (Norwich, 1993), p. 85). Sites are shown against a background of modern soil grades, demonstrating that there is no clear link between poor-quality soils and desertion or good-quality soils and survival.

ask what it was about these places that resulted in their failure rather than their survival. In particular, the data now exists to begin to compare and contrast the fortunes of villages and hamlets. That such a task can be attempted is surely indicative of how far this field of study has come since 1948.

In some regions of England, extensive field surveys and the interpretation of aerial photographs have led to the location of deserted sites in such significant numbers that the geography of desertion has had to be radically reconsidered. In Devon, Beresford and Hurst's gazetteer of deserted villages, as known in 1968, listed only 15 places; the county's sites and monuments record now contains 142 entries relating to deserted settlement sites, to which a further 21 examples of shrunken settlements can be added (Figure 2.1).[5]

In other parts of the country, patterns of desertion have not altered to the same extent. In Norfolk, for instance, the total has risen less dramatically from the 148 sites of 1968 to stand at 199 (Figure 2.2).[6] Nevertheless, this still represents a 33 per cent rise in the number of settlement sites which can now be mapped. It has been the identification and recording of smaller settlement sites in the intervening years that largely accounts for these increased figures. In the ever-growing literature, the deserted village has now been joined by the deserted hamlet and the deserted farmstead.

Problems of terminology

Of course, these classifications are not without their problems. When, for instance, does a farmstead morph into a hamlet, or a large hamlet become a small village?[7] The formula – a village comprises 6 to 60 households, 30 to 300 people – pertains for the majority, but some places that are certainly to be classed as villages would escape such definition at both ends of the spectrum.[8] Some scholars have placed the village threshold at 15 or 20 households depending on landscape context, but this only shifts the problem rather than resolving it.[9] Similarly, we might ask how close farmsteads need to stand together before they are considered to make up part of a hamlet rather than independent units in their own right. Despite many attempts to solve these issues no consensus has emerged and the distinction between village and hamlet remains as problematic as it has always been.

The term 'deserted' is no less challenging. Why, for instance, is the term traditionally applied only to medieval settlements? Why does the archaeological literature not abound with references to 'deserted Iron Age hillforts' or to 'deserted Roman villas'? By limiting its usage the implication seems to be that there is something different or special about the deserted medieval village or

5. DMVS, pp. 185–6.
6. J. Everett (ed.), *An historical atlas of Norfolk* (Norwich, 1993).
7. B.K. Roberts, *Rural settlement in Britain* (London, 1977), p. 159; B.K. Roberts and S. Wrathmell, *An atlas of rural settlement in England* (London, 2000), p. 11; B.K. Roberts, *Landscape, documents and maps: villages in northern England and beyond AD 900–1250* (Oxford, 2008), pp. 2–6.
8. C. Lewis, P. Mitchell-Fox, and C. Dyer, *Village, hamlet and field. Changing medieval settlements in central England* (1997, Macclesfield, repr. 2001), p. 5.
9. P. Allerston, 'English village development: findings from the Pickering district of North Yorkshire', *Transactions of the Institute of British Geographers*, 51 (1970), pp. 95–108; J. McDonnell, 'Upland Pennine hamlets', *Northern History*, 26 (1990), pp. 20–39.

hamlet that is not shared by settlements of other periods; or that the term is deemed inappropriate to describe the fate of places in other temporal contexts. What may be a quirk of terminological use in fact serves to highlight the more fundamental absurdity of using the modern uninhabited state of these places as a defining characteristic at all, for this too leads to confusion. Gainsthorpe in Lincolnshire, famed as the first medieval village earthworks to be photographed from the air in 1925, is still occupied by a single farm which bears its name. Might we justifiably ask whether this is a true deserted village or just a case of severe shrinkage? Equally ambiguous is the status of those seemingly empty settlements whose houses and inhabitants have gone but whose churches have continued to function.

Essentially what this exposes is the long-standing obsession historians, archaeologists and geographers have had with physical form as the principal means of categorising rural settlement.[10] The ancient and modern appearance of these places, reconstructed from documents, maps, earthworks and standing buildings, very quickly generated a particular vocabulary now enshrined and perpetuated as standardised terms appropriate for the searches of electronic databases.[11] But as interest has shifted over time from forms to processes, and from the recording of the static to the investigation of the dynamic, this vocabulary now appears to belong to a bygone age. As many of the contributions in this volume show, the focus of deserted settlement studies has moved from the identification and recording of sites *already* deserted (although this remains of fundamental importance) towards the investigation of the routes by which these places *came to be* abandoned. More widely, rural settlement studies are also showing how settlement plans and layouts could change over time, further undermining the utility of form as a classificatory tool.[12]

To exacerbate further an already difficult situation, while the terms used to describe abandoned medieval settlements may have been standardised, how they are applied has not. There may now be a wealth of available evidence relating to deserted villages, hamlets and farmsteads, much of it entered on county sites and monuments records or historic environment registers, but any nationwide analysis is hampered by the notable lack of consistency in how the physical remains of

10. M. Widgren, 'Is landscape history possible? Or, how can we study the desertion of farms?', in P. Ucko and R. Layton (eds), *The archaeology and anthropology of landscape. Shaping your landscape* (London, 1998), pp. 94–103.

11. For example, http://thesaurus.english-heritage.org.uk/ and http://www.fish-forum.info/ inscript.htm (both accessed 9 September 2009).

12. M. Page and R. Jones, 'Stable and unstable village plans: case-studies from Whittlewood', in M. Gardiner and S. Rippon (eds), *Medieval landscapes in Britain* (Macclesfield, 2007), pp. 139–52; R. Jones, C. Dyer and M. Page, 'Changing settlements and landscapes: medieval Whittlewood, its predecessors and successors', *Internet Archaeology*, 19 (2006) at http://intarch.ac.uk/journal/issue19/jones_index.html (accessed 9 September 2009).

desertion are recorded. We find that some county datasets do not separate out deserted villages and hamlets, the two being subsumed under the term 'village', or the neutral tag of 'settlement', where they are joined by single farmsteads and small towns. In counties such as Nottinghamshire a helpful distinction is drawn between deserted, shrunken and shifted sites, but this is not the case elsewhere, where a living village preserving, let us say, a short row of tofts and crofts as earthworks might be described as 'deserted'. Such inconsistency leads to inevitable confusion when trying to make sense of this morass of information, and precludes easy quantitative comparison between counties which might reveal desertion hot spots or areas where desertion was less common. It certainly hinders the making of any meaningful assessment of the fate of hamlets as opposed to villages or vice versa.

Redefining villages and hamlets

If we are to compare and contrast the fortunes of villages and hamlets we must be able to distinguish one from the other. If a hamlet is just an alternative form of a village, or a village just another type of hamlet, then there is no comparison to be drawn. In everyday speech 'village' and 'hamlet' carry such clear meanings that it is difficult to envisage the two ever being mistaken or conflated. Precise definition, however, is more elusive. If, as we have argued, size and layout can be questioned as valid criteria for separating out these two categories of rural settlement, then we are forced to look at other facets of their functioning and organisation to determine difference. Examination of the varying levels of social complexity supported in certain places, or the levels of economic independence or dependence exhibited, or the range of services they provided, seems to offer some scope for resolving the problem.[13] Likewise, differentiation might possibly be sought in terms of whether or not particular places were centres of secular and ecclesiastical administration.

Treated separately, each of these aspects of settlement carries with it the same problems associated with size and layout. The economic activities, social organisation and administrative functions of village and hamlet have a tendency to merge, but if taken in combination the place where a line can be tentatively drawn can be suggested.[14] Just as historians of the early town have identified traits that might reveal urban status (while acknowledging that they do not all need to be

13. G. Jones, 'Multiple estates and early settlement', in P. Sawyer (ed.), Medieval settlement. Continuity and change (London, 1976), pp. 15–40; McDonnell, 'Upland Pennine hamlets', pp. 20–1.
14. M. Biddle, 'Towns', in D. Wilson (ed.), The archaeology of Anglo-Saxon England (London, 1976), pp. 99–150.

present), so we should look at the balance of 'village' or 'hamlet' characteristics to categorise a particular place.

It is suggested that the term 'village' should be applied only to those settlements that had become, usually by the end of the Middle Ages, the local centre of secular and ecclesiastical authority, and recognisable as the primary place of a particular manor and parish. These places will have been recognised by the state as a separate vill for tax and judicial purposes. They will usually have housed the largest concentration of people within their overlapping secular and religious jurisdictions, but not always. They will have exploited their territory either independently or together with other settlements but they will demonstrate no signs of social, economic or religious dependency upon these. They will have generally offered, where these are known, a wider range of services and supported a more complex mix of social groups than other places within their orbit. Hamlets, on the other hand, may have been the centres of secular lordship but not always. They may have been recognised as separate vills, and certainly will have been independently named, giving them a discrete identity, but might equally have been returned for tax with another place. They may have farmed their own fields but these will have lain within the wider territory whose administrative centre lay elsewhere. They will always have exhibited some signs of social, economic or religious dependence on another place; for instance, they may not have had access to independent ecclesiastical provision but may, rather, have maintained a chapel of ease. They will have been made up of two or more farmsteads, but generally will have offered a narrow range of services and have had a more simple social hierarchy.

The effects of this redefinition are four-fold. First, an insistence on signs of dependency being a feature of the hamlet increases the numbers of hamlets nationwide by reassigning settlements currently deemed villages to this category. Secondly, and reassuringly, the notion, recognised by Elizabethan antiquarians and Victorian scholars alike, that parts of England such as the south-western counties essentially represent a 'land of hamlets' is reinforced.[15] Thirdly, and as importantly, the number of hamlets in the central belt of England, the so-called 'land of villages', is increased, in line with more recent scholarship which has begun to show that even in areas where nucleated villages dominate, hamlets and farmsteads are not necessarily totally absent.[16] Fourthly, the new model allows settlements to change status over time: farmsteads may develop into hamlets,

15. William Harrison quoted in Roberts and Wrathmell, *An atlas of rural settlement*, p. 15; F.W. Maitland, *Domesday Book and beyond* (1897, London, repr. 1960), pp. 38–9.
16. For example, H. Fox, 'The Wolds before c. 1500', in J. Thirsk (ed.), *Rural England* (Oxford, 2000), pp. 50–61.

dependent hamlets may gain independence and become villages and, of course, the reverse may happen.

How this plays out on the ground can be shown by examples drawn from Devon and Northamptonshire. The famous deserted village of Hound Tor, on the south-eastern fringes of Dartmoor, was assessed as a separate manor in Domesday Book with a recorded population of two villeins, four bordars and two serfs. Four thirteenth-century longhouses, four other smaller houses and three barns with corn driers formed the main settlement, beyond which stood a separate farmstead. Terracing as well as the corn driers demonstrate that the community cultivated its own fields.[17] In terms of size, manorial status and social make-up, then, Hound Tor might be categorised as a village. But it lay within the parish of Manaton, with which its later history is entwined, and possessed no church of its own. Based on the criteria set out above, Hound Tor should more properly be described as a hamlet and as such joins a much larger group, such as those places in Okehampton Park to the north of the moor, that would also be deserted.[18]

In south-west Northamptonshire, the medieval manor of Deanshanger, first mentioned in 1299, lay within Whittlewood Forest and was then in the king's hands. A field book of 1566 describes its three open fields and by 1608, when first mapped, the main settlement is shown with 28 houses. Today the civil parish covers 2,468 acres. Its absence from the Domesday survey can be accounted for by the fact that it lay, until 1951, in the parish of Passenham, where the inhabitants of Deanshanger went to church until the building of a new chapel of ease in Deanshanger itself in 1854.[19] Medieval and early modern Deanshanger was subordinate to Passenham and thus, despite its size, should be considered a hamlet. Medieval Wicken, its neighbour, contained two manors in Domesday Book, later differentiated as Wick Hamon and Wick Dive. Both maintained separate fields and despite their proximity both, from the early thirteenth century at least, possessed their own church. Archaeological evidence points to two capital messuages on these separate manors. Their associated ecclesiastical parishes survived as separate entities until their unification in 1587. Both warrant the description of village (although they are no larger than Deanshanger) in the later Middle Ages, although a case could be made for calling Wick Hamon a hamlet after the amalgamation of the two manors and parishes at the end of the sixteenth century. Within their territory two additional hamlets developed during the course of the Middle Ages: Dagnall in Wick Dive, and Elm Green in Wick Hamon. A

---

17. G. Beresford, 'Three deserted medieval settlements on Dartmoor: a report on the late E. Marie Minter's excavations', *Med. Arch.*, 23 (1979), pp. 98–158.

18. C.D. Linehan, 'Deserted sites and rabbit-warrens on Dartmoor, Devon', *Med. Arch.*, 10 (1966), pp. 113–44.

19. *VCH, Northamptonshire*, 5 (Woodbridge, 2002), pp. 208–44.

separate field system was farmed at Dagnall, but in all other respects these satellite communities remained entirely dependent upon their parochial centres. Neither appears to have had independent manorial status.[20]

For the purposes of this survey, then, it is the status of a place at the point of desertion which matters and which dictates whether it is an example of village or hamlet failure. To make sense of hamlet desertion rates in Northamptonshire would require that the demise of sites such as Dagnall and Elm Green be viewed against the background of survivals such as Deanshanger. In what follows two county surveys are employed to explore what they have to say about the desertion of these newly defined settlement types. Despite the inherent problems of such an approach, it is the closest proxy we have for revealing local and regional patterns of desertion. These will be fleshed out by looking at 'settlement families', groups of places sharing the same name elements, in an attempt to identify broader patterns.

Village and hamlet desertion

Our survey might usefully begin with England's smallest county, Rutland (Figure 2.3).[21] Domesday Book names fifty manors here. These need not, of course, equate to actual villages or hamlets, for the survey provides no clues to where, or in what types of settlement, the assessed population lived. But in all likelihood we are dealing here with permanent resident populations living within bounded estates. Certainly by the thirteenth century all had developed recognisable settlement foci. Of these fifty, only six would be deserted, and of these six only one, Horn, would become a parish centre and thus, according to our terms of reference, a village. Four villages, which do not appear in Domesday Book, but which later gave their names to parishes, survive as no more than a single house; these are Gunthorpe, Leighfield, Martinsthorpe and Normanton. And a further twenty settlements whose names are recorded in documentary sources before 1500 do not appear in the 1086 survey, or give their names to parishes, or survive as anything more than a single house. In terms of patterns of desertion, then, the evidence from Rutland points in four directions. First, settlements which took shape during the Middle Ages, becoming both villages and hamlets, could fail; desertion was not an experience limited to one or other of these categories of places. Secondly, it would appear that villages and hamlets that formed late, or at least have their names recorded late, were more prone to desertion than those that were established early

20. *Ibid.*, pp. 413–38.
21. The statistics that follow are taken from the introduction to B. Cox, *The place-names of Rutland*, EPNS, 67–9 (Nottingham, 1994), pp. lv–lvi.

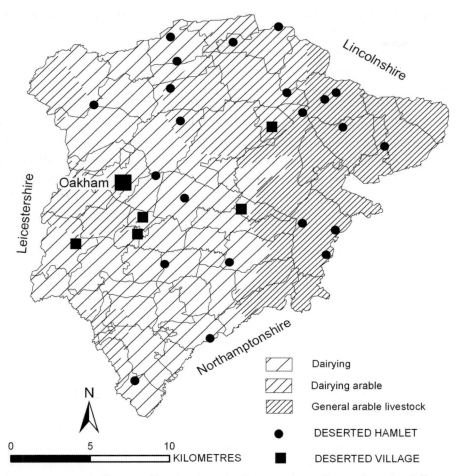

Figure 2.3 Deserted villages and hamlets in Rutland seen against soil types favouring different types of agricultural economy – dairying, dairying and arable, and arable with livestock rearing. The distribution of abandoned settlements shows that none of these zones were immune to desertion, although there are hints that dairy/arable soils suffered less depopulation and settlement loss than the other two areas.

– hence the large number of later sites, unrecorded in Domesday Book, that were deserted. In this, however, we may be on less certain ground, for we know that some settlements that certainly did exist in 1086 fail to appear in the survey. Absence from this record, therefore, cannot be taken as definitive proof of later creation. In particular, small, dependent places may have remained below the radar of the assessors, or their assessment may have been subsumed with that of the head manor. Archaeological evidence from Martinsthorpe, for example, proves that a small nucleated settlement had developed by the early eleventh century despite the silence of Domesday Book, a case perhaps of a dependent hamlet gaining its own independence in the century or so after the survey. Stemming from this, we might argue, thirdly, that it was the smaller communities that tended to be more prone to desertion than their larger counterparts. And finally, and here there is more certainty, by far the majority of failed places fall into our category of hamlets.

How can this pattern of desertion be accounted for? Was it the case that because the land units associated with hamlets were generally smaller than the parish centres, and their populations were small too, these places were particularly vulnerable to demographic and economic downturns or the actions of aggressive lords? Did these places exist just above the level of sustainability in the good times, bad times quickly taking them under the critical threshold at which their social structures would disintegrate and farming the land would become impractical, pushing them into a self-feeding cycle of decline? For the moment we will leave these questions open, noting only that there is no clear correlation in Rutland between the quality of soils (and the farming regimes that they could support) and levels of desertion and survival (see Figure 2.3), and turn to another English region to see whether the patterns of desertion here are a localised phenomenon or part of a more widespread experience.

County Durham is historically and topographically different from Rutland. It offers an interesting contrast but also methodological problems, notable among them the fact that Domesday Book does not cover the county. Instead, we have to look to the Bolden Book, compiled in 1183, supplemented by evidence from the *History of St Cuthbert* (dated to *c.* 1040) and the Yorkshire folios of Domesday Book which, owing to the altering of administrative boundaries, include places now found in the southern part of the county.[22] Here we might note that of the seventy-seven deserted sites in the county recorded on the sites and monuments record, only twenty-two (28 per cent) are named in the Bolden Book. Again, we must be careful not to assume that the remaining fifty-five that were not recorded were necessarily founded later than 1183, although this may have been the case for some. As the example of Martinsthorpe has shown, places might have a long undocumented existence before their first formal written record revealed their presence in the landscape.

That many were not very early arrivals in the landscape is indicated, however, by the smattering of names in *new* among the known deserted settlements, such as Newton Cap, recorded both in *c.* 1040 and in the Bolden Book.[23] There are also

22. T. Johnson South (ed.), *Historia de Sancto Cuthberto: a history of St Cuthbert and a record of his patrimony*, Anglo-Saxon Texts, 3 (2002).

23. V. Watts, *A dictionary of County Durham place-names* (Nottingham, 2002), p. 85.

significant numbers of names in -*leah*, generally considered a later stratum of naming than -*tun* and perhaps suggestive of colonisation into wooded areas.[24] Other secondary name elements – *worths*, *wics* and *thorps* – are prominent among the deserted settlements of this region, and there are plenty of other names which suggest either dependency or secondary status, such as Black Hurworth, Little Burdon and Low Stainton, all of which carry qualifiers which differentiate them from the main centre. Even Preston-le-Skerne, the priest's *tun*, first recorded 1091–2, began life not as an estate or manorial centre, but rather as a satellite.[25]

Taken together, the weight of the evidence suggests that many of County Durham's deserted sites were founded relatively late, that few became centres of local administration, but rather remained as dependent townships, and that most stayed small. That is to say, the desertion of villages and hamlets in County Durham follows much the same model as that in Rutland. From the outset, settlements that would be deserted were apparently disadvantaged in terms of size and status. Location may have been more important here than in Rutland: in a county with greater extremes of topography and soil quality, later arrivals were often forced into marginal areas with poorer soils, higher rainfall and shorter growing seasons, none more so than County Durham's two deserted places called Unthank, names which we see first recorded in the thirteenth and fourteenth centuries and which point towards the unforgiving nature of the local soils or their origins as squatter settlements.[26]

The examination of desertion patterns using place-name 'families' is one way to break out of the county-based surveys. Place-names in -*thorp* are particularly useful in this context for, as a sub-group, they contain both villages and hamlets.[27] Most work on *thorps* has to date concentrated on their origins and their place in the developing settlement hierarchies of the tenth and early eleventh centuries, but their later histories are equally informative. A survey of *thorps* in the east midlands shows that by far the majority remained hamlets, with only 18 per cent developing into parochial centres (Figure 2.4). The number of these places which subsequently became abandoned is also striking: almost 46 per cent of those for which we have documentary evidence. If we look at the cognate -*throp*, the name form more commonly encountered in those parts of England beyond the Danelaw,

24. M. Gelling, *Place-names in the landscape* (London, 1993), p. 198. But see J. Baker, *Cultural transition in the Chilterns and Essex region, 350 AD to 650 AD*, Studies in Regional and Local History, 4 (Hatfield, 2006), pp. 217–36.

25. Watts, *County Durham*, p. 97.

26. Ibid., p. 128.

27. P. Cullen, R. Jones and D. Parsons, *Thorps in a changing landscape* (Hatfield, forthcoming).

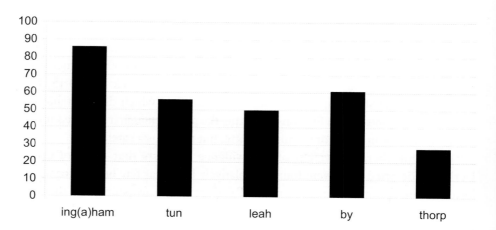

Figure 2.4 Percentage of east midland settlements with particular place-name generics recorded before 1500 that became parishes.

attrition rates are lower but nevertheless significant. Of 142 recorded places, 37 (or 26 per cent) no longer survive. Armed with these statistics we can compare the levels of *thorp/throp* desertion and abandonment against other place-name generics (Figure 2.5). Here it is clear that they fared less well than other groups, particularly against the name forms considered to be of an earlier naming stratum, such as -*ingham* and -*tun*.[28] Places so named were far more likely to develop into centres of local power and authority than were *thorps*.

We are encouraged to conclude, then, that larger places and those with a high standing within the settlement and administrative hierarchy were more likely to be insulated against desertion. As a corollary, the smaller the place, the less significant it was, and perhaps the later it was founded, the more likely it was to fail. This was equally true within the *thorp* group, where the majority of those *thorps* which became parish centres would survive, while those that remained dependent on other places were much more likely to be lost.

Causes and chronologies

So far we have considered neither the reasons that lay behind desertion nor the timing of desertion. Of course, the reasons for village and hamlet desertion are diverse and many are eye-catching. As Beresford and Hurst showed forty years

28. M. Gelling, 'Towards a chronology for English place-names', in D. Hooke (ed.), *Anglo-Saxon settlements* (Oxford, 1988), pp. 59–76.

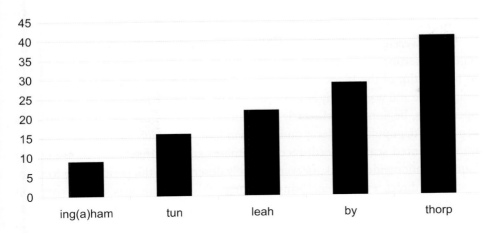

Figure 2.5 Percentage of east midland settlements with particular place-name generics recorded before 1500 that have been subsequently 'lost'.

ago, settlements were prone to desertion throughout the Middle Ages. We might think, for example, of William the Conqueror's clearance of a large part of Hampshire to make way for the New Forest in the late eleventh century, although contemporary accounts might have exaggerated the reality.[29] Better documented is the removal of settlements in the twelfth century by Cistercians seeking isolation for their religious houses.[30] Marine transgressions in the late thirteenth century, such as those vividly described by Matthew Paris which affected the areas around Wisbech in Cambridgeshire,[31] probably account for the loss of both major and minor settlements along the North Sea coastline in Norfolk and the Fens. Places were also lost to the sea along the Yorkshire coast.[32] In the fourteenth century places such as Mortham in County Durham suffered, and were perhaps partially destroyed, during Scottish border raiding in 1346.[33] French incursions along the south coast during the Hundred Years War led to several villages, such as Exceat in East Sussex, being abandoned. Finally, natural causes did for Kynaston, a hamlet in Much Marcle parish (Hereford.), destroyed on 17 February 1571 by a landslip

29. K. Mew, 'The dynamics of lordship and landscape as revealed in a Domesday study of the Nova Foresta', Anglo-Norman Studies, 23 (2000), pp. 155–66.
30. R.A. Donkin, The Cistercians: studies in the geography of medieval England and Wales (Toronto, 1978).
31. Everett, An historical atlas of Norfolk; the relevant passages from Matthew Paris are translated in H. Hallam, Settlement and society. A study of the early agrarian history of South Lincolnshire (Cambridge, 1965), p. 127.
32. S. Neave and S. Ellis (eds), An historical atlas of East Yorkshire (Hull, 1996), pp. 6–7.
33. E. Miller (ed.), The agrarian history of England and Wales, 3, 1348–1500 (Cambridge, 1991), p. 51.

which was said to have 'thrust before it highways, houses and trees', and which became known as 'the Wonder'.[34]

These were extraordinary events, but more generally the causes of village and hamlet desertion were more prosaic. Even Tusmore in Oxfordshire, once thought to be a victim of the Black Death, is now known to have been in serious decline long before and was already half-abandoned in 1341.[35] The piecemeal enclosure of open fields, beginning in the early fifteenth century, certainly led to an attenuated process of depopulation, decay and site abandonment which eventually reached an unprecedented scale. Indeed, recent estimates suggest that many thousands of hamlets nationwide shrank, or were entirely deserted, in the period 1370 to 1520, many as a direct result of enclosing, although this outcome was a more common experience at the end of this period than at the beginning (see below, pp. 28–32).[36] Emparkment and landscaping associated with the construction of the country seats of seventeenth- to nineteenth-century nobility and gentry accounted for many others, as this often involved the clearance of existing settlements, regardless of size or status, and the rehousing of their populations on other parts of the estates (although see Williamson, this volume).

Again we might profitably look at places in -thorp as a means of tracing these trends. The hamlet of Beesthorpe (Notts.) was removed to make way for a Cistercian grange of Rufford Abbey as early as the twelfth century.[37] In 1437 it was reported of the village of Dunsthorpe (Lincs.) that '... the lack of parishioners, the fewness of peasants, their low wages, the bareness of the lands, the lack of cultivation, pestilences and epidemics with which the Lord afflicts his people for their sins ...' had so reduced the viability of the place that the glebe income was 'hardly sufficient for their eighth part of the salary of a stipendiary chaplain much less of a Rector...'.[38] The church of Thorpe-by-Newark (Notts.) was disappropriated in 1455 owing to 'the fewness and poverty of the inhabitants as a result of which land once fertile and arable are now sterile and fallen back to grass ...'.[39] Late-fifteenth-century enclosure at Thorpe-by-Norton (Northants.) forced inhabitants to move away.[40] Enclosure and emparkment accounted for

---

34. Herefordshire SMR no. 2242.
35. D. Miles and T. Rowley, 'Tusmore deserted village', *Oxoniensia*, 41 (1976), pp. 309–15; C. Dyer, 'Deserted medieval villages in the west Midlands', *Economic History Review*, 2nd series, 35 (1982), pp. 19–34
36. C. Dyer, *Making a living in the Middle Ages. The people of Britain 850–1520* (London, 2002), p. 350.
37. M. Barley, 'Cistercian land clearances in Nottinghamshire: three deserted villages and their moated successor', *Nottingham Medieval Studies*, 1 (1957), pp. 75–89.
38. LVE, p. 171.
39. Ibid.
40. Ibid., p. 74.

Wilsthorpe (Yorks.), where in 1514 it was reported that the lord '... dydd cast doune the town of Willistrop, destroyed the corn feldes and made pasture on theym, and hath closed in the common and make a parke of hytt'.[41] In Norfolk, where Henry Fermor was engaged in similar activities, he was said to have 'let down the houses at Thorpland and allowed a number of houses to decay ... to the destruction of the said town'.[42] Considering the earthworks at Gainsthorpe (Lincs.), a local vicar wrote in his diary in 1697:

> ... Gainstrop was once a pretty town, though now there is nothing but some of the foundations. Being upon the place I easily counted the foundations of about two hundred buildings and beheld three streets fair ... Tradition says that that town was, in times of yore, exceedingly infamous for robberies and that nobody inhabited there but thieves; and that the country having for a long while endured all their villanies they at last, when they could suffer them no longer, rose with one consent, and pulled the same down about their ears ... But I fancy that the town has been eaten up with time, poverty and pasturage.[43]

The demise of the Nottinghamshire village of Thorpe-in-the-Glebe, undoubtedly the victim of eighteenth-century private enclosure, can be charted with some precision. By 1790 only the derelict church occupied the site, although this had still been in use in the 1730s. Seven years later Robert Thoroton reported that:

> ... inclosing the lordship, as it doth in all places where the soil is anything good in this county for certain, hath so ruined and depopulated the town, that in my time there was not a house left inhabited in this notable lordship (except some part of the hall, Mr. Armstrong's house) but a shepherd only kept to sell ale in the church.[44]

We can be equally certain about the fate of other places. Hothorpe and Althorp (both Northants.) and Williamstrip (Gloucs.) are only three of a much larger number of -thorp settlements cleared to make way for the houses and parks of the elite.[45]

Overall, it is difficult to avoid the conclusion that the damaging effects of lordly action were particularly acutely felt where these were targeted against the kind of smaller settlement which places taking -thorp generally remained. But equally it would be wrong to overstate the fragility of hamlets. Take, for example, desertion chronology. If villages were more resilient than hamlets, then we might expect

41. Ibid., pp. 301–6.
42. Ibid., p. 316
43. Ibid., p. 94.
44. Quoted in A. Cameron and C. O'Brien, 'The deserted mediaeval village of Thorpe-in-the-Glebe, Nottinghamshire', *Transactions of the Thoroton Society*, 20 (1981), p. 56.
45. RCHME, *North-west Northamptonshire* (London, 1981), pp. 1–2, 141–2.

their desertion histories to follow different trajectories. Villages, we might posit, would tend to survive longer than hamlets because, with larger populations and more diverse economic bases, they were able to cushion quite large exogenous and endogenous shocks, while we might expect even quite small shocks to affect so severely the fabric of diminutive hamlet communities that they would stumble and fail more easily. With such a model, we would perhaps expect to find that attrition rates of hamlets would be far higher, to take just two examples, in the aftermath of the agrarian crises of the early fourteenth century or following plague in the mid-century; on the other hand, villages would survive, albeit perhaps in shrunken form, only to succumb later to depopulation following enclosure or clearance as a result of emparkment.

Precise dates for desertion, of course, are often difficult to establish. Far too few villages and especially hamlets have been excavated to provide a meaningful sample; and while references in tax-lists and feudal surveys help to track the fortunes of particular places in the Middle Ages, and the hearth tax returns offer another horizon into the early modern period, it is often only possible to offer a vague 'time-after-which' a particular place was deserted. While it is impossible to provide precise statistics – indeed, with the current state of knowledge any attempt to do so might itself be considered foolhardy – no clear patterns that differentiate between the timing of village and hamlet desertion seem to emerge. Early desertions are not dominated by hamlets, later desertions are not dominated by villages.

By way of example we can look at a number of settlements situated on either side of the Buckinghamshire–Northamptonshire county boundary.[46] Lamport (Bucks.), a separate township within the parish of Stowe, showed signs of contraction as early as the thirteenth century. Inquests in 1341 revealed it to be suffering from agrarian problems and a decline in grain growing, as on the eve of the Black Death one of its lords sought to avoid payment of rents on land. Yet despite shrinkage, and the land's lack of productivity, Lamport survived and was recorded as having sixteen resident households in the sixteenth century. In fact it was the parochial centre itself, the village of Stowe, that was the first to disappear from the landscape, as its population was removed by the Temple family to make way for the landscape gardens surrounding their new mansion. At the moment when Lamport was returning sixteen residents, the Northamptonshire village of Furtho, five miles (8km) to the east, a centre of manorial lordship, and the main settlement of the parish, is recorded as having only three taxpayers. Its demise had begun in the fifteenth century when the Furtho family began to consolidate their demesne holdings and convert arable to pasture, a process probably completed by

46. Jones and Page, *Medieval villages*.

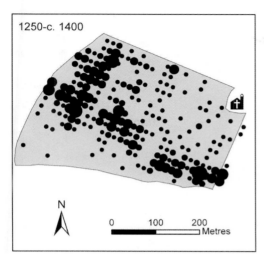
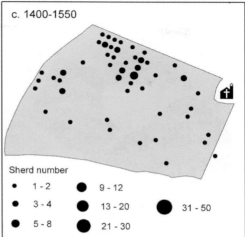

Figure 2.6 Evidence for desertion at Lillingstone Dayrell, Buckinghamshire. The village had expanded rapidly during the thirteenth and early fourteenth century. Pottery evidence from the fifteenth and the early part of the sixteenth century shows large-scale shrinkage over this period and the probable abandonment of all the houses along the main east–west street, and probably along one leading north off this.

1571–2. Similarly, at Lillingstone Dayrell, just to the north in Buckinghamshire, the lord is recorded engrossing eight peasant holdings in 1491, thus displacing perhaps forty people. Lillingstone Dayrell's initial decline can be dated by fieldwalking evidence to the second half of the fourteenth century, at which time it seems that one third of the village, including a whole village street, was abandoned (Figure 2.6). When its lord, Thomas Dayrell, moved to enclose the parish he was clearly preying upon a weakened community. By 1611 the whole parish and manor, here coterminous with each other, had been enclosed and the village reduced to a church and two cottages (but see below, pp. 133–4). Two parishes away, in Wicken (Northants.), village shrinkage can be charted from the mid fourteenth century, although decline here was not terminal, while the hamlets of Dagnall and Elm Green, which lay within the same parish, respectively shrank to a single farm and were lost entirely by 1717 when the first estate map was drawn up (Figure 2.7).

Conclusion

From the foregoing stem some observations on which we might conclude. First, it could be suggested that it would be an error to equate the small size of a settlement with weakness and large size with strength. As recent studies have shown, hamlets were found, and can be shown to have flourished, within every

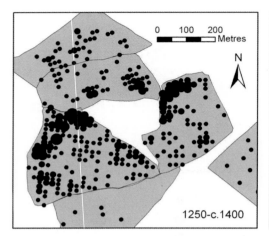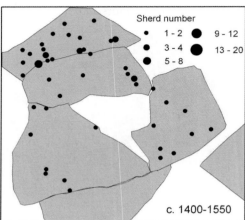

Figure 2.7 Evidence for abandonment at Elm Green, Wicken, Northamptonshire. The hamlet appears to have been created in the twelfth century, before growing into a loose and unplanned collection of domestic buildings. By the middle of the sixteenth century, the hamlet had been entirely deserted and had reverted to woodland unsurveyed (central section) and agricultural land (hence the few sherds of pottery deposited at this period in farmyard manure).

English region.[47] Even in the central belt, so-called 'village country', hamlets are interspersed among the more nucleated larger villages. Hamlets have proved to be one of the most adaptable forms of, and most favoured solutions to, communal living and the exploitation of the land. In many ways they are better suited for this purpose than larger villages, explaining perhaps why the distribution of villages is, by comparison with hamlets, so restricted. And just as hamlets were able to take shape in almost all medieval landscapes, the majority proved capable of surviving the late medieval economic and demographic depressions. It could be argued, then, that versatility and adaptability, resilience and tenacity, mark out the English hamlet community. Of course, many suffered and a proportion succumbed. But hamlets were not intrinsically weaker in this respect than villages, many of which were shrinking and failing at the same time. Size became an issue only in the face of aggressive lordly action. Hamlets, it would seem, were particularly vulnerable where they were held in single ownership. These were the places where enclosure could be driven through without significant resistance, and which would be cleared to make way for new country estates. But by the same token this also applied to those villages reduced by events in the later Middle Ages whose populations were yet to recover. In terms of size, at least, many of these villages now resembled hamlets. The bonds that held together their social structures had been broken, mirrored by the collapsing coherence of their physical layouts.

47. Roberts and Wrathmell, *An atlas of rural settlement*.

Throughout the course of the long medieval period, settlements were both constantly forming in and disappearing from the landscape; indeed, this process of creation and demise was often taking place in the same landscapes at the same time. The process of desertion was neither period-specific, nor regionally specific, nor restricted to a particular form of settlement. It was a common, if not universal, experience. The thousands of hamlets that can be identified as being on the decline in the period 1400–1600 may suggest high levels of vulnerability and proneness to desertion among the smaller settlements, and maps of desertion such as the one that can now be drawn for Devon also appear to carry the same message. But in many senses both are misleading. One of the defining features of Devon is the number of farmsteads and hamlets that survive to carry names found in medieval documentation.[48] Likewise, taken as a percentage of their total, the number of deserted hamlets may not be proportionally too dissimilar to that of villages. Just as it has been stated that 'it is difficult to kill a village', so this would appear to be true for hamlets too. In the final analysis, just as there is no single model for village and hamlet origins (and now considerable evidence to suggest that they might be end-products of similar processes and thus difficult to differentiate) so there is no one model for their desertion, and grounds to suggest that neither of these two forms of settlement were more or less prone to desertion than the other. While sharing some common elements, of which enclosure and emparkment are perhaps the most obvious, the realities of desertion varied from place to place, independently of whether villages or hamlets were at risk. In the current state of knowledge it would be unwise, if not impossible, to draw any great distinction between the two. As for the precise timing and causes of desertion, these almost invariably need to be sought locally and it is here, too, that much more work remains to be done.

---

48. J.E.B. Gover, A. Mawer and F.M. Stenton, *The place-names of Devon*, EPNS, 8–9 (Cambridge, 1931–2).

3

Villages in crisis: social dislocation and desertion, 1370–1520

CHRISTOPHER DYER

Economic historians, wearing boots as advocated by R.H. Tawney, discovered deserted villages, and historians still have a role in interpreting them. This essay aims to demonstrate the continued historical importance of village desertions. If we revisit the subject, beginning with the academic recognition of village sites in 1948, new answers to the question 'why were medieval villages deserted?' can be offered, and new insights gained into past societies and economies.

The scholars who visited Leicestershire deserted villages in June 1948 included M.M. Postan, Professor of Economic History at Cambridge, who must have had in mind the paper on declining population that he would deliver at an Economic History Society meeting in May 1949.[1] In the absence of census figures, Postan showed that between 1350 and 1460 wages rose, and land values and rents fell, which were trends compatible with a reduction in the number of people. He ended with now famous phrases which referred to the 'honeymoon' of expansion in the thirteenth century being succeeded by recession when the 'marginal lands ... punished the men who tilled them'. He believed that deserted villages supported his argument that population declined and cultivated land was abandoned in the period 1350–1460. W.G. Hoskins had already published a paper in 1946 which showed that many desertions had occurred in Leicestershire; he believed that they were caused by enclosure in the sixteenth and seventeenth centuries, but by 1955 he gave more prominence to the abandonment of marginal land.[2] M.W. Beresford had discovered deserted villages independently in Warwickshire, and was developing the argument to be published in 1950 and 1954 that there had been a surge of depopulating enclosures in the period 1450–1520.[3]

---

1. M.M. Postan, 'Some agrarian evidence of declining population in the late Middle Ages', *Economic History Review*, 2nd series, 2 (1950), pp. 221–46.
2. W.G. Hoskins, 'The deserted villages of Leicestershire', *Transactions of the Leicestershire Archaeological Society*, 22 (1946), pp. 241–64; idem, *The making of the English landscape* (London, 1955), pp. 89–95.
3. M.W. Beresford, 'The deserted villages of Warwickshire', *Transactions of the Birmingham Archaeological Society*, 66 (1950), pp. 49–106; LVE.

Between 1952 and 1968 the Deserted Medieval Village Research Group listed sites, resulting in a gazetteer and map with 2,263 deserted villages. In the forty years after 1968 the subject expanded to cover hamlets and farmsteads, both in the western and south-eastern regions, which were excluded by the original focus on villages. Meanwhile, beginning in the 1950s, archaeologists took advantage of the research potential of accessible and well-preserved remains of settlements, and explored new dimensions such as peasant material culture, village origins and village planning.[4]

Causes of desertion

While village studies have broadened to embrace a thousand years of the rural past, the original question 'why were they deserted?' remains without a complete or precise answer. According to the documentary research published in 1971 a small proportion had been abandoned before 1350, and desertion continued after the seventeenth century, but the loss of most villages lay between 1350 and 1700.[5] It was believed that the bulk of these late medieval and early modern desertions were caused by depopulation to make way for sheep pastures. Literary evidence supported this, from John Rous, the Warwickshire priest writing in the 1480s, and Thomas More and the 'commonwealth men' in the sixteenth century, to the play *Pericles* in about 1607.[6] The 'depopulation hypothesis' cannot be applied in all regions, however; in Northumberland and elsewhere desertions were caused by reorganisations of farms in the seventeenth and eighteenth centuries.[7] The most often cited causes of desertion other than depopulation are 'plague' and the abandonment of poor land. The survival of many to-be-deserted villages until 1377–81 (when the poll taxes were collected) disproves any simple connection with the Black Death of 1348–9, and the 'retreat from marginal land' is unlikely to apply to the midland lowlands, where most deserted villages are congregated.[8] Here the focus will be on the period 1370–1520, and on villages in west midland counties, but some of the findings may be applicable in other regions.

Any modern view must take into account the new appreciation that the

4.   J. Hurst, 'The medieval countryside', in I. Longworth and J. Cherry (eds), *Archaeology in Britain since 1945* (London, 1986), pp. 197–236; C. Gerrard, *Medieval archaeology. Understanding traditions and contemporary approaches* (London, 2003), pp. 99–107, 138–42 and 186–8.

5.   DMVS, pp. 12, 35, 66.

6.   T. Hearne (ed.), *J. Rous: Historia regum Angliae* (Oxford, 1745), pp. 122–6; E. Surtz and J.H. Hexter (eds), *The complete works of St Thomas More* (New Haven, 1965), pp. 64–9; F.D. Hoeniger (ed.), *Pericles* (Arden edition, London, 1963), pp. 43–4.

7.   See Wrathmell below, pp. 117–18.

8.   DMVS, pp. 8–10; M. Bailey, 'The concept of the margin in the medieval English economy', *Economic History Review*, 2nd series, 42 (1989), pp. 1–17.

ordinary people of the countryside had an influence on their own destinies. Because the lords' records and monuments have survived, the aristocrats and wealthy churchmen are too often assumed to have been the agents of all significant changes, such as enclosures and depopulations. Even Beresford, the principal advocate of the 'depopulation hypothesis', showed that the smaller and poorer villages were the most vulnerable to desertion, which suggests that at least part of the answer lies in the nature of the communities. Many of them lay near to other villages, and were not the principal settlement in their parish.[9]

Documents such as manorial court rolls, compiled in the years before the villages were deserted, allow us to identify various internal problems. In the period 1380–1480 some villages adapted clumsily to the shift of at least part of their production from arable to pasture, which created tensions because some villagers broke the rules governing open-field farming. As the population dwindled, wealthier tenants were able to take on extra land, which set up potential divisions. The peasant engrossers often became the peasant graziers, and their conversion of land to pasture and overstocking of the commons threatened the harmony of the village. The demesne farmer was also anxious to graze more land, and to exclude village livestock from his many acres. All villages had a migratory population, but in some the pace of change became rapid, and those going out exceeded the incomers. In view of the generally low population, those who moved could easily find vacancies elsewhere.[10]

These internal problems are not incompatible with the depopulation hypothesis, as a lord or his agents, observing the decline in rents from a decaying village, might decide to encourage the departure of the tenants in order to use the land more profitably. This explains why the commissions enquiring into depopulation in 1517 often found that a relatively small proportion of households had been abandoned at each village that they investigated. For example, at Compton Wyniates (Warks.) three households were said to have been allowed to decay in 1502 and 1513, but before 1349 it is known to have had twenty-seven tenants.[11] Of the other twenty-four households, some had no doubt migrated before 1485, beyond the scope of the 1517 inquiry. There is still an important difference between those who emphasise depopulation, and those who focus on villages' inherent weaknesses. If modern inquests were held into the death of these villages, a jury might be persuaded by advocates of the depopulation hypothesis to bring a verdict of 'murder', while those influenced by an alternative

9.   DMVS, pp. 20–29.

10. C. Dyer, 'Deserted medieval villages in the west Midlands', *Economic History Review*, 2nd series, 35 (1982), pp. 19–34; idem, *An age of transition?* (Oxford, 2005), pp. 66–85.

11. I.S. Leadam, *The domesday of inclosures 1517–1518*, 2 (Oxford, 2005), pp. 417–18; T. John (ed.), *The Warwickshire hundred rolls of 1279–80* (Oxford, 1992), pp. 194–6.

view would favour 'misadventure', 'natural causes', or occasionally 'suicide'. A verdict of 'mercy killing' is not available to a modern coroner, but some settlements may have been put out of their misery.

While the majority of village desertions occurred in the central province, where nucleated villages and open-field agriculture were most evident, it is worth emphasising that desertion was part of a universal social, economic and cultural transformation. The processes of moving from arable to pasture, from subsistence cultivation to specialised production for the market, from open field to enclosures, from peasants to farmers are all part of the 'grand narrative' of the transition from feudalism to capitalism.[12] The desertion of villages was one of the side effects of the rise of individualism at the expense of communities, and the weakening of peasant cultivation in preparation for the large commercial farms of the agricultural revolution. According to another grand narrative of economic fluctuations, villages enjoyed their heyday in the boom of expanding economy and population of the thirteenth century, and some of them suffered a loss of people in the 'crisis of the fourteenth century', as population growth was checked before the Black Death. Many more fell victim during the demographic trough of the period 1380–1520.[13] Population grew again in the sixteenth century, and levelled off in the seventeenth, but villages continued to succumb, so clearly there was no simple equation between general population decline and the fate of villages.

While we should be aware of these universal trends, the experience of individual communities in particular places should concern us. Why did some villages survive and others die at this stage of the emergence of capitalism and the long-run rhythm of population change? If it depended on the estate management policy of particular lords, as the depopulation hypothesis would suggest, desertions should be concentrated on particular estates. The lands accumulated by the Spencers of Hodnell (Warks.) and later of Althorp (Northants.) between 1461 and 1522 included eight former village sites, but that was partly because successive members of the family acquired an interest in villages that were already deserted or decaying for use as pastures, rather than because they had depopulated them.[14] Nor did the desertions congregate on the manors of particular types of lord, but they are found on estates of all kinds, from those of acquisitive gentry (who are often linked with depopulation) to conservative church institutions.

12. R.H. Hilton (ed.), The transition from feudalism to capitalism (London, 1976); R.J. Holton, The transition from feudalism to capitalism (London, 1985); T.H. Aston and C.H. Philpin (eds), The Brenner debate. Agrarian class structure and economic development in pre-industrial Europe (Cambridge, 1985), pp. 46–9, 58–9.

13. R.M. Smith, 'Human resources', in G. Astill and A. Grant (eds), The countryside of medieval England (Oxford, 1988), pp. 188–212.

14. H. Thorpe, 'The lord and the landscape', Transactions of the Birmingham Archaeological Society, 80 (1962), pp. 38–77, at 55–9.

The alternative to the 'depopulation hypothesis' would be to give pride of place to environment and economics. One could argue that villages suffered from a sickness induced by their previous commitment to cereal production in open fields, and that problems would have been most acutely felt in champion country, in the centre of the Warwickshire Feldon, or in the Vale of Evesham in south-east Worcestershire, which was described by John Leland in *c.* 1540 as 'clean champain'.[15] Here before 1348 almost every village grew corn on clay soils in open fields, often worked on a two-field system, with little wood or permanent pasture. Most of these communities lost a high proportion of their people and houses in the period 1350–1550, but they survived. Deserted sites were concentrated on the western side of the Feldon, rather than in its centre, and in Worcestershire the abandoned villages are found around the edges of the Vale, which was almost devoid of desertions (Figure 3.1). There seems to be no deterministic alternative to the depopulation hypothesis, or at least not one based on a simple connection between open-field farming on heavy clays and vulnerability to desertion.

Having expressed doubts about some of the conventional approaches, henceforth we will examine some new evidence, mostly documentary, to throw light on the dating and causes of desertion.

New light on the problem: the Register of the Stratford guild

New information on the chronology of desertion comes from the Register of the Holy Cross Guild in Stratford-upon-Avon (Warks.).[16] The book was kept by a religious fraternity which had origins in the thirteenth century, but which was refounded in 1403. The institution, which employed clergy to pray for the souls of departed members and organised impressive funerals, played a central part in town life, and performed many functions of government.[17] It attracted members from the surrounding countryside, accounting for about a half of the 8,000 admissions to the fraternity in 1406–1535. Numbers fluctuated from year to year, usually with between 20 and 80 each year up to 1444, and then more than 100 in some years 1444–81, but falling below 80 in most succeeding years.[18]

---

15. L. Toulmin Smith (ed.), *The itinerary of John Leland in or about the years 1535–1543*, 2, part 5 (London, 1964), p. 52.
16. M. Macdonald (ed.), *The Register of the Guild of the Holy Cross, Stratford-upon-Avon*, Dugdale Society, 42 (2007).
17. Ibid., pp. 1–13; R.H. Hilton, *The English peasantry in the later Middle Ages* (Oxford, 1975), pp. 93–4; C. Carpenter, '"Town and country": the Stratford guild and political networks of fifteenth-century Warwickshire', in R. Bearman (ed.), *The history of an English borough. Stratford-upon-Avon, 1196–1996* (Stratford, 1997), pp. 62–79.
18. Macdonald, *Register*, pp. 16–22.

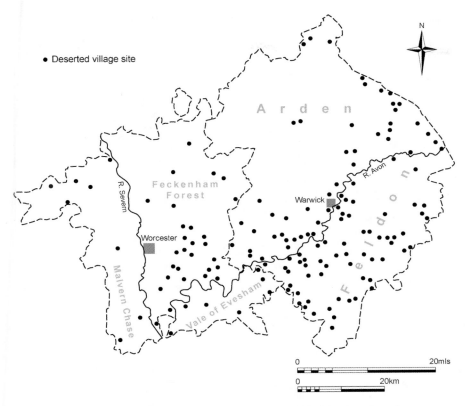

Figure 3.1 Deserted village sites in Warwickshire and Worcestershire (based on the Warwickshire County Council SMR, modified by the author, and for Worcestershire, lists and distribution maps compiled by the author and C.J. Bond, see C.J. Bond, 'Deserted medieval villages in Warwickshire and Worcestershire', in T.R. Slater and P.J. Jarvis (eds), *Field and forest: an historical geography of Warwickshire and Worcestershire* (Norwich, 1982), pp.147–71, and works cited there in note 6).

The Register's ability to throw light on deserted villages was recognised by a local antiquary annotating the document in 1605. He noticed that 'John Mortemere of Milcote was admitted [in 1406–7] by which it is apparent that then there was a village town at Milcote'.[19] We can go beyond identifying deserted sites as he did, as the numbers joining the fraternity reflect the size of a settlement's population, and in particular the better-off inhabitants who would be able to afford the admission fee of 6s 8d, 10s or 13s 4d per person. Only the more commercially and socially ambitious would seek links with Stratford. A 'normal' pattern is indicated by selecting three villages which were not deserted at Hampton Lucy, Quinton and Welford (Figure 3.2 and Table 3.1). Each provided between twenty and forty admissions to membership. These were most numerous before 1460, but

19. Ibid., p. 461.

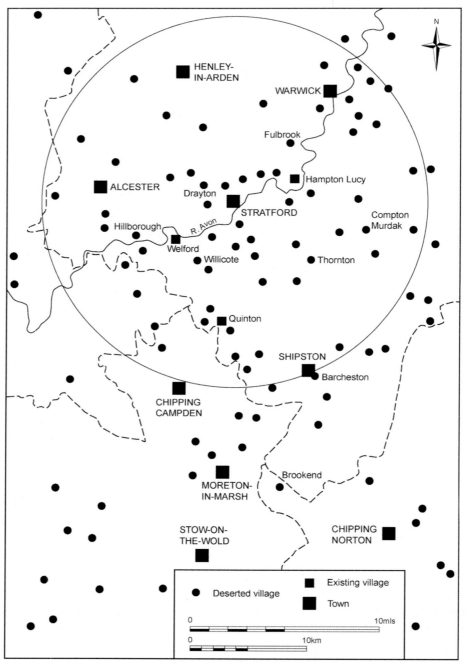

Figure 3.2 Map to illustrate the information gained from the Stratford guild register, marking the radius of 10 miles (16 kilometres) around the town, and showing the location of places mentioned in the text (for the source see note 16).

Table 3.1 Recruitment to the Stratford guild from selected villages

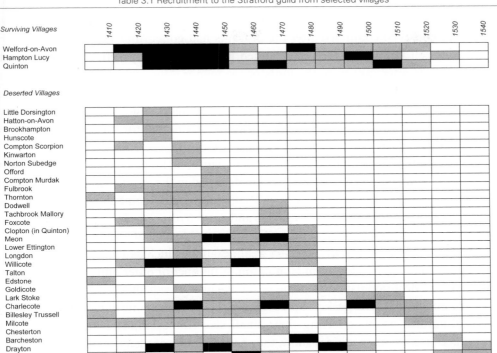

Each entry refers to people joining the fraternity, both as individuals and as married couples. The enrolment in the fraternity of a couple therefore is treated as a single recruitment, so that the figures reflect as much as possible the number of households in the village. The villages selected all lie within a radius of ten miles (16km) (for the source see note 16). 1 or 2 entries to the fraternity over the period shown in grey; 3 or more entries to the fraternity in black.

continued until the early sixteenth century. These villages shrank in size and experienced problems, but survived and provided a flow of recruits to the fraternity.[20]

Of the thirty deserted villages for which admissions to the fraternity can be analysed (Figure 3.2 and Table 3.1), all of which lay within a ten-mile (16km) radius of Stratford, eleven have no inhabitants recorded in the Register after 1460, another eight ceased to provide recruits in the next twenty years, three more were apparently defunct by 1490, and eight continued into the early sixteenth century. These figures tend to understate the number of villages that lost their ordinary

20. C. Dyer, 'Were late medieval English villages "self-contained"?', in idem (ed.), The self-contained village? (Hatfield, 2007), pp. 6–27, at 9; Dyer, Age of transition, pp. 78–85.

inhabitants in the early and mid fifteenth century, because new fraternity members from some villages in the later phases were parish clergy, gentry, or demesne farmers who continued after the peasants had gone. After 1442 members of the Trussell family and the rector joined from Billesley Trussell, and both Milcote recruits after 1481 were the lords of the manor. Most of the fraternity members from Fulbrook were officials, notably parkers, and there is nothing in the Register to suggest that the village survived long after 1400. Members of the Colchester family, the farmers of the lord's demesne, accounted for three of the four new admissions to the guild from Lark Stoke after 1462.

Some villages were abandoned even before the Register's entries began: most of the inhabitants of Hatton-on-Avon departed in the 1370s and 1380s, but two of the farmers of the pasture which occupied the site, John Scheperd and Thomas Rolf, joined the fraternity in 1415–16 and 1425–6 respectively.[21] Early desertions are also under-represented, because if a village had lost all of its population by 1406 it would not appear in the Register at all; examples include Hillborough in Temple Grafton and Broadmoor in Honington. A number of other omissions may reflect the modest population of some of the villages; Heathcote, for instance, had few families even at its peak.[22] Other villages produced only one or two entries into the fraternity, again reflecting their small size (for example, Hunscote) but also because, as other sources show, they had lost most of their inhabitants by the late fifteenth century. This was certainly the case at Compton Murdak, once a large village.[23]

Some villages show a pattern that is compatible with the depopulation hypothesis. Willicote was a source of thirteen admissions (in each case a married couple) to the fraternity until 1473, and from Drayton there were twelve entries in the Register, but recruitment stopped in 1500. The cessation of admissions may point to a sudden loss of tenants. We can sometimes link a village's fortunes as depicted in the Register with records of depopulating enclosure. For example, a number of people from Meon joined the Stratford fraternity in the mid fifteenth century, and we know from the enclosure commissions that houses were being made 'ruinous', 'desolate' and 'deserted' there in 1513.[24] Welcombe, near Stratford, from which a few people appear occasionally throughout the Register, is

21. C. Dyer, 'Population and agriculture on a Warwickshire manor in the later Middle Ages', *University of Birmingham Historical Journal*, 11 (1968), pp. 113–27.

22. W.F. Carter (ed.), *The subsidy roll for Warwickshire of 6 Edward III (1332)*, Dugdale Society, 6 (1926), pp. 8–9.

23. C. Dyer, 'Compton Verney: landscape and people in the Middle Ages', in R. Bearman (ed.), *Compton Verney. A history of the house and its owners* (Stratford, 2000), pp. 90–1.

24. I. Gray, 'A Gloucestershire postscript to the "Domesday of Inclosures"', *Transactions of the Bristol and Gloucestershire Archaeological Society*, 94 (1976), pp. 79–80.

known from other sources to have been still inhabited in the early sixteenth century, and the end came a century later.[25]

On the other side of the argument, some places for which depopulating enclosure is recorded were clearly not very populous or prosperous before the final coup de grace. For example, Clopton, near Quinton, suffered enclosure between 1481 and 1522, but the four villagers who joined the fraternity in the middle of the fifteenth century were all called Yonge, and there may have been only a remnant of the village, even a single household, in the decades before 1481.[26] Barcheston looked a little healthier before 1480 judging from entries in the Register, although it declined drastically before the last inhabitants were removed in 1509 by William Willington, the lord of the manor. The last Barcheston person to join the fraternity, in 1529–30, was, ironically, none other than William Willington.[27]

Finally, one of the sample of villages may never have been totally deserted. Charlecote, which was reported to have been emparked in about 1485, and which has left earthworks located in a field called 'Old Town', seems to have been relocated to a new site at the edge of the park, which it still occupies. Certainly the entrants to the fraternity from Charlecote continued steadily throughout the period.[28]

The evidence from the Register suggests variations in the timescale of decline, which probably points to different circumstances of desertion. It shows that more than half of the communities had gone before the mid fifteenth century, and the small numbers of recruits and their sporadic appearance suggests that villages experienced a process of shrinkage, which is sometimes supported by other sources. Three or four suffered a more abrupt fate around 1500, which would accord with the depopulation hypothesis.

Desertion seen from within the community

A modern approach to the medieval countryside sees the villagers not just as victims of the various misfortunes handed out by impersonal economic changes or estate management but as active participants in the life and death of their own communities.[29] We can attempt to enter their world to glimpse their perspective and even their psychology. The modern label of 'sink villages' implies a

---

25. VCH, Warwickshire, 3 (London, 1945), pp. 264, 267–8.
26. Gloucestershire Archives, D5626/1/71.
27. See below pp. 40–2.
28. DMVS, plate 1.
29. M. Bourin and R. Durand, Vivre au village au moyen age. Les solidarités paysannes du Xe au XIIIe siècles (Rennes, 2000).

resemblance to run-down housing estates on the edge of modern cities.[30] This is not an exact analogy, because the people in the decaying villages were not necessarily poor and they were not unemployed in the modern sense. The villages resembled 'sink' housing estates in their dilapidated houses and dysfunctional communities. The depressed inhabitants suffered from anti-social behaviour, and their low levels of self esteem prevented them from developing a positive sense of identity.

We can follow the process of desertion of villages, both those of the 'sink' type and others, by close analysis of such sources as manorial court records. One place with high-quality documents is Brookend (Oxon.), which lay at the northern end of the parish of Chastleton and belonged to Eynsham Abbey. At its height, in 1279, the sixteen tenants mostly cultivated a standard yardland holding of thirty-two acres (12.8ha). The Black Death seems to have had only a limited impact, as in 1363 there were fourteen tenants of yardlands and half-yardlands. The village fell apart in the period 1380–1440, with unfree tenants reported as leaving and many complaints of buildings falling into ruin. For the rest of the fifteenth century just four tenants remained, which suggests a total population (including servants) of about twenty people.[31]

In 1441 Richard Faukener's goods at Brookend were seized by the lord's officials in order to pay for building repairs, and they show that the yardland from which they were taken was being run as a traditional mixed farm, with twelve acres (4.8ha) under crops (not greatly less than the sixteen acres (6.4ha) that should have been sown each year following a two-field system) together with two horses and two foals, three cows and two calves, and sixty sheep.[32] Such a farming system was difficult to sustain when the holdings had grown to two or three yardlands (64–96 acres (25.6–38.4ha)), with one tenant who had 8.5 yardlands at one time, in a settlement that was chronically short of wage workers. With no official cottage holdings, houses or land for houses seem not to have been sublet to potential labourers, as happened in other villages.[33] Labourers could have walked from nearby Moreton-in-Marsh and Little Compton, and households would have contained servants, but Brookend must always have had a labour problem. One choice, typical of the age, which was, according to early sixteenth-century records,

30. I am grateful for the encouragement of Stephen Fisk and for the benefit of his website on 'abandoned communities'. For sink villages, Dyer, 'Late medieval English villages', p. 20.

31. T. Lloyd, 'Some documentary sidelights on the deserted Oxfordshire village of Brookend', *Oxoniensia*, 29/30 (1964/5), pp. 116–28; H.E. Salter (ed.), *Eynsham cartulary*, Oxford Historical Society, 2 (1908), pp. xxv–xxix.

32. BL, Harleian Roll, B11.

33. H. Fox, 'Servants, cottagers and tied cottages during the later Middle Ages: towards a regional dimension', *Rural History*, 6 (1995), pp. 125–54.

made by Peter Barton was to acquire a flock of about 450 sheep which occupied a sizeable proportion of his former arable, now converted to grass. This pastoral option was probably taken in varying degrees by all of the tenants after 1440.[34]

The amalgamation of the former yardlands and half-yardlands into larger holdings had made many houses redundant and ruinous; the lord sought to have these rebuilt or repaired, but this campaign was abandoned in 1479, by which time the village must have consisted of four sets of occupied buildings standing among the still-visible foundations of a dozen houses with their barns and outbuildings. Beyond the remains of the settlement stretched the fields, with the ridge and furrow of the original arable largely covered with grass. Some land was still cultivated, to provide grain for the four households and fodder for their livestock, but one imagines islands of cultivated strips surrounded by pasture. Tenants had no need for strong rules of cultivation, as was normal in a well-populated village. Their main concern must have been to agree a fair allocation of grazing, as they could not all have kept as many as 450 sheep. The yardlands were still preserved as units of tenure not for their theoretical acreage of arable in the fields, which lost meaning as many of the unused strips were forgotten, but for the sake of the stint of animals and especially sheep, to which each yardlander was entitled. The grassy fields, which cannot have been closely guarded, tempted people from neighbouring Chastleton and Moreton-in-Marsh to graze their animals within Brookend's boundaries. The farmer of Chastleton, John Fletcher, also carried off hay and diverted a watercourse.[35]

This small rump of a community experienced a range of frictions, as their relatively large quantities of land promised wealth but also posed problems. Labour was scarce, they no longer practised the routines of common-field husbandry, their livelihood was threatened by outsiders and they inhabited a depressing environment of ruined buildings and neglected land. A succession of tenants with no less than twelve surnames are recorded in possession of the four holdings at Brookend during the forty years between 1460 and 1499, so the mean length of a tenancy was thirteen years.

The James family, unusually, stayed for the whole forty years, and their anti-social behaviour created a troubled atmosphere. At some time before 1469 Richard James died and his three-yardland holding, paying a rent of 30s 9d, came into the hands of his widow, Agnes James. The right of free bench gave a widow tenure of her husband's holding for life, as long as she did not remarry. Most widows of course valued this security for themselves, and the holding would later go to their

---

34. Westminster Abbey Muniments, 12258, fos. 2v, 6v. This document records the purchase of wool from Peter Barton from which an estimate of the size of his flock can be calculated.
35. BL, Harleian Roll B13, B14.

son or daughter. But a Brookend holding was not a prize without drawbacks, and a few years earlier Joan Fowler, eligible to take on a large quantity of land, 'immediately after the death of her husband, refused to hold it', and repeated the same rejection later before the lord's steward.[36]

Unlike Joan, Agnes James became a tenant, but found it difficult to keep good relations either with the lord or her neighbours. Like everyone else she neglected building repairs. More unusually, she was repeatedly and persistently accused of being a gossip and disturbing 'the people of the lord king, her neighbours, and the lord's tenants'. In 1482 'she disturbed people with her tongue' and broke the pinfold, presumably because her animals had been impounded there for wandering on to other tenants' land. In 1484 she was threatened with forfeiting her holding if she did not stop scolding, but she broke the pinfold again, did not pay rent and cut down trees (which on customary land needed the lord's permission). In 1488, after more complaints from the 'homage' – that is, her three neighbours – she was evicted, and her holding granted to John Davys. She refused to accept this loss, and in 1491 was reported to have occupied a holding (presumably her family's former home) 'by force and arms'. This was a conventional legal phrase which did not necessarily mean real physical violence, although one imagines that Davys and her unfortunate neighbours suffered some strong verbal abuse.[37]

By 1499 Agnes had been replaced by Thomas James, presumably her son, but he had evidently inherited her mental instability, as he was described as a 'lunatic, is furious and has a mind possessed ... not believing in the catholic faith and is not able to hold the aforesaid tenure'.[38] Such a description of a tenant is very unusual, even unique. James's reported denial of Christianity may mean that he sympathised with the Lollard heresy, but it is more likely that he just expressed hostility to religion along with much else. Life in a depressing and stressful place like Brookend might have been linked with mental illness, but the presence of a family like the Jameses must have been an added burden in such a small community. It can be objected that our sources are fallible, and that Agnes and Thomas James suffered unjust accusations. If this was the case, such a persecution pursued over twenty years would still be evidence of social and psychological disorder in the village.

The final stages of Barcheston (Warks.), a few miles to the north of Brookend, can be glimpsed in court records and deeds. In about 1300 it consisted of about fifteen households, ten of them with a yardland of twenty-two acres (8.8ha) each,

36. BL, Harleian Roll, B11.
37. BL, Harleian Roll, B13.
38. BL, Harleian Roll, B14.

and five cottages. In the late fifteenth century most tenants had gone and their houses had collapsed, leaving five or six tenants, most with two yardlands each.[39] The loss of two-thirds of the households left an already small village in a very fragile state. The quality of life declined when the brewing and sale of ale ceased. In 1450 the ale taster presented that John Grymes had brewed and broken the assize for the last time, and without a village ale house Barcheston people had to walk half a mile (1km) across the river into the town of Shipston-on-Stour.[40]

The rules governing the use of Barcheston's fields were often broken. The villagers were said to have grazed their sheep on the pasture reserved for larger beasts, and did not put their cattle into the keeping of the common herdsman. Wayward pigs caused damage. These offences are found in many villages at this period, but they seem to have been mentioned at Barcheston more often in the 1470s and 1480s than might be expected in such a small community. Barcheston was troubled by the relentless encroachment by people from nearby Shipston, who drove their animals on to the fields, grazed their geese and dug stones out of the causeway which led to the town. Barcheston's few families must have felt threatened and defenceless as they faced the acquisitive inhabitants of a lively and populous town.

An unusual feature of Barcheston was the personal and violent antagonism between the villagers and the lords of the manor. It was of course very common for tenants to attempt to reduce their rents or improve the conditions of their tenure, and the inevitable differences between them and their lords were often settled by negotiations. The Durants at Barcheston were a minor gentry family, one of whom filled a lesser county office in the 1460s. They were resident on their only manor, and suffered from debt and family quarrels.[41] Far from being shown respect by their tenants, the Durants suffered a series of verbal and physical assaults. In 1473 Thomas Turche 'ill treated' the lord with 'many opprobrious and scandalous words' in the manor court before the steward, and was amerced the very large sum of 6s 8d. The Turches, an aggressive family, also quarrelled, sometimes violently, with other villagers, although in 1483 William Turche was said to have been assaulted by William Jones, the constable, an official who was also accused of assaulting William Durant, the lord, for which he was amerced the surprisingly modest sum of 12d. Also in 1483 Richard Haukes, the tithing man, 'ill treated the lord', and both he and Jones were removed from office. In the following year a dispute between William Turche and William Durant over two acres of land and

---

39. WRO, CR580/1 – CR 580/8; CR580/9/31.

40. WRO, CR580/3; the plentiful supplies of ale available in Shipston are shown in Worcester Cathedral Library, E 74 (court roll of 1483 recording 12 brewers).

41. C. Carpenter, *Locality and polity. A study of Warwickshire landed society, 1401–1499* (Cambridge, 1992), pp. 146, 496, 501 and 507; WRO, CR 580/9/31; CR580/9/9; CR580/11.

the payment of heriot (death duty) went before an arbiter, which resulted in a judgement (unusually) in favour of the tenant.[42] This settlement did not bring peace, as Matilda Turche was said to have scolded the lord in 1487. In 1503 the farmer's servant was accused of assaulting Agnes, the lord's daughter, who must be the same Agnes Durant who was attacked so that her knees bled in 1487. Also in 1503 two sons of the lord, Henry and Nicholas Durant, were apparently assaulted by two servants of a townsman from Shipston. The Durants appear as weak lords, who were treated by their tenants as if they were troublesome neighbours.[43]

We cannot hope to unravel the stories behind these official presentments, and we must keep an open mind to the possibility that the Turche family and others were unjustly accused. But the persistent allegations are enough to suggest a very bitter and quarrelsome community – if the Turches were innocent, their neighbours must have been very malicious! A document listing complaints made by Henry Durant against his father William refers to a contract probably in the 1490s with a man from Chelmscote, in nearby Brailes, for 400 sheep to be grazed at Barcheston, and also for negotiations for the leasing of the manor to graziers, either Robert Hunks of Evesham or John Bradwey of Chipping Campden, in about 1500.[44] The Turches and the other tenants may have been suspicious that their lords were acting against the interests of the village.

They were right to feel trepidation after 1505 because in that year William Willington, a wool merchant on the make, leased the manor, and soon afterwards bought the lordship outright from the impecunious Durants. In 1509 Willington 'permitted' the remaining five houses to be devastated and the arable land was converted into pasture, and Barcheston's existence as a village ended.[45]

There were various reasons why villagers might lose confidence in themselves and in their neighbours, and feel disenchanted with the places in which they were living. Many of the villages under threat, which were often not the main settlement in the parish, looked to their chapel as a community asset. Villagers had often contributed to the chapels' construction and endowment, and although the parish church retained official rights of burial, some chapels nonetheless had a cemetery. They are poorly documented and often are mentioned at the point when their upkeep could no longer be afforded, like the chapel at Brookend, which had fallen into ruin by the 1430s.[46] The chapel which served Thornton (Warks.) must have

42. WRO, CR580/7; CR580/9/1.
43. WRO, CR580/7; CR580/8.
44. WRO, CR580/11.
45. WRO, CR580/9/9; CR580/9/15; CR580/9/16; CR580/9/17; CR580/9/18; CR580/9/19; CR580/9/21; CR580/9/22; CR580/9/23; CR580/9/24; Leadam, *Inclosures*, pp. 416–17.
46. Salter (ed.), *Eynsham cartulary*, p. xxix.

been especially valued by the villagers, as attendance at the parish church of Ettington involved a round journey of more than four miles (6.4km). In 1407 the lord's court heard that the weathercock and two clappers were in the hands of John Hancok, and another tenant was in possession of two bells. The tower had evidently fallen into ruin, and these items had been salvaged. Later a tenant was allowed to take away two wall plates (horizontal timbers) from the chapel, so the nave roof must have gone.[47] The decay of the chapel took away one of the props of the community's sense of identity, and Thornton went downhill in the next generation. A recent study of Bishops Itchington, again in Warwickshire, has shown how the village was in a state of serious decline in the late sixteenth century, and its parish church's ruin must have contributed to the villagers' loss of morale.[48]

The formal structures on which villages were based apparently survived after decay because the documents still refer to the messuages and tofts that made up the settlement, the yardlands as units of tenure, and the selions and furlongs into which the open fields were divided. This is partly because of the survival of the institutions, such as the manor court, which continued to use the old vocabulary. As we have already seen, the chief value of a yardland, which in theory contained around thirty acres of arable, lay increasingly in the pasture rights attached to it. In some villages the old structures disintegrated, however. At Compton Murdak (later called Compton Verney (Warks.)) in the early years of the fifteenth century (as is known from the main archive of its lords) yardland holdings had been split up and reassembled into new, irregular units of landholding.[49] In the fields selions had been brought together in groups, and the former two-field division was abandoned. Merestones which marked the otherwise invisible boundaries of the open fields were being moved, and outsiders put their animals to graze on Compton's fields. A newly discovered rental of 1407 shows that Compton then had twenty-two tenants (compared with more than forty a century earlier), but one of them lived in neighbouring Chadshunt, and another was described as a tenant's servant.[50] So there may have been twenty households, paying a great variety of rents, from 6d to 35s 8d, the last being owed by John Cole, who had the largest holding. No trace was left of the standard holdings with uniform rents and services. Tenants tended to have a main piece of land and in addition fractions of an acre or a garden, which came from the disintegration of former yardlands.

47. WRO, CR1911/2.
48. P. Upton, 'The lost parish church of All Saints, Bishops Itchington', *Warwickshire History*, 13 (2007/8), pp. 217–25; *eadem*, 'Thomas Fisher and the depopulation of Nether Itchington in the sixteenth century', *Local Historian*, 39 (2009), pp. 3–12.
49. Dyer, 'Compton Verney'.
50. WRO, CR580/349/2.

Parcels of pasture suggest the conversion of former ploughland, explicit in a 'pasture of four acres of tenant land lying frisc'. Not just the physical landmarks in the fields but also the old rules which defined the differences between arable and pasture, and the underlying framework of tenurial units, had all been disrupted. People who had learnt in youth to observe and respect merestones, furlongs and rules of crop rotation must have been disorientated by the changes which were dissolving their once-ordered world.

Conclusion

We cannot identify a single cause of village desertion. Settlements were abandoned at different times and in varied circumstances, and we now think of piecemeal processes rather than cataclysmic events.

This essay has revealed that, in addition to succumbing as a result of a series of underlying factors and immediate causes of desertion, villages sometimes moved traumatically towards their final collapse in the period 1370–1520. Depressed and quarrelsome communities were abandoned by their demoralised inhabitants, and newcomers were discouraged from taking their places. Lords and their agents took advantage of the decay to graze large flocks and herds, and eventually established an enclosed pasture. Ingredients in villagers' lack of cohesion and sense of belonging included the break-down in formal rules of husbandry, the social claustrophobia of living in settlements greatly reduced in size, anti-social behaviour, the predatory threat from surrounding villages and towns, and the loss of community facilities such as the ale house and the chapel.

This picture of villages in their last days might reinforce a negative interpretation of the rural economy of the later Middle Ages. Barcheston, Brookend, Thornton and Compton Murdak could be seen as characteristic of more widespread ills, as arable farming became unprofitable, the demand for land slumped, population densities were reduced by high mortality and low fertility, migrants moved restlessly from village to village and the stability of society was weakened.

But changes within villages were also connected to more positive trends, as this was an age of freedom, prosperity, technical innovation and a thriving market. Increased individual liberty allowed people, and especially the young, to leave their lord (if they were serfs) and escape the ties of family and community. Most villages and towns lost and gained people in approximate balance. Some suffered net emigration, but cloth-making settlements increased their populations. We rightly think of the later Middle Ages as a period when a minority of peasants accumulated land and prospered as yeomen. We have encountered them already in the deserted villages – people such as Peter Barton and John Cole – but they established themselves everywhere, and although they represented a new individualism they could still work within a common-field system, which was by no means inflexible. The switch from a specialism in arable to mixed farming with more pasture had many general benefits, and reflected a demand for meat from better-nourished consumers. In many villages the increase in pasture was accommodated by changes in the fields (introducing leys, or grassed-over strips, for example) which did not destroy the discipline and balance of the whole community. Both weak lords (like William Durant) and ruthless lords (such as William Willington) had a place in rural England. The latter could kill off villages and turn them into specialised pastures, but that was sometimes a continuation of a process, not a new departure.

Commerce was already well established before 1350, so we should not follow John Rous in his condemnation of avarice as a new sin in the fifteenth century. Rather we should recognise that profit-seeking throughout village society, not just among the lords and big farmers, but also the peasants, was motivated by a desire to gain rewards in the market for wool and meat.

4

Dr Hoskins I presume! Field visits in the footsteps of a pioneer

PAUL EVERSON AND GRAHAM BROWN

In June 1948 a party of eminent historians and archaeologists motored from Cambridge to Leicester and made field visits to a series of sites of deserted medieval villages lying closely east and south of the city. The party was led by W.G. Hoskins, who was then forty years old and in his second spell of teaching at Leicester, and the young Maurice Beresford also attended.[1] It was these two 'young Turks' among economic historians – rather than archaeologists – who took the lead in the identification and documentation of the phenomenon of deserted villages in the English countryside. And it was their fellow economic historians whom they were most concerned to convince of the interest and relevance of the field evidence, as a confirmation and extension of what could be teased from the documentary sources. Both men embraced the value of getting outdoors and looking on the ground. In Beresford's evocative descriptions of visits with Keith Allison to Thorpe in Nottinghamshire or alone to Calcethorpe in the Lincolnshire Wolds, one reads the pleasurable excitement of the determined explorer into dark and distant lands, uncertain of the destination, of the temper of the natives or of the discoveries awaiting.[2] 'No traveller comes easily to a lost village ... You must be friend to mud, to green lanes and unused footpaths, to rotting footbridges and broken stiles, to brambles and barbed wire.'[3]

The outing in 1948 visited Knaptoft and Ingarsby and Hamilton, but not – in Beresford's memory – Great Stretton (alias Stretton Magna). What they made of the humps and hollows that they walked over, or saw from the roadside, is difficult to conjecture. Nothing much in detail, one suspects. Nucleated village sites are some of the most complex and densely detailed of all categories of archaeological field remains, whose form and structure are often difficult to grasp, except through the process of making a surveyed plan, or unless one has a surveyed plan

1. M.W. Beresford, 'Professor Sir Michael Postan', *Medieval Village Research Group Annual Report*, 29 (1981), p. 4.
2. LVE, pp. 272–3.
3. Ibid., p. 27.

in hand. Moats, as substantially visible features, presumptively identifiable as residences of local manorial lords, have long been depicted on published Ordnance Survey maps; but the settlement remains alongside them have not. The village remains at Wharram Percy in the Yorkshire Wolds are famous, and exceptional, for their early and knowledgeable depiction. One of us recalls how, as late as the 1970s, the fine clayland village remains at Rand in Lincolnshire were categorised by the Ordnance Survey as 'miscellaneous drainage ditches' and only the moated platform of the manorial site was depicted on large-scale maps and categorised as an antiquity.[4]

It was typical of Hoskins's acuity that, as the Ordnance Survey's archaeological branch began to depict deserted medieval settlements – a newly authorised site type – more systematically in its post-war revision of large-scale mapping, he obtained the use of a group of such depictions to form the basis of renewed exposition of deserted settlements in Leicestershire.[5] As he himself noted, this paper followed up, with more detail, including the new plans, his own two previous papers on the county's lost settlements.[6] But this may not be simple recognition of a serendipitous opportunity. In fact, there was probably a reciprocal influence and effect. It is likely to have been the case that Ordnance Survey field staff were more willing to depict these Leicestershire remains because there was an 'authority' here, who, by his publications, had validated their character and historical context.

These Ordnance Survey diagrams, as published by Hoskins, continue to be very useful to all who travel in his footsteps; not least because the published coverage of Leicestershire's earthworks through new surveys by Fred Hartley has stopped short of this sector of the county,[7] apart from Hamilton, which features in the 1989 volume.[8] But Hoskins himself made little of plans: as he commented in publishing them, 'Little can be usefully said about the interpretation of the plans of these

4. NMR, TF17NW1; P.L. Everson, C.C. Taylor and C.J. Dunn, *Change and continuity. Rural settlement in north-west Lincolnshire* (London, 1991), pp. 153–5.
5. W.G. Hoskins, 'Seven deserted village sites in Leicestershire', *Transactions of the Leicestershire Archaeological and Historical Society*, 32 (1956), pp. 36–51. Reprinted in idem, *Provincial England* (London, 1963), pp. 115–30.
6. W.G. Hoskins, 'The deserted villages of Leicestershire', *Transactions of the Leicestershire Archaeological Society*, 22 (1946), pp. 241–64; 'The deserted villages of Leicestershire', in idem., *Essays in Leicestershire history* (Liverpool, 1950), pp. 67–107, was a revised version of this paper.
7. R.F. Hartley, *The medieval earthworks of Rutland*, Leicestershire Museums Publications, 47 (1983); idem, *The medieval earthworks of north-west Leicestershire*, Leicestershire Museums Publications, 56 (1984); idem, *The medieval earthworks of north-east Leicestershire*, Leicestershire Museums Publications, 88 (1987); idem, *The medieval earthworks of central Leicestershire*, Leicestershire Museums Publications, 103 (1989).
8. Hartley, *Central Leicestershire*, pp. 8, 16.

Leicestershire sites since none has been excavated.'[9] And the paper, when re-read, remains a juxtaposition of two separate forms of evidence: the documentary, largely for the medieval era, and the field archaeology, which is by implication generally assumed to reflect and illustrate the documents. Dialogue between the two is absent. Several generations of field archaeologists since Hoskins who have specialised in the investigation of earthworks through plan-making allied to interpretation – notably those working in the traditions of the Royal Commissions on Historical Monuments – would disagree with his pessimistic assessment of the primary evidential value of earthworks, and there is now a considerable body of work in print that has altered perceptions and revolutionised thinking by working with such evidence.[10]

Nevertheless, it was with these plans in hand as guides, and without new surveys or newly researched studies, that the field visit of the Leicester 2008 conference ventured out on a fine Sunday in June to walk over the earthworks at, in turn, Hamilton, Ingarsby, Stretton Magna and Knaptoft. We did not encounter Dr Hoskins in the flesh, but very much in spirit and in places he knew and in what he understood about them! The same strong sense of place, notably at Ingarsby, on the wolds, caused us to recall with sorrow at his recent death the absence from our party of Harold Fox, a friend to many of us. The following accounts are effectively notes about what was seen and said and discussed on site. If the result appears to be more questions rather than confident interpretations it may be as well to recall that identifying problems and possibilities is a critical stage in developing more robust understandings.

Hamilton (Figure 4.1)

Beresford recommended the remains at Hamilton, in company with Ingarsby and Knaptoft, as clear deserted medieval village sites suitable for visiting, presumably on the basis of the 1948 outing.[11] Yet, as Hoskins' paper reminds us, Hamilton in documentary terms was a hamlet within the parish of Barkby Thorpe with only 374 acres attached to it and very small taxable values and recorded population.[12]

It is informative to approach the site from the north-west (Figure 4.1 'a') by a shallow holloway heading directly downslope between ridge-and-furrow furlongs. Along the right-hand (west) side of this road is an elongated earthwork platform or close, which may have been an encroachment on the routeway and/or the

9.   Hoskins, 'Seven deserted village sites', p. 37.

10. C. Taylor, *Fieldwork in medieval archaeology* (London, 1974); M. Aston, *Interpreting the landscape: landscape archaeology in local studies* (London, 1985); M. Bowden (ed.), *Unravelling the landscape: an inquisitive approach to archaeology* (Stroud, 1999).

11. LVE, p. 360.

12. Hoskins, 'Seven deserted village sites', pp. 44–5.

Figure 4.1 Hamilton, aerial photographic view looking west (NMR 23751/21, 26 October 2004),
© English Heritage. NMR. The perambulation described starts in the top right-hand corner (a).
The holloway (b) and village properties lying between it and the stream form one element of the
settlement. (c) identifies the irregular closes on the flood-plain. The manorial complex lies on
the north-facing slope, centre left (d), and is cut by the curving by-road; and (e) identifies plots
alongside that curia and apparently related to it.

fieldland, perhaps taking the form of a roadside cottage. As the way enters the
settlement, it branches. Ahead, and broadly marked, it curves down to run along
the stream, which it soon crosses, emerging on a similar scale on the south side.
There is a single large property to the west of the way and north of the stream, with
a clear sunken yard and adjacent platforms for buildings.

Striking off at right angles eastwards at the point of junction, is a narrow, quite
straight way (Figure 4.1 'b'), which is terraced into the slope and has the ridge and
furrow of arable ploughing upslope on its north side and a series of village tofts
and crofts downslope of it with the stream forming their rear boundary. There are
three clear properties here of nearly identical widths which are closely integrated
with the way and slight changes in its alignment. Where the way kicks off north-
east (presumably to go off to Beeby), there may be a fourth property to the east,
although features plotted as scarps at the far east end – east of the modern through
road – are the ends of arable selions on the slope. The three clear properties have
the slight earthworks of yards and building platforms within them. Their
regularity and accommodating relationship to the north–south arable furlong
upslope and the sinuous stream which gives them such irregular back boundaries
raises the possibility that this group of properties was developed over the end of

the arable furlong. It might have continued in cultivation, but ploughed to a shorter length. This is a characteristic type of proposition that arises from non-excavational field survey, and to which an intelligent survey process can typically afford an answer. Even if the superseded arable ridges do not survive residually within the crofts, the relationship of the way to the former arable, the presence (or not) of a developed headland, or the correspondence of the croft boundaries to bundles of arable ridges might inform that view.

In contrast to this run of properties north of the stream with their clear evidence of organisation and occupation, a run of plots along the south flank of the stream and occupying the narrow flood plain (Figure 4.1 'c') – although presented in the Ordnance Survey's planning as if every bit as much village crofts – are less clear-cut in their significance. At the least, they are different. They are large, they are very irregular, they exhibit precious little unequivocal sign of occupation. From the west, the first above 'c' with two sides framed by the right-angled hedge line (shown as outside the settlement envelope on Hoskins's plan) contains broad north–south ridging; in the next, ridging is narrower and lies east–west. Only to the east of the modern by-road does the close appear to be subdivided and possibly to contain settlement traces in the form of platforms. Perhaps, then, there is a chronological difference in the occupation of this zone; or, even, this zone was not occupied plots after all, but open space. It is bounded on the south by what presents on plan as a holloway, but this is in parts very broad and very wet. It would be worthwhile to give some consideration to the possibility that the stream once had alternative courses or was once braided, and that the village streets, in crossing, used short stretches as extended fords. In May 1972 the Ordnance Survey's field investigator noted that 'earlier in the year the major portion of the site was under flood, apparently a regular annual occurrence; suggesting that the village was possibly only summer occupied'![13]

The north-facing slope has the largest extent of earthworks, and occupying its eastern half lies the most substantial and clearly marked. Here, identified as 'Moated Area and probable site of Manor House', is what is undoubtedly a manorial complex (Figure 4.1 'd'). It is centred on what is probably better described as a prominent ditched platform rather than a 'moat', as the southern, upslope side of this feature, together with the eastern and western flanks, are no more than substantial channels in which water could not be made to stand. By contrast the downslope, northern arm was broader and was intended to hold water; and it formerly extended westwards into what survives as a notably rectangular pond in use, lying on the same orientation, and eastwards into what seems to have been another pond or water feature, the residual earthworks of

13. NMR, SK60NW14.

which are difficult to make out since they are smashed through by the alignment of the modern by-road, which passes on a causeway.

This arrangement immediately surrounding the house platform is fed by a system of channels upslope of the platform; and these in turn divide this area into regular-sized rectangular compartments. Within these is uniform ridging, which – if it underlies the layout, as appears to be the case, rather than occurring only within the compartments – implies that this complex is set on former arable cultivation and is at best late medieval in date. The house platform (or 'moat') sits quite centrally within an almost square enclosure, which is defined by a bank that is massive – broad as well as high – on the south and east sides, and somewhat less so on the west. Particularly on the south, it could have served as a raised garden walk. On the east, the modern by-road slices through this bank, thereby both degrading it and reducing the coherence of the whole complex. The earlier course of a road to Scraptoft, passing round the north-east corner of the house-and-garden complex and following the length of its eastern side, outside, is visible as a holloway not mapped by the Ordnance Survey. The notable symmetry of this complex seems to extend to the house platform itself. In contrast to the available Ordnance Survey field plan, which is of limited use because of the scale at which it is drawn, the north side of the platform – although damaged – seems to have a recessed central section with projections to east and west, in a quite symmetrical arrangement. There are surface traces of what appear to be large building ranges lining at least the three other sides of the platform. As field remains, the layout described in this way might quite naturally be thought likely to be post-medieval in date, although it might have developed from late medieval origins. Documentary evidence, interrogated with this archaeological assessment in mind, should have something to contribute, but Hoskins' focus had a narrower perspective in this case. Whether this residence originated in the late medieval period or was new-built later, the question arises about its setting at that juncture: was there any contemporary settlement nearby? Was it perhaps modestly emparked? There was a house with two hearths at Hamilton in 1664, and even as late as Prior's county map of 1777 there was a single house at 'Hambleton', south of the stream and west of the road to Scraptoft, that was worth mapping and naming.[14]

Finally, lying along the western side of the house-and-garden complex, there is a block of closes that extends up the north-facing slope (Figure 4.1 'e'). They have a rather regular, rectangular overall arrangement and are accessed axially via a short north–south dead end holloway. There are signs of buildings or building platforms and hollowed yards. So, despite the fact that the two southernmost

14. LRO, L 929.3 SR2; J.D. Welding (ed.), Leicestershire in 1777. An edition of John Prior's map of Leicestershire with an introduction and commentary by members of the Leicestershire industrial historical society (Leicestershire, 1984), p. 38.

closes (one reckoned within and one without the village envelope on Hoskins' map) are filled with ridging, these may be a group of village tofts and crofts. But the rectangularity of plan and overall conformity of the block with the manorial/'big house' complex to its east raises the possibility that it forms a part of the manorial curtilage. At the least, one might anticipate a link, tenurially or chronologically, with the neighbouring element in the settlement plan.

Hoskins himself tried excavating at Hamilton in 1948 when he put a small trench across a depression near the south-west corner of the moat; but he reportedly judged the attempt 'best forgotten'.[15] There were also excavations by a local group in the early 1960s. Three small trenches were cut in the toft on the east side of the modern road, and two of them revealed evidence of a cobbled surface.[16] Both the foregoing account and considerable experience now accumulated from excavating deserted medieval settlements for more than half a century tend to demonstrate that there is little profit or intelligible result likely from such ventures without a strategy or research questions, which intelligent investigation of the earthworks can help to develop and articulate.

Ingarsby (Figure 4.2)

Ingarsby is located in the steeply hilly terrain of Leicestershire's wolds, a stretch of countryside which contains numerous well-preserved medieval settlement remains. Ingarsby itself has been described as 'one of the outstanding deserted village sites in Britain, with the watermill, streets, boundary ditches, and house sites clearly identifiable'.[17] Field remains here are more extensive and more massive in scale than at any of the other sites visited. That observation itself might make one anticipate that there is more than solely and simply a deserted medieval settlement in this landscape. Hoskins' storyline was that Leicester Abbey engrossed and deserted the village, converting its lands to grazing and creating an extensive network of paddocks and closes around its moated grange for this purpose. He took parts of Ingarsby Old Hall (Figure 4.2 'a') – notably the generically Perpendicular detailing of the surviving south wing (the so-called chapel) – to be a late medieval survival of the abbey's tenure.[18]

15. D.T.-D. Clarke, 'Archaeology in Leicestershire 1939–1951', *Transactions of the Leicestershire Archaeological Society*, 28 (1952), p. 47; NMR, SK60NW14; M. Beresford and J. Hurst, *Wharram Percy deserted medieval village* (London, 1990), p. 27.

16. Anon., 'Archaeology in Leicestershire and Rutland 1963–1966', *Transactions of the Leicestershire Archaeological and Historical Society*, 41 (1965–6), p. 67.

17. N. Pevsner with E. Williamson, *The buildings of England: Leicestershire and Rutland* (Harmondsworth, 2nd rev. edn, 1984), p. 186.

18. Hoskins, 'Seven deserted village sites', pp. 46–7; Pevsner, *Leicestershire*, p. 185; Listed Building Listing description.

Figure 4.2 Ingarsby, aerial photographic view looking north-east (NMR 21907/23, 5 February 2003), © English Heritage. NMR. The medieval settlement remains lie centre right on the facing slope, its main terrace-way running from (b) to (c) and probably, originally, beyond in both directions. The hall is to the left (north) in its polygonal enclosures (a); the deep linear earthwork (g) is the drive to the house, from a junction of public roads at its east end. The lake along the valley at the bottom, with a main dam to the left (f), is bounded by a tree line. The large triangular mound at (h) and angled banks at (i) have the appearance of formal ornamental features. The aerial viewpoint is directly above the so-called Monk's Grave.

Everything about the field remains that comes to light on a first encounter – their scale, their location and articulation, their content, and even a series of straightforward stratigraphic relationships – urge that it is not only a medieval story that they tell, but one with a substantial post-medieval component that has its own value and interest.

The principal medieval earthworks are based on a gently curving, well-defined, broad terrace-way (Figure 4.2 'b' to 'c') orientated north–south and sitting high on the slope that falls away westwards down to the stream named 'Ingarsby Hollow'. Uphill from the terrace-way, two good holloways strike off at right angles, giving access to crofts and tofts with hollowed yards and building platforms, which are double-banked above the terrace. Below it, further properties front the lower side. These may be further peasant crofts and tofts, but there may be a much larger property here (Figure 4.2 'd') with its extensive curtilage extending downslope in a series of compartments or paddocks to the modern by-road. In purely earthwork terms this might be a candidate for a manor or 'grange'.

At the north and south ends of this core layout, two long, broad and deep hollows curve down the slope on converging alignments. It seems possible – especially upslope of the terrace-way of the village's main street – that these are on the lines of medieval streets, but as encountered they are clearly later features; broader and much deeper than the medieval features, they slice at right angles through the terrace-way at 'b' and 'c', leaving it hanging a clear step above their base. The southern most of them, dropping down the slope from 'h', was mapped as a road in the nineteenth century.[19]

Going northwards again from 'c', the vestige of the terrace-way narrows and becomes ragged and then is blocked by an oval mound at 'e'; this is perhaps a 'pillow mound', or rabbit warren mound, but at any rate is a development that is clearly stratigraphically later. Beyond that, the way is barely traceable, having been smoothed by differential land use here compared with that which has affected the village site further south.

The moated enclosure surrounding Ingarsby Old Hall stands rather separate from these medieval earthworks, occupying an extraordinary location set high on the end of the ridge and looking down both westwards into the valley of 'Ingarsby Hollow' and northwards into a second stream valley, which forms a confluence to the north-west of the Hall. The moat does not form a complete circuit, occurring only on the north, west and south-west, and is varied in form, with the long, straight northern arm being especially broad and requiring an impressively massive bank or dam to retain it against the slope. While the south side of the residential complex seems to have been a wall on the line of the mapped boundary – which gives a length and orientation mirroring the south-west moat arm – the east side was a mere ditch and cross-feeder channelling water into the east end of the northern moat. Overall this 'enclosure' is exceptionally large, measuring about 170 by 215m, and curiously – clearly purposefully – geometric in configuration. One would say that it structures the designed setting of the Old Hall in a post-medieval rather than medieval manner. Significantly, the *Buildings of England* entry conjectures that the old south range of the Hall complex was in fact built by the Cave family in the 1540s.[20] The Caves were the sole residents in the village in 1563, and there is a surviving fireplace with the Cave arms dated 1579. A stylish country residence was perpetuated in the seventeenth century following purchase successively by Sir Robert Bannister and Lord Maynard;[21] only a substantial

19. J.B. Harley and R.R. Oliver, *The Old Series Ordnance Survey maps of England and Wales*, 7 (Lympne Castle, 1989), p. 91.
20. Pevsner, *Leicestershire*, p. 185.
21. For the Cave family and their local connections, see S.T. Bindoff, *History of Parliament: the Commons 1509–1558*, 1 (London, 1982), pp. 594–6; P.W. Hasler, *History of Parliament: the Commons 1558–1603*, 1 (London, 1981), pp. 563–5.

rebuilding in the early eighteenth century seems to have reduced a former great country house to the present more manageable size.[22] This simplified understanding clearly offers scope for proper research.

Previous commentary and the present archaeological record identify the dam below the Hall in 'Ingarsby Hollow' as a medieval feature. While there may have been a medieval mill or mills on this stream, the huge earthwork we see, with its elaborate bypass channel and very extensive angled former water sheet (Figure 4.2 'f') has an integrated place in an ornamental landscape around the Hall. This is emphasised by the circumstance that the former water sheet of the main dam has a finished, squared back, which proves on examination to be a further, low dam capable of creating a second pond behind – the effect perhaps being comparable (if on a smaller scale) to the fine flight of lakes at Fawsley (Northants.), with their illusionist effect of a continuous water sheet.[23]

Further features, although not hitherto noted, fit with this context. For example, in the run of closes north of and below the eastern end of the principal moat arm, visible from the by-road, are not only an outflow channel from the moat but also a number of low mounds. They look like so-called pillow mounds and may thus indicate the presence of a rabbit warren of a type that is known from both archaeological and cartographic evidence as an adjunct of early post-medieval country houses.[24]

The modern by-road from the north now dog-legs up to Ingarsby Old Hall. In doing so, it carves improbably through both the massive dam and the bed of the northern moat arm. This clear stratigraphic relationship must mark a change in the road pattern and access routes to the Hall. Previously this road must have skirted rather than penetrated the Old Hall's designed setting; it very probably climbed the hill along its east side by continuing more or less straight ahead, outside the envelope depicted on Hoskins' published diagram. Indeed, its appearance in the diagram appears to be marked by a big holloway about halfway up the eastern side of the surveyed plan. From this point – a junction of holloways – a broad deep way (Figure 4.2 'g'), perhaps the most strongly marked feature in earthworks, curves back towards the Old Hall. This is without doubt the former main entrance drive to the Hall in its post-medieval configuration, and it, too, was mapped as a public road in the nineteenth century.[25] The massive bank along its

22. NMR, SK60NE10; Listed Building Listing description. There were seventeen hearths recorded at Ingarsby in 1664, eight in the principal dwelling; and an inventory of 1698 itemises the rooms of the Hall and their contents and mentions a malt mill valued at £1 5s: LRO, L929.3 SR2; 14 D 60.

23. M.W. Beresford, *History on the ground* (London, 1957; rev. edn, 1971), pp. 110–13; RCHME, *North-west Northamptonshire* (London, 1981), pp. 88–91.

24. For a convenient overview, see T. Williamson, *Rabbits, warrens and archaeology* (Stroud, 2007), pp. 155–75.

25. Harley and Oliver, *Old Series Maps*, p. 91.

northern side forms both a feature within the gardens in front of the Hall and a screen, allowing the Hall to be revealed to the arriving visitor in a contrived manner.

Other features of this post-medieval designed landscape represented in the earthworks – although not previously thought about in that context – are probably the huge triangular mound at the south-east corner of the earthworks (Figure 4.2 'h'), whose formal shape and prominent location suggest some form of viewpoint, perhaps including a garden building, and the angled embanked alignments that define the southern edge of the earthworks (Figure 4.2 'i'), which recall formal features with a military aspect (such as bastions or angled earthworks) sometimes found in garden layouts.[26]

With these outline interpretations in mind – of a landscape at Ingarsby wholly recast in a developed ornamental garb through the sixteenth and seventeenth centuries – the possibility arises that the mound known as the Monk's Grave was another feature in this scheme. Although it is traditionally – if perhaps rather improbably and without any context – categorised as an 'adulterine castle' originating in the twelfth-century Anarchy, its location on the opposite side of the valley of 'Ingarsby Hollow' affords an excellent view back to the full extent of the designed, formal landscape that we have sketched out.[27] It might therefore have been a viewing point, part of but external to that scheme.

Stretton Magna (Figure 4.3)

The settlement remains of Stretton Magna (Great Stretton) are, among those visited during our 2008 outing, the most characteristic of midland England's deserted medieval villages. They are not unusual, too, in that desertion was evidently gradual and not completed in the medieval period, since five hearths in four properties were still recorded here in 1664.[28] In addition, the earthworks are grouped around a medieval church site, St Giles, which has not succumbed to the loss of resident population, although it is now on the brink of redundancy. It appears to be largely a rebuild of 1838, with iron-framed windows, but it incorporates architectural fragments of its medieval predecessor in its outside walls in a notable antiquarian display.

Yet despite its characteristic appearance as village earthworks grouped around a church, there are several significantly odd aspects to this settlement. The parish is now 'Little Stretton', but Little Stretton has its own surviving medieval church within that separate settlement and, although the two were often assimilated in

26. W.H. Adams, *The French garden 1500–1800* (London, 1979), p. 38, fig. 30.
27. D.J. King, *Castellarium Anglicanum* (London/New York, 1983), p. 254.
28. LRO, L929.3 SR2.

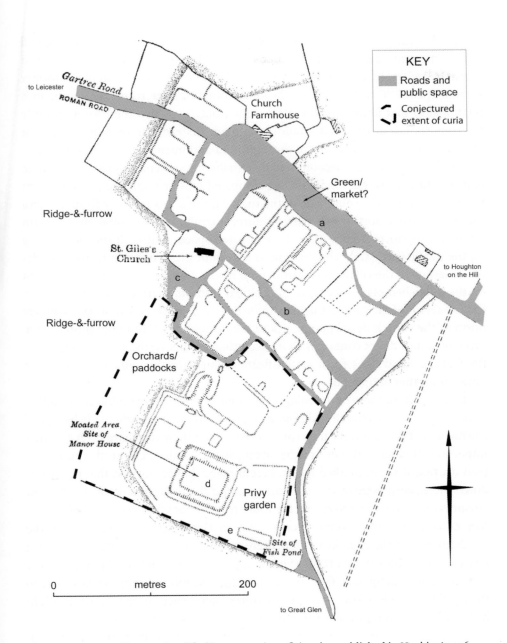

Figure 4.3 Stretton Magna: simplified interpretation of site plan published in Hoskins' 1956
paper 'Seven deserted village sites in Leicestershire'.

medieval documentation, Great Stretton was certainly a separately tithed unit still in the nineteenth century.[29] The settlement itself lies hard against the north-west parish boundary. In addition, it is situated adjacent to the alignment of the former Roman road – 'Gartree Road' – heading into Leicester from the south, in a relationship that underpins the place-name; but, as is also the case with Little Stretton, its layout does not straddle the road. Instead, the remains lie almost entirely to the south-west of the through road alignment. This makes it easy to ignore this route and to discount it in discussing the settlement's layout. Yet there is in the earthwork plan a distinctive elongated close containing no settlement traces lying along the south side of the road (Figure 4.3 'a'). It may formerly have extended further north-west, where Church Farmhouse of *c.* 1800 and its farm buildings appear to occupy a similar elongated space, as if perhaps encroaching on the public way. Might this have been a form of green or trading space on the road? Several of the village crofts front onto it, and a holloway – only partly shown on the published plan – seems to have exited from its south-east corner into the eastern sector of the village. But also, quite distinctively, several short cross streets north of the church lie at right angles to the through road, bringing more village properties into direct contact with it. According to this strand of thinking, then, the Gartree Road does form a significant element of this village, even if it is physically rather peripheral.

By contrast, the core of the village lies along a well-marked holloway extending south-east from the churchyard (Figure 4.3 'b') and lined on either side by typical earthworks of peasant tofts and crofts. It seems that there may have been a further important, 'hidden', element of the layout, which is absent from the published plan because it is not marked by a coherent mappable earthwork: that is, a route down the eastern edge of the settlement, along the western side of the shallow stream valley. This was effectively the route from Great Glen to Houghton, and it would have provided linking access between Great Stretton's streets. By the southern edge of the churchyard, too, there are small triangles of interlinked street spaces, resembling small greens (Figure 4.3 'c'). Immediately to the west, where former arable – defined by fine spreads of ridge and furrow – approaches close to the church, there is a low mound or platform encroached on the arable. It might be the site of a cottage or quasi-public building such as a priest's house.

The other principal component in this village plan is the moat (Figure 4.3 'd'), which is sited on lower ground to the south of the ridge that the village occupies. This peripheral location not only places this manorial residence at a clear distance from the church, in contrast to the relationship at Little Stretton, for example, but also removes it out of sight of the through road. Here, it is easy to concentrate on

---

29. Hoskins, 'Seven deserted village sites', pp. 42–3; tithe award of 1849 in LRO.

the exceptionally well-marked moated platform – without doubt the location of major residential buildings. But on its eastern side there is also a formal rectangular pond (or 'fish pond', Figure 4.3 'e'), fed from the west and forming the south side of a rectangular close which contains traces of low terracing and has a circular mound at its north-west corner – if not the site of a dovecot then plausibly a prospect mound. In short, all the elements of a formal privy garden, situated below the private wing of the house. To the west and north the earthworks consist of a series of rectangular closes which neither abut any village street nor contain any sign of yards or buildings such as the peasant crofts typically have. Indeed, several contain ridging, which has caused them to be excluded from the settlement envelope as outlined in the published plan. This might, however, indicate an extension over former arable or even use as orchards. Much – perhaps all – of this is no doubt within the bounds of the manorial curia, and the issue is where the curia stops and the peasant properties of the village begin. Both our understanding of the extent and the significance of the fine details in the field archaeology of this manorial complex are affected if Hoskins was right to suggest that the capital messuage of Great Stretton continued in occupation on this site until the end of the sixteenth century, and perhaps well into the next.[30] Stretton Hall, situated half a mile (1km) away to the south, post-dates the enclosure of the parish between 1640 and 1670 and in its core dates architecturally to the first or second decade of the eighteenth century.[31]

Knaptoft (Figures 4.4 and 4.5)

Knaptoft lies more distantly south of Leicester. It was not included in Hoskins' 1956 article, but did form part of the famous 1948 visit.[32] Despite this emblematic role and the reiteration of the site's interpretation by several subsequent commentators, including its formal protection as deserted village remains, the difficulty at Knaptoft is actually to identify any village earthworks at all.[33] The complex at Hall Farm includes the fragmentary but impressive remains of a very substantial sixteenth-century country house, now forming parts of the farm's outbuildings (Figure 4.4), and, to its east, the site and ruins of the medieval church of Knaptoft.[34] The field lying on the northern side of the east–west valley immediately to the south of Hall Farm is traditionally indicated as the location of

30. Hoskins, 'Seven deserted village sites', p. 42.
31. Pevsner, *Leicestershire*, p. 169.
32. See p. 47 n.5.
33. English Heritage, unpublished revision of scheduling information for RSM no. 17103 (29 July 1994).
34. J. Nichols, *The history and antiquities of the county of Leicester*, 4, part 1 (London, 1807), pp. 217, 220–1; J.G. Cooke, *The lost village of Knaptoft* (Leicester, c. 1958); Pevsner, *Leicestershire*, p. 195.

Figure 4.4 Knaptoft, remains of sixteenth-century house and MSRG visitors, 22 June 2008.

the village remains. The opinion of the Ordnance Survey's archaeological field investigator visiting in June 1960 was articulate and negative: 'the major part of this field has been worked for sand and gravel, and apart from a few short lengths of non-surveyable enclosure banks amongst the quarries, there are no extant remains of the village'.[35]

Unsurprisingly in the light of that assessment, no antiquity model or published map depiction which Hoskins might have used in publication was produced at any stage by Ordnance Survey field staff.[36] It also seems quite uncertain that ponds in the valley bottom just to the south-west, although labelled as 'fish ponds', are anything other than modern adaptations of gravel pits.

In another context the field investigator's commentary is excessively severe. For in fact the 'non-surveyable enclosure banks' form a wholly coherent pattern of terraces and rectangular compartment boundaries of an extensive formal garden layout. This is precisely what one would anticipate accompanying a substantial post-medieval country house such as Knaptoft Hall in the occupation of county gentry such as its owners, the Turpin family.[37] Although rather cut about by quarrying into the valley side, the earthwork layout is intelligible and finely

---

35. NMR, SP68NW6.
36. An 'antiquity model' was the manuscript survey diagram of a field monument at basic map scale produced on site by the Ordnance Survey investigator, often including notes, measurements and sections. This was edited – typically simplified, with small-scale details and annotations omitted – to produce the published map depiction. These finely drawn paper records, usually stored as an adjunct to Ordnance Survey Record Cards, have become vulnerable to oversight or loss with the textual digitisation of archaeological records. See generally, J.B. Harley, *Ordnance Survey maps: a descriptive manual* (Southampton, 1975), pp. 145–51.
37. Bindoff, *The Commons 1509–1558*, 3, pp. 492–3; Hasler, *The Commons 1558–1603*, 3, pp. 535–6.

Figure 4.5 Knaptoft, aerial photographic view looking south (NMR 21460/34, 26 November 2001), © English Heritage. NMR. Probable settlement remains (a) around the head of the minor valley lie to the south-east of the medieval church site, which is in the trees at bottom right. Remains of the hall (see Figure 4.4) lie further right; the miscellaneous earthworks (b) are the edge of its formal gardens cut through by piecemeal sand and gravel quarrying. Ridge and furrow and a well-preserved mill mound are at (c).

detailed. But in 1960 earthworks of post-medieval formal gardens were scarcely recognised as the common survivals that they actually are, and they were not legitimate antiquities for Ordnance Survey mapping.[38]

The combined extent of a garden layout accompanying even quite a modest house of a county family, plus the farmyard complex of its modern successor, might quite easily mask a medieval settlement site, as at Harpswell or Knaith in Lincolnshire, for example.[39] Or it might render any piecemeal and peripheral remains very difficult to recognise without the sort of careful survey that records and seeks to explain all features encountered through their field relationships. This may be the circumstance here at Knaptoft: namely that later land use has hidden the site and remains of the village. But in addition there are some indications, newly recognised through aerial survey, of what may be a group of settlement tofts and crofts situated apparently detached and about 350m to the south-east of the church, near to the source of the stream in this valley (Figure 4.5 'a'). This evidence raises

38. C. Taylor, *The archaeology of gardens* (Princes Risborough, 1983); English Heritage, *Post-medieval formal gardens*, single monument class description for the Monuments Protection Programme of English Heritage (1997), see http://www.eng-h.gov.uk/mpp/med/intro2.htm#a9.
39. Everson *et al.*, *Change and continuity*, pp. 107–9, 116–17.

several possibilities, which we cannot immediately resolve. For example, it may represent peasant settlement displaced from a historic location near the church and manor. Alternatively, it might indicate that, contrary to traditional expectation, the historic settlement pattern at Knaptoft was not that of a single nuclear settlement, but rather, perhaps, one of a manor and church complex plus one or more hamlets.[40] There is no doubt that medieval settlement studies have become more aware of the range of forms that settlement patterns may take, and of their potential for dynamic change, even in the midland counties.[41] There certainly seems scope for renewed and rewarding research on Knaptoft, freed of the strait-jacket that Hoskins imposed on our understanding sixty years ago.

Conclusion

This group of visits – superficial enough in themselves compared with a systematic programme of original fieldwork – nevertheless brought forward a number of themes. Principal amongst them, perhaps, was how much approaches to plan-making of deserted medieval settlements and survey and interpretation generally have changed. It is only fair to recall that the plans printed in Hoskins' 1956 article were made for the specific purpose of map depiction of antiquities within large-scale Ordnance Survey printed map sheets. There were limitations imposed by scale, expectations of the ready visibility of features by laymen, issues of an expected level of intelligible coherence. Perhaps most importantly, description and interpretation went little further than 'here be medieval settlement remains'. This is what the external authority, in the person here of Hoskins, had indeed asserted; and it was as little more than illustrations of that phenomenon that he too was inclined to view the earthworks. A latter-day approach, informed by the skills of influential practitioners such as Bowen and Taylor, is (as it has been described) an inquisitive one. Questioning relationships, conformity and non-congruity by careful observation of detail on the site, and recording accordingly; perhaps most distinctively, anticipating change rather than stability; looking to explain what the earthworks indicate – often through dynamism in the landscape up to the present day – rather than comfortable pigeon-holing into simple archaeological categories such as 'deserted medieval village'.

A second theme was clearly to do with the 'last phases' of these sites. It was writ largest at Ingarsby and Knaptoft, where substantial parts of the earthworks

40. As Tony Brown advises us (pers. comm.), there are some places in Leicestershire where the demesne, manorial set-up and servile tenants had a separate settlement and sometimes field system from the free tenants, all within the parish. But the tenurial position at Knaptoft was not of this sort: tenancies within this parish were overwhelmingly villein ones.
41. B.K. Roberts and S. Wrathmell, *An atlas of rural settlement in England* (London, 2000).

seem most plausibly to be post-medieval and related to the development of country houses on or near the medieval sites. In one way this sort of observation is a natural consequence of the more alert, archaeologically more confident, survey approach noted in the previous paragraph. It chimes with points about the end of these settlements made by several other contributions in this volume. Ingarsby illustrates especially well that the presence of deserted settlement remains in and among those of a later designed landscape does not automatically demonstrate that the creation of the latter caused the desertion of the former (see also Williamson, this volume). These episodes may be separated in time. Indeed, the excellent survival of the village remains may itself be evidence that this was so, since levelling the settlement site was not included within the works of design.

A third issue, perhaps surprising to those unfamiliar with field remains as primary evidence, are the hints of changes within the lifetime of villages, such as expansion over ridge and furrow cultivation. Such cultivation remains often afford a key benchmark in interpretation, commonly indicating that an antiquity is clearly post-medieval or modern, but sometimes that a change lies within the medieval era and is highly significant to our overall understanding.[42] Practically, this makes observation and recording on the periphery of settlement complexes and with regard to their relationship to the surrounding landscape at least as important as in their core.

A fourth issue, only tangentially touched upon on this occasion, concerns settlement form. The field evidence that we saw at Knaptoft underlines that it cannot be assumed, even in Leicestershire, that most village-dominated of all the Central Province counties, that the settlement is a single nucleation.

Hoskins might have been impressed with such outcomes from a small sample of sites and a single day's outing.

Acknowledgements

We are very grateful to a series of owners and tenants who allowed us, as a party of more than 60 participants, to walk over their land: namely Mr Tim Pick at Hamilton, Mr Brian Henton at Ingarsby, Mr Nick Padwick at Stretton Magna and Mr Neville Hall at Knaptoft. In several cases they were additionally very helpful in facilitating parking in constrained circumstances. Special thanks are owed to the incumbent and church warden of St Giles church at Stretton for ensuring that it was open for us and allowing us to use it as the base for our picnic lunch.

42. Taylor, Fieldwork, passim; idem, 'Aspects of village mobility in medieval and later times', in S. Limbrey and J.G. Evans (eds), The effects of man on the landscape: the lowland zone, CBA Research Report, 21 (1978), pp. 126–34.

5

Houses and communities: archaeological evidence for variation in medieval peasant experience

SALLY V. SMITH

Archaeological investigation of deserted villages of the medieval period has been in progress for more than half a century and in that time great strides have been made in using data from these sites to add to our knowledge of medieval settlement forms and material culture.[1] Much less attention, however, has been paid to the way in which deserted villages can advance our knowledge of the experiences and mentalities of the medieval peasants who occupied them. This is hardly a failing only of the archaeologists who investigate these settlements: medieval archaeology as a whole has been more concerned with determining the variation, chronology and function of material culture types than with investigating any meanings they may have expressed or produced. Historians, on the other hand, have discussed aspects of the lived experience of the medieval peasantry but, insofar as they do not deal with the material aspects of these lives, their accounts will inevitably be partial.[2]

While close, contextual study of individual villages can reveal specific features of the peasantry's experience which are not observable when villages or the peasantry are studied *en bloc*, attempts to obtain a nuanced archaeologically rooted sense of peasant social lives can also be achieved by widening the field of vision to

1. For example Hinton, this volume.
2. For example, E. Britton, *The community of the vill: a study in the history of the family and village life in fourteenth-century England* (Toronto, 1977); C. Dyer, 'Power and conflict in the medieval English village', in D. Hooke (ed.), *Medieval villages: a review of current work* (Oxford, 1985), pp. 27–32; P.J.P. Goldberg, 'Masters and men in later medieval England', in D.M. Hadley (ed.), *Masculinity in medieval England* (London, 1999), pp. 56–70; J. Murray, 'Individualism and consensual marriage: some evidence from medieval England', in C.M. Rousseau and J.T. Rosenthal (eds), *Women, marriage and family in medieval Christendom: essays in memory of Michael M. Sheehan C.S.B.* (Kalamazoo, 1998), pp. 121–51; M. Pimsler, 'Solidarity in the medieval village? The evidence of personal pledging at Elton, Huntingdonshire', *Journal of British Studies*, 17 (1977), pp. 1–11; M. Müller, 'A divided class? Peasants and peasant communities in later medieval England', in C. Dyer, P. Coss and C. Wickham (eds), *Rodney Hilton's Middle Ages, Past and Present* Supplement no. 2 (2007), pp. 115–31.

consider a number of settlements at once.[3] Such a scale allows us to consider patterns of consistency and diversity and thus to advance our general understanding of peasant perceptions.

This essay, therefore, considers the evidence from three of Buckinghamshire's deserted villages to obtain a comparative view of peasant experience in late medieval England. The three settlements in question – Great Linford, Tattenhoe and Westbury – were chosen because of the extensive excavations undertaken at each and because they are all located within seven miles (11km) of one another, thereby allowing us to investigate variations within a tight geographical area.

These three settlements were all surveyed and excavated as part of the archaeological investigations carried out in advance of the development of the city of Milton Keynes (Figure 5.1). Great Linford was excavated between 1974 and 1977 with some further work undertaken in 1980. The main areas excavated were crofts on the south side of the village green and the east side of the main street, as well as the manor house, church and windmill. In addition, the field system was recorded prior to development in 1972.[4] Approximately 10 per cent of the village of Tattenhoe was excavated in 1988 and again in 1990. Material from the late eleventh to the sixteenth centuries was discovered. Field boundaries, holloways, ponds and individual buildings were investigated.[5] Westbury-by-Shenley was very substantially investigated between 1984 and 1990, with over 75 per cent of the earthworks being excavated. Considerable amounts of material were recovered from late medieval contexts.[6]

A comparative approach to these three settlements reveals significant differences in the material world of the peasants who lived within them which would have, it can be argued, profoundly affected their experiences of the social world. This essay will concentrate on two aspects of these settlements which can broadly be encapsulated by the terms 'community' and 'household'. I will first outline the evidence pertaining to each of these themes and will then suggest some social 'meanings'.

3. S.V. Smith, 'Towards a social archaeology of the medieval English peasantry: power and resistance at Wharram Percy', *Journal of Social Archaeology*, 9 (2009), pp. 391–416.
4. D.C. Mynard, R.J. Zeepvat and R.J. Williams, *Excavations at Great Linford, 1974–80*, Buckinghamshire Archaeological Society Monograph Series, 3 (1991), p. 47
5. R. Ivens, P. Busby and N. Shepherd, *Tattenhoe and Westbury. Two deserted medieval settlements in Milton Keynes*, Buckinghamshire Archaeological Society Monograph Series, 8 (1995), p. 15.
6. Ibid., p. 53.

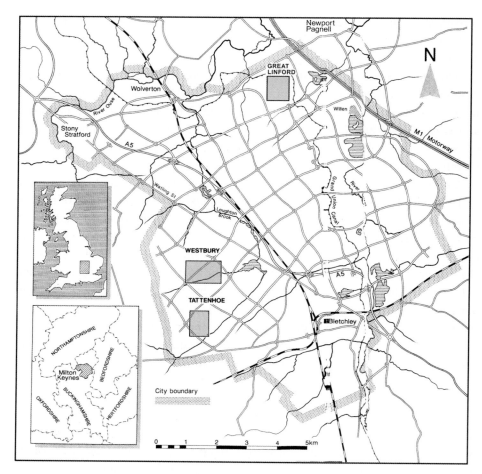

Figure 5.1 Map showing location of sites in relation to modern Milton Keynes (adapted from Ivens *et al.* and reproduced by permission of the Buckinghamshire Archaeological Society).

Community

General morphology

An initial very obvious difference between these three settlements is their degree of nucleation. Great Linford was a nucleated village in the medieval period which had developed around a green and, by the late thirteenth to fourteenth century, 'the village plan with regularly laid out crofts ... was fully developed'.[7] Tattenhoe was also a nucleated village but of a slightly more 'straggling' form.[8] Westbury, on the

7.   Mynard *et al.*, *Great Linford*, p. 17.
8.   Ivens *et al.*, *Tattenhoe and Westbury*, p. 211.

other hand, was a dispersed settlement with houses or house-sites positioned at road intersections, around greens and irregularly along roads and holloways.[9] Its constituent parts have been described as a group of 'hamlets' and as a 'loosely connected group of farmhouses'; there was never a 'fully functioning village community' here.[10]

That such varied settlement forms could exist within a relatively small geographical region has been noted by both historians and archaeologists.[11] The former (most notably Dyer) have outlined some of the aspects of peasant social life which may have differed between these types of settlement. Dyer has argued that the residents of dispersed settlements may have been more individualistic and rebellious than their counterparts in nucleated villages, for example.[12] Archaeological research on these different settlement forms, on the other hand, has been much influenced by the discipline of historical geography, and effort has therefore largely been expended on investigating patterns of settlement distribution.[13] Archaeological work on dispersed settlement has most often been concerned with questions of origin, whether these settlements appeared later or earlier than nucleated villages, what forces caused them to appear, and whether these forces were different from those which led to nucleation.[14]

While these questions are of undoubted importance, they are not the only ones which can be investigated. The differences between these types of settlement would also have been meaningful in the lives of the peasants themselves. Space, architecture and boundaries provide a structure for human action, allowing or encouraging some interactions and activities and barring or discouraging others, and therefore impacts on social meaning. Lefebvre, for example, has drawn attention to the way that 'space commands bodies, prescribing or proscribing

9. Ibid., p. 79.
10. Ibid., pp. 134, 178.
11. For example, C. Dyer, *Hanbury: settlement and society in a woodland landscape*, (Leicester, 1991); C. Taylor, 'Dispersed settlement in nucleated areas', *Landscape History*, 17 (1995), pp. 27–34.
12. Dyer, *Hanbury*, p. 48; C. Dyer, 'Dispersed settlements in medieval England: a case study of Pendock, Worcestershire', *Med. Arch.*, 34 (1990), pp. 97–121.
13. For example, B.K. Roberts and S. Wrathmell, *Region and place: a study of English rural settlement* (London, 2002).
14. For example, R. Jones and M. Page, *Medieval villages in an English landscape: beginnings and ends* (Macclesfield, 2006), pp. 231–42; T. Williamson, *Shaping medieval landscapes: settlement, society, environment* (Macclesfield, 2003); C. Taylor, 'Nucleated settlement: a view from the frontier', *Landscape History*, 24 (2002), pp. 53–71; A.E. Brown and C.C. Taylor, 'The origins of dispersed settlement; some results from fieldwork in Bedfordshire', *Landscape History*, 11 (1989), pp. 61–81; S. Rippon, R. Fyfe and A. Brown, 'Beyond villages and open fields: the origins and development of a historic landscape characterised by dispersed settlement in south-west England', *Med. Arch.*, 50 (2006), pp. 31–70.

gestures, routes and distances to be covered'.[15] These actions – gesturing, travelling along routes – are part of the way people evoke (or revoke) meaning in their lives so that as they move through landscapes certain basic values are relived, social categories are given meaning and material form and social relations are made concrete.[16] Space, therefore, is a potentially fruitful source for an archaeological investigation of experience.

Turning to our Buckinghamshire examples, it can be seen that medieval peasants' movement through Great Linford and through Westbury would have invoked quite different meanings and that the spatial 'terms' articulated by each settlement would have created quite different social lives.[17] The morphology of the latter would not have served to evoke feelings of cohesion (Figure 5.2). Because of the scattered topography of this settlement, the daily round of activity for most medieval men and women would have included only limited close contact with others – they would have seen, encountered and interacted with their fellows much less frequently than would the inhabitants of nucleated settlements such as Great Linford.

Agricultural practices

Experiences of the morphology of their settlement, however, would not have been the only aspect of peasants' lives which affected their sense of community. Social practices involved with farming are also important in this regard. At Great Linford, the field system – which overlay the middle Saxon settlement at Pennyland – was probably laid out at the same time as the village, and was certainly well established by the tenth and eleventh centuries. The arable land here was allocated to the villagers in what is often regarded as the 'classic' medieval fashion, with each tenant farming individual strips which were scattered through two large fields.[18] In addition to arable land being divided in this way and subject to communal disciplines, a fifteenth-century document shows that meadows were divided into various lots called 'doles' and 'swathes', and a document dated to 1567 suggests that grazing too was strictly controlled here.[19]

---

15. H. Lefebvre, *The production of space*, trans. D. Nicholson-Smith (Oxford, 1991), p. 143.

16. H. Moore, 'Bodies on the move: gender, power and material culture: gender, difference and the material world', reprinted in J. Thomas (ed.), *Interpretive archaeology: a reader* (London, 2000 [1994]); M.L.S. Sørensen, *Gender archaeology* (Cambridge, 2000), pp. 146–56; E.W. Soja, 'The spatiality of social life: towards a transformative retheorisation', in D. Gregory and J. Urry (eds), *Social relations and spatial structures* (Basingstoke, 1985), pp. 90–127.

17. D. Miller and C. Tilley, 'Ideology, power and prehistory: an introduction', in D. Miller and C. Tilley (eds), *Ideology, power and prehistory* (Cambridge, 1984), pp. 1–15.

18. Mynard *et al.*, *Great Linford*, p. 8; R.J. Williams, *Pennyland and Hartigans. Two Iron Age and Saxon sites in Milton Keynes*, Buckinghamshire Archaeological Society Monograph Series, 4 (1993).

19. *Ibid.*, p. 9.

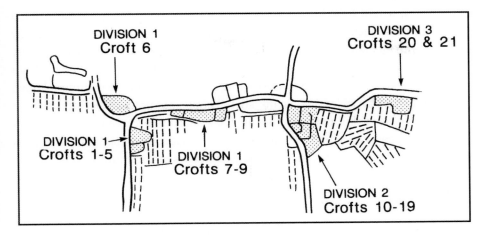

Figure 5.2 Spatial arrangement of the settlement of Westbury (reproduced by permission of the Buckinghamshire Archaeological Society).

At Tattenhoe, there is evidence for open fields containing ridge and furrow in the late medieval period.[20] There is no additional evidence about these fields or their use but it would not seem unreasonable to assume that they were also worked in some communal way, as most fields associated with nucleated villages were. At Westbury, however, quite a different story emerges. Everson's detailed survey of the earthworks draws attention to evidence for 'ploughing of a medieval type *within* crofts and closes' (my emphasis).[21] Everson comments that 'no two or three large open common fields are revealed in the documentation, and it seems probable that if open arable fields existed ... they were both small and numerous.'[22]

These contrasts in farming practices between Great Linford and Tattenhoe on the one hand and Westbury on the other suggest differences in the constitution of peasant communities at these three sites. The residents of non-nucleated settlements such as Westbury certainly would have needed to employ some agreement between neighbours to effect satisfactory field management.[23] It is widely accepted, however, that the classic open-field agricultural system in which each tenant held strips in scattered fields would have necessitated and reproduced a strong sense of village community – the practices of negotiation between adjacent strip-holders, as well as the familiarity gained by working side-by-side in

20. Ivens *et al.*, *Tattenhoe and Westbury*, pp. 26, 38.
21. Ibid., p. 80.
22. Ibid., pp. 82–3.
23. Dyer, 'Dispersed settlements', p. 113.

all weathers, would have forged a strong communal bond.[24] Ingold has argued that 'in the resonance of movement and feeling stemming from people's mutually attentive engagement in shared contexts of practical activity, lies the very foundation of sociality'.[25] This suggests that social interaction would have been more intense at Tattenhoe and Great Linford, where work in the communal open fields would have provided a constant 'shared context of practical activity', than at Westbury, where a limited quantity of such sharing occurred. The different farming practices we see in these three proximate medieval settlements, therefore, alert us to differences in the practices and experiences of community.

Intra-site variability

Turning back to the remains of the settlements themselves, there is further evidence of variation between both individual crofts and houses within each settlement. In Great Linford, all of the excavated medieval houses were remarkably unvarying in their construction, with walls largely being the same thickness (*c.* 0.5m), and displayed consistent dimensions – most were 5 to 5.5m (16 to 18 feet) in width, were comprised of bays of a uniform length and were associated with external cobbled surfaces.[26] The crofts, too, which expanded along the south side of the green in the late twelfth century, were all of similar size, averaging 39m wide and 135m deep (128 by 443 feet). By contrast, the crofts at Tattenhoe varied in size and were arranged in an irregular fashion.[27] But *within* them (four out of eight were excavated) all were much the same in layout and shape, being more or less rectangular, often defined by ditches and contained rectangular timber buildings facing small cobbled surfaces.[28]

Westbury presents us with a very different situation. Crofts here varied significantly in size and shape.[29] For example, Croft 15B, which dates to the late thirteenth century, was 25m north–south by 48m east–west (82 by 157 feet), while Croft 17, which belongs to a similar period, measured at least 98m north–south by 57m east–west (321 by 187 feet). Similarly, the positioning of buildings within individual crofts varied quite considerably, with structures found in the corners of crofts, along edges and placed centrally; courtyard and T-shaped forms were also in evidence.[30]

24. For example, P.R. Schofield, *Peasant and community in medieval England* (Basingstoke, 2003), p. 72.
25. T. Ingold, 'The temporality of the landscape', reprinted in J. Thomas (ed.), *Interpretive archaeology: a reader* (London, 2000 [1994]), p. 518.
26. Mynard *et al.*, *Great Linford*, p. 50.
27. Ivens *et al.*, *Tattenhoe and Westbury*, p. 11.
28. Ibid., pp. 50–1.
29. Ibid., pp. 213–14.
30. Ibid., p. 215.

We can see that peasants at Great Linford would have lived in an environment in which all members of the community resided in fundamentally similar-looking houses, whereas at Westbury such dwellings were markedly heterogeneous in appearance. These contrasts would have effected a difference in these peasants' experience of community as the knowledge created by encounters with the material world at each settlement varied.[31] At Great Linford, the spaces and houses of the village spoke of similarity and cohesion and thereby the sense of a collective. At Westbury, by contrast, the materiality of the settlement evoked a quite different world – of household distinctiveness, separation and perhaps independence from the forces of community.

Change over time

In addition to variation in both general topography (in terms of dispersion and nucleation) and settlement layout, the temporal dynamics of these settlements appears to have varied and this would also have affected the inhabitants' experience of community.

Great Linford developed steadily from the late twelfth to the early fourteenth century with regular crofts on the east side of the main street being laid out over this period. During the fourteenth and fifteenth centuries various small changes took place, although 'most of the excavated crofts appear to have been continuously occupied until the mid–late seventeenth century'.[32] The impression given by a comparison of the reconstructions of the village from the late twelfth and early fourteenth centuries with the pre-enclosure estate map of 1641 is of slow growth and small changes occurring within a fairly regular pattern.

The evidence for morphological change at Tattenhoe differs from that at Great Linford. In the late thirteenth century the settlement underwent a major reorganisation in which the primary field boundaries were laid out and the nucleated settlement was established, replacing an early settlement which was perhaps polyfocal but for which there is little evidence.[33] What is particularly striking about the nucleated village is that, of the crofts that were excavated, 'little or no development [occurred] within [them] … over time and they appear to have remained very much as established until their abandonment'.[34] All the crofts seem to have been laid out at one time and experienced almost no subsequent modification.[35]

31. See J.C. Barrett, 'Agency, the duality of structure and the problem of the archaeological record', in I. Hodder (ed.), *Archaeological theory today* (Cambridge, 2001), pp. 141–64.
32. Mynard *et al.*, *Great Linford*, p. 17.
33. Ivens *et al.*, *Tattenhoe and Westbury*, p. 24.
34. Ibid., p. 28.
35. Ibid., p. 47.

The situation at Westbury was, again, very different, and a 'dynamic of property creation and abandonment' is apparent here, a dynamic which involved, among other things, changes in land use.[36] Crofts often overlay former ridge and furrow, which was the case, for example, with Croft 3, which expanded to encompass both another croft (Croft 2) and ridge and furrow to the east and north during the mid thirteenth to mid fourteenth century.[37] Similarly, at some point between the fourteenth and sixteenth centuries Croft 6B expanded over an existing trackway, and there are numerous other examples of late medieval crofts overlying ridge and furrow or incorporating previously existing crofts.[38] The crofts themselves at Westbury were also remarkably dynamic and changeable. For example, it was very quickly after Crofts 4 and 5 were established in *c.* 1250–1350 that one of them (Croft 5) was abandoned. Similarly Croft 7, which was probably laid out in the mid fourteenth century, had grown sufficiently by the early sixteenth century to absorb both Crofts 8 and 9.[39] Similar dynamism can be seen in another area of the site (Division 2), which is illustrated in Figure 5.3 (late medieval phases are *c.* 1250–1600). As a whole, Westbury was a settlement which displayed enormous fluidity and mutability, where major reorganisations seem to have occurred at fifty- or sixty-year intervals. This volatile character is in strong contrast to Tattenhoe and the other Milton Keynes villages that have been excavated.[40]

What do these differences in the stability of the settlements and the amount of changeability tell us about peasant experience of community? Variety in medieval settlement morphology is most commonly discussed by historians and archaeologists in terms of *initiative* – who drove settlements along their trajectory towards nucleation or dispersion, lords or peasants?[41] The Tattenhoe excavators encapsulate this concern when they state that, in the replanning of the settlement, 'it is difficult not to see the hand of some authority at work',[42] although 'it could ... have been a lower level decision made by the vill'.[43] This concern with initiative is consistent with medieval rural archaeology's preoccupation with the *origins* of both villages and field systems, rather than with any social meanings their features may allow us to identify.

36. *Ibid.*, p. 82.
37. *Ibid.*, p. 17.
38. *Ibid.*, p. 114.
39. *Ibid.*, p. 85.
40. *Ibid.*, p. 214.
41. For example, Dyer, 'Power and conflict'; C. Lewis, P. Mitchell-Fox and C. Dyer, *Village, hamlet and field. Changing medieval settlements in central England* (Macclesfield, 1997); C. Taylor, *Village and farmstead: a history of rural settlement in England* (London, 1983); P.D.A. Harvey, 'Initiative and authority in settlement change', in M. Aston, D. Austin and C. Dyer (eds), *The rural settlements of medieval England* (Oxford, 1989), pp. 31–43.
42. Ivens *et al.*, *Tattenhoe and Westbury*, p. 47.
43. *Ibid.*, p. 213.

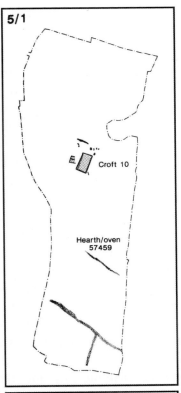

5/1

Croft 10

Hearth/oven
57459

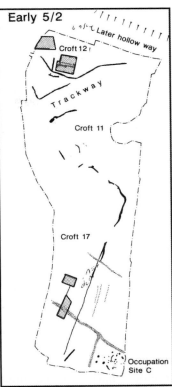

Early 5/2

Later hollow way

Croft 12

Trackway

Croft 11

Croft 17

Occupation
Site C

Figure 5.3 Development of
Division 2 at Westbury (adapted
from Ivens *et al.*, *Tattenhoe and
Westbury* and reproduced by
permission of the
Buckinghamshire
Archaeological Society).
5/1: 10th–early 13th centuries
5/2: mid 13th–mid 14th
   centuries
5/3 mid 14th–16th centuries

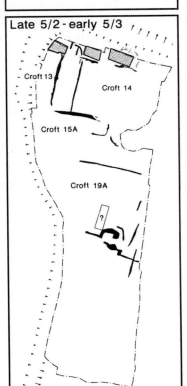

Late 5/2 - early 5/3

Croft 13

Croft 14

Croft 15A

Croft 19A

?

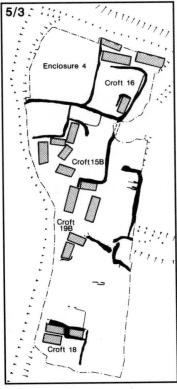

5/3

Enclosure 4

Croft 16

Croft 15B

Croft
19B

Croft 18

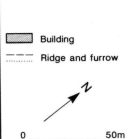

Building

Ridge and furrow

N

0   50m

What we can say is that there was a significant amount of variation in the fluidity and dynamism of the three settlements under consideration – ranging from Tattenhoe, in which crofts seemed unchanging for up to two centuries, to Westbury, in which major organisational change appears to have occurred every fifty to sixty years.[44] Clearly these differences can be explained in various ways, including, possibly, variation in lordship; but, in addition, many different experiential effects would have arisen from them. As an example of one such effect, let us consider the evidence of paths. Tilley has pointed out the way in which the greater the number of people who share the 'purpose' of a path, the more important the path becomes and the more it is able to create a sense of linear order.[45] Late medieval peasants at Tattenhoe trod the same paths as their parents, and would doubtless have expected their children to do the same. The sense of the longevity and 'embedded-ness' of the social order created by these paths, therefore – of the relationships reflected and produced by the settlement's spatial relationships of which the paths were a part – would surely have been greater here than at Westbury. In addition, we know how important local geography as a structure of remembrance for peasants was at this time; the mutability of such places would, therefore, have affected inter-generational memory and the accompanying sense of community.[46] At Tattenhoe, the continuity of what could reasonably be considered to be 'the village community' would have been strong (as it would also have been at Great Linford to some degree) but the dynamism of the settlement at Westbury would have made such a sense much weaker there.

Four aspects of these settlements have been considered here – general morphology, evidence for agricultural practices, extent of intra-site variability and degree of temporal dynamism. Dyer has previously noted that community is likely to have been weaker in medieval dispersed settlement.[47] Similarly, Roberts has argued that it is only in nucleated settlement that all the forces of 'communality' would have been operative.[48] It is clear that the evidence from the Milton Keynes settlements outlined here supports these statements insofar as distinctions between Great Linford and Tattenhoe (nucleated or semi-nucleated settlements) on the one hand and Westbury (a dispersed settlement) on the other

44. *Ibid.*, p. 47.
45. C. Tilley, *A phenomenology of landscape: places, paths and monuments* (Oxford, 1994).
46. J. Bedell, 'Memory and proof of age in England 1272–1327', *Past and Present*, 162 (1999), pp. 3–27; J. Fentress and C. Wickham, *Social memory* (Oxford, 1992), pp. 112–13.
47. Dyer, *Hanbury*, p. 48.
48. B.K. Roberts, 'Nucleation and dispersion: towards an explanation', *Medieval Village Research Group Annual Report*, 31 (1983), pp. 44–5.

are apparent.

Unlike historians and historical geographers, archaeologists have only rarely utilised their evidence to comment on peasant community, and those who have done so have tended to stress the way that village layout and other aspects of peasant material culture *bolstered* a peasant sense of cohesion and corporate identity.[49] While this might be the case in some villages, the universality of these conclusions can be disputed. The examples outlined here demonstrate both the specific ways in which the material world contributed to variations in the peasant experience of community (to which Dyer and others have pointed) and also that a real patchwork of such experiences and understandings of social life could exist within a small geographical area.

Houses and households

The second half of this paper considers the excavated houses of these three settlements. The relevant archaeological material will be described first, and then the possible meanings of the evidence will be discussed.

Hearths

Hearths are very commonly found during the excavation of medieval peasant buildings and therefore it is important to consider the meanings they may have represented and helped construct. It must first be noted that it is my intention here to comment on peasant *houses* – that is, their domestic structures. Attributing function to medieval peasant buildings, however, is notoriously difficult – buildings changed function throughout their lives, from agricultural or industrial to domestic. Consequently, diagnostic features such as hearths and byre drains may be robbed out and so forth. A fairly standard method used to deal with these uncertainties is to assume that the presence of a hearth, if not associated with significant evidence that suggests an agricultural or industrial function (such as large amounts of slag or carbonised grain residues), indicates that the building in question, at least at some point during its life, fulfilled a domestic function.[50] While not infallible, it is the method followed here.[51] The settlement of Tattenhoe produced solid evidence for the position of a hearth in only one building, so the

49. M. Johnson, *An archaeology of capitalism* (Oxford, 1996), p. 76; D.A. Hinton, *Archaeology, economy and society: England from the fifth to the fifteenth century* (London, 1990).
50. For example, Ivens et al., *Tattenhoe and Westbury*, p. 215.

subsequent discussion will focus on the evidence from Great Linford and Westbury.

Information exists about the location of hearths in approximately nine buildings from the thirteenth, fourteenth and fifteenth centuries at Great Linford. These hearths tended to be made of stone or limestone slabs. While some of these hearths do occupy central positions – at least centrally within a bay (for example, Building 3 in Croft A, Building 8 in Croft C and Building 17 in Croft F) – variety exists even in this small dataset. Two hearths backed on to cross-passages (Building 5 Croft B and Building 16 Croft F), one was located along a wall (Building 22 Croft H) and one was positioned in the south-east corner of the bay (Building 12 Croft D). It is even possible that one building had three hearths and an oven in its central 'hall' room, although the function of this building (Building 27) is debated.[52]

At Westbury the position of hearths is known from approximately eleven buildings, all but one of which dates to the mid fourteenth to sixteenth century. It is worth outlining the evidence from these in tabular form, so that the variation may become clear (Table 5.1). It must be borne in mind that not all buildings were excavated completely so that it is always possible that additional hearths may have been in use in these buildings. Throughout the period hearth position, number and construction clearly exhibited a very large amount of variation.[53] Bearing this in mind, let us turn to other features of the excavated houses in these three settlements.

51. So, for example, Building 53513 in Croft 7C at Westbury was not considered to have a domestic function despite the presence of a hearth owing to its small size and very narrow doorway, features which led to this building being interpreted as a workshop. Also note that the very interesting 'pot hearths' that were found throughout this site have also not been considered to be domestic features and therefore their presence has not been sufficient to categorise a building as 'domestic'. This is because pottery analysts pointed out that similar structures at West Cotton had been interpreted as being associated with non-domestic functions such as dyeing or fulling. See Ivens et al., *Tattenhoe and Westbury*, p. 271.

52. Mynard et al., *Great Linford*, pp. 88, 125.

53. Hearth position has often been understood by students of vernacular architecture in chronological terms. It is thought that increasingly sophisticated methods developed to manage smoke that led to the replacement of the central hearth by, initially, hearths which were positioned alongside a cross-passage or wall below a smoke bay or a smoke hood, before developing over time into fully fledged internal chimneys. See R.W. Brunskill, *Traditional buildings of Britain: an introduction to vernacular architecture* (London, 1981), pp. 101–2; E. Mercer, *English vernacular houses: a study of traditional farmhouses and cottages* (London, 1975), pp. 20–1; J. Grenville, *Medieval housing* (London, 1997), p. 146. Such a chronological distinction, however, does not appear to explain the range of variation we see in all aspects of hearth construction from these three settlements.

Table 5.1 Details of hearths from excavated buildings at Westbury, Bucks.

Building Ref	Number of hearths	Hearth construction	Hearth position within building
55820 (Croft 3C)	5	Burnt areas	Near centre
55864 (Croft 3C)	1	Limestone roof slate	Just east of doorway
50782/50765 (Croft 3C)	1	Burnt area	Near centre (in terms of width of building; length of both buildings unknown)
55822 (Croft 4)	5	1 pot hearth, 4 burnt areas	1 hearth located in southern bay (burnt area) not central – 'random' position 4 in northern bay scattered across building. 3 'burnt area' hearths appear to form a line
53542 (Croft 8)	1	Mix of potsherds and burnt cobbles. Regular sides	Near to or against north wall
52261 (Croft 9)	3	1 mix of potsherds and burnt cobbles with regular sides 2 pot hearths	'Marginal position' but precise location unclear
53515 (Croft 7C)	3	1 area of red clay (first phase of building) 1 pit with limestone block base (second phase of building) 1 selection of limestone slabs	Not central – 'random' position Not central – 'random' position Central
77005 (Croft 7C)	1	Tightly packed and reddened small stones	When in use, probably central
57409 (Croft 18)	1	Oven structure	Central
59602 (Croft 20)	2	1 pot hearth 1 single large sandstone block with kerb	N/A Not central – 'random' position

Building longevity

One of the most striking differences between the houses at these three settlements is their archaeological visibility. At Great Linford, the local stone was used extensively in house construction (Figure 5.4).[54] All of the houses had limestone rubble-built walls that were mostly about 0.5m wide but were sometimes as thick as 0.8m (as in Building 5 Croft B), and their layout was therefore very clear. In sharp contrast, the houses at Tattenhoe and Westbury were often identifiable only as gaps in cobbled yards, or through the presence of drainage ditches or lines of postholes – at the very best, the occasional stone plinth appears. While these are contrasts obvious to the archaeologist, we must be cautious in assigning them too much meaning when considering peasant experience. From the perspective of their inhabitants, the differences in construction may have been fairly immaterial. While the bases of the walls at Great Linford are clearly visible to us today, the

54. Mynard *et al.*, *Great Linford*, p. 3.

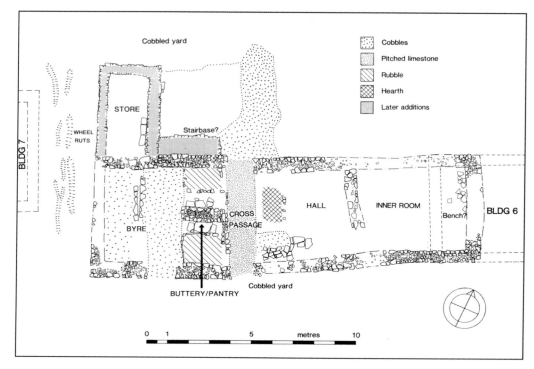

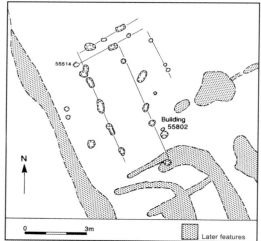

Figure 5.4 Contrasting archaeological remains of houses at Great Linford (above) and Westbury (below) (reproduced by permission of the Buckinghamshire Archaeological Society).

superstructures consisted of timber framing and wattle and daub infill, and timber framing was similarly used at Tattenhoe and Westbury.[55] Contemporaries probably would have hardly noticed the material on which these walls rested, however different they appear to us.

While the materials themselves may not be of much significance in our investigation of peasant experience, there does appear to be a potentially meaningful difference in the longevity of the buildings at these sites. The excavators of Westbury noted that 'from the middle of the thirteenth century there was a great expansion in the size of the settlement and over the following 150 years the site [underwent] repeated changes and developments ... Such reorganisations were noted right across the excavated settlement but are most clearly seen in Division 2'; these are illustrated in Figure 5.3,[56] which demonstrates that from the middle of the thirteenth century to, at the very maximum, the early sixteenth century (a 250-year period) three very different configurations involving the appearance and disappearance of a variety of buildings can be observed at this site.[57] In fact no house remained in use throughout all of these three 'versions' of Division 2.[58] A similar situation is observed in the development of another area of this site, Crofts 1 to 3. Here, within the same 250 years, we see four different configurations during two of which no buildings were in use at all.[59] One building (in Croft 2) was definitely domestic, while the function of that in Croft 1 could not be determined. Neither was extant in the latter part of this period, so they only survived for approximately fifty years.

The evidence regarding the longevity of the houses at Tattenhoe is inconclusive. The excavators note that the modification to one of the excavated structures might suggest that they were relatively long-lived but also wrote that 'given the character of the surviving remains it is possible for a complete rebuild to have occurred leaving no structural trace of its predecessor'.[60]

In contrast to the situation at Westbury, Great Linford houses appear to have been occupied over long periods of time. Here, while buildings certainly

55. Ibid., p. 50.
56. Note that the building in the west of Division 2, while being on the same site in Croft 12 as in 13, was not the same structure (ibid., pp. 141, 145). It must also be noted that even if all houses in 5/3 were occupied throughout this entire period, it is only of 150 years' duration.
57. Ivens et al., Tattenhoe and Westbury, p. 177.
58. In making this statement, I confront the same problems of attributing a 'domestic' function to these buildings as mentioned above. While the building in Croft 13 was definitely domestic, a typical comment on the structures in this area is as follows: 'It may be that all of these buildings were agricultural barns, stables and so forth... [but] houses or specialised craft-shops ... are possible explanations': ibid., p. 144.
59. The earliest evidence for medieval occupation at this site was Period 5 Phase 2.
60. Ivens et al., Tattenhoe and Westbury, p. 47.

underwent alteration and modification, the primary structures were often occupied for centuries. For example, Building 5 in Croft B dated from the fourteenth century and continued in use into the third quarter of the seventeenth century – a period of approximately 300 years.[61] Similarly, Building 8 in Croft C was constructed in the middle of the fourteenth century and continued in use until the seventeenth.[62] The main period of use of Building 10 in Croft E stretched from the twelfth to the fifteenth century,[63] while Building 12 in Croft D was probably constructed in the thirteenth century[64] and continued in use until the seventeenth century – some 400 years. [65]

It is possible to suggest, therefore, that there was a significant difference between the longevity of the domestic buildings of Great Linford and Westbury, with many buildings in the latter settlement being in use for no longer than half a century (with 150 years being the very maximum length of use for others) while those at Great Linford were in use for much longer periods.[66]

Spatial differentiation

Finally, and perhaps most tentatively, it may be possible to suggest that differentiation in domestic space varied most markedly between the two settlements of Westbury and Great Linford. This contrast is not as stark as that connected to length of use and it is important not to overstress the point, largely because it is very difficult to make positive statements about the internal arrangements of the houses at Westbury owing to the nature of the soils and building materials. The excavators merely commented that 'a characteristic of many of the buildings is opposed doorways in the long sides which so often marks

---

61. Mynard *et al.*, *Great Linford*, p. 56.
62. Ibid., p. 60.
63. Ibid., p. 67.
64. Ibid., p. 65.
65. Ibid., p. 63.
66. A shift in opinion about the general longevity of peasant housing has taken place over the last twenty years. Up until the 1980s, it was thought that peasant houses were flimsy and were rebuilt perhaps every generation (e.g. J.G. Hurst, 'A review of archaeological research (to 1968)', in DMVS, pp. 76–144). It is now thought that many were semi-permanent and that the evidence for numerous wall rebuilds does not indicate a lack of robustness of the house itself (e.g. B. Harrison and B. Hutton, *Vernacular houses in North Yorkshire and Cleveland* (Edinburgh, 1984); S. Wrathmell, 'The vernacular threshold of northern peasant households', *Vernacular Architecture*, 15 (1984), pp. 29–33; S. Wrathmell, *Wharram. A study of settlement on the Yorkshire Wolds, VI. Domestic settlements 2: Medieval peasant farmsteads*, York University Publications, 8 (1989); C. Dyer, 'English peasant buildings in the later Middle Ages 1200–1500', *Med. Arch.*, 30 (1986) pp. 19–45). An in-depth discussion of variation in longevity of peasant houses is, however, yet to be done.

the provision of a cross-passage dividing two functionally different ends'.[67] Further divisions could have been maintained, however, by more ephemeral architectural means. The room divisions at Great Linford were, owing to the stone wall bases, much easier to recognise than at Westbury.

However, if we take the archaeology at face value and assume that the major divisions are observable within these houses, there does seem to be a greater differentiation of space at Great Linford than at Westbury. For example, at Great Linford, Building 5 (of the fourteenth century) was a longhouse with a byre, a buttery/pantry, a cross-passage and a hall. Building 26 (according to the most probable reconstruction) comprised a square hall, a cross-passage and another room at the lower end.[68] Building 10 (dating from the twelfth to fifteenth century) consisted of four rooms – a hall, a cross-passage, a kitchen with an oven and a pantry/dairy. Building 6 (Croft F) in its Phase 2 arrangement (dating from the mid–late thirteenth century to the late fourteenth–early fifteenth century) was even more elaborate, consisting of a garderobe, a byre, a cross-passage, a hall and a parlour.

It can be suggested that, while the archaeology admits no distinction to be drawn between the *nature* of the partitions from the point of view of the inhabitants (they were all of timber, those at Great Linford simply having stone bases), there does appear to be some difference in the *number* of the divisions. Given the evidence available, we can only say that many of the houses at Westbury were divided into two rooms, a byre and a domestic end.[69] At Great Linford, on the other hand, many of the excavated houses have evidence for more than this simple division, with examples of butteries, pantries and parlours being present. Domestic spatial differentiation, it seems, was more elaborate here than at Westbury.

The meanings of domestic architecture

Various differences in certain features of the medieval houses both within and between the three settlements under consideration have been noted in the foregoing discussion; such variation is often overlooked by medieval archaeologists. Tringham makes a useful point in this regard: 'In the process of discovering explanatory general principles, individual variability is understood as exceptional and of secondary relevance. In such generalising, the 'microscale' interpretation of house histories … and the small inequalities between

---

67. Ivens *et al.*, *Tattenhoe and Westbury*, p. 215.
68. Mynard *et al.*, *Great Linford*, p. 125.
69. For example, Building 55822. Ivens *et al.*, *Tattenhoe and Westbury*, p. 108.

households ... tend to be undervalued as irrelevant.'[70] A concern with establishing such general principles and an accompanying lack of concern with individual variation between houses is typical of medieval rural archaeology. It is therefore quite possible that many would think that the differences in hearth position, for example, represent only a relatively trivial contrast, and that it is not plausible or useful to attempt to attach much significance to what may have been simply the idiosyncratic choice of medieval people.

Such differences can be argued to have been distinctly non-trivial and should not be subsumed in attempts to seek, for example, functional explanations for regional variation. Many archaeologists as well as researchers in other disciplines have stressed the fundamental importance that domestic space plays in shaping and forming people's ideas about themselves and the world. A key focus of many of these studies is the way in which domestic space replicates and reinforces general classificatory principles. So, for example, Brück writes of Scottish Iron Age houses that 'the categorization and subdivision of space within the buildings perhaps reflects a more general concern with processes of social classification ... social differences were given material form through architecture.'[71] The particular place that houses have in naturalising such classifications and divisions, moreover, has also been seen as tying domestic space intimately into the deployment of power and the maintenance of ideological systems.[72] In addition, wider social cosmologies are also thought to be reflected in the layout of domestic architecture. Anthropologists point out, for example, that hearths are often conceived as pivotal points which may symbolise the centre of the world and cardinal points are also often meaningful, with east/sun/life often being juxtaposed in the symbolism and use of the house with west/dark/death. Modern English homes have similarly been analysed according to these principles, with distinctions being drawn between front/public/'clean' rooms and back/private/'dirty' rooms.[73]

70. R. Tringham, 'Archaeological houses, households, housework and the home', in D.N. Benjamin, D. Stea and D. Saile (eds), *The home: words, interpretations, meanings and environment* (Aldershot, 1995), p. 95.

71. J. Brück, 'The architecture of routine life', in J. Pollard (ed.), *Prehistoric Britain* (Oxford, 2008), p. 262; and see also C.P. Graves, 'Social space in the English medieval parish church', *Economy and Society*, 18 (1989), pp. 297–322; B. Hillier and J. Hanson, *The social logic of space* (Cambridge, 1984).

72. T.L. Sweely, 'Introduction', in idem (ed.), *Manifesting power: gender and the interpretation of power in archaeology* (London, 1999), pp. 1–14; M. Johnson, 'Houses, power and everyday life in early modern England', in J. Maran, C. Juwig, H. Schwengel and U. Thaler (eds), *Constructing power: architecture, ideology and social practice* (Hamburg, 2006), p. 285.

73. For an archaeological discussion of this literature see M. Parker Pearson and C. Richards, *Architecture and order: approaches to social space* (London, 1994). It should be noted that interpretation of archaeological remains according to these kinds of binary divisions has been challenged recently for being too simplistically 'structuralist' — see Brück, 'The architecture' and R. Pope,

Those few archaeologists who have commented on the 'meaning' of the late medieval peasant house have tended to stress the way in which they seemingly display a layout similar to those of elite social groups. This consistency in form is seen to reveal a 'cultural unity', or 'underlying unity', which existed throughout medieval society.[74] Johnson, for example, has suggested that this layout reflected the principles of medieval patriarchy.[75] One of the assumptions inherent in these various statements is that of a basic homogeneity of peasant houses themselves – they are all put into the same category and then compared with and found similar to those of the medieval elite. An example of this tendency can be found in various statements from Johnson: 'the late medieval peasant house in much of England and Wales was centred round a central hall open to the roof';[76] 'peasant households opted *invariably* for a space that was cold, draughty, full of smoke, because of the central importance of what it meant to them and for their view of the world' (my emphasis).[77]

While the general degree of 'sameness' seen to be revealed within any group of buildings is inherently debatable, the houses of the three settlements examined in this essay have revealed clear evidence for variation in the position and construction of hearths, in general longevity and (possibly somewhat less clearly) in the spatial differentiation their layout represented. Given the role that domestic architecture plays in categorisation, the production of ideology and general cosmology, the evidence suggests that medieval peasants experienced a complex array of social understandings of the world. For the occupants at Building 8 at Great Linford, for example, with its very long period of use and central hearth, such understandings may have been associated with the permanence of the family unit or with fundamental conceptual divisions such as 'upper' and 'lower', as suggested by Johnson. But whatever the precise nature of these meanings, they would have been quite different from those produced and reflected by Building

73 (cont)
    'Ritual and the roundhouse: a critique of recent ideas on the use of domestic space in later British prehistory', in C. Haselgrove and R. Pope (eds), *The earlier Iron Age in Britain and the near Continent* (Oxford, 2007), pp. 204–28.

74. Hinton, *Archaeology, economy*, p. 163; M. Gardiner, 'Vernacular buildings and the development of the later medieval domestic plan in England', *Med. Arch.*, 44 (2000), pp. 159–79.

75. M. Johnson, *Housing culture: traditional architecture in an English landscape* (London, 1993), p. 55; Johnson, *Archaeology of capitalism*, p. 81.

76. Johnson, *Archaeology of capitalism*, p. 79.

77. M. Johnson, 'Houses, power', p. 289. Johnson often states that he is referring to 'peasant' houses, as in the quotes above, but at times he also suggests that he is only concerned with the 'middling' sort who occupied surviving standing buildings of the late medieval period. His comments nevertheless comprise the only substantial interpretation of the meaning of any non-elite architecture from late medieval England and are therefore relevant in this context.

53542 at Westbury, with its hearth positioned along the wall and much shorter length of use.

Conclusion

What this essay has attempted to explore and elucidate is the evidence for variation in the social experience of the peasants of late medieval England, particularly in their experiences of their communities and households as viewed through the material evidence. 'Experience' is a difficult concept to pin down definitively when the time period under discussion is manifestly greater than that of one generation – it could be argued that to elide the differences between the 'experiences' of a peasant of the earlier thirteenth and the late fifteenth centuries, for example, is illegitimate. The workable scale of analysis for all archaeologists, however, is dictated by their data to a large degree, so that many prehistorians, for example, will create narratives and interpret past lives on the basis of data encompassing half a millennium or more, while archaeologists of the very recent past can do so with material dated to within a decade. Medieval rural archaeologists usually confront evidence that can be dated to perhaps between fifty years (in the case of some house rebuilds) and a few centuries (in the case of many settlement plans and field systems). It is my contention that it is warranted to attempt to discuss peasant 'experience' within such a timeframe, even if the experience under question was undergone by a number of generations of individuals and will therefore necessarily have varied somewhat between them.

The material evidence from the three settlements under consideration here seems to have expressed and produced very difference experiences of community and household. In drawing this conclusion it is implicit that much archaeological thinking on such topics has been too simplistic and generalising. Instead of envisaging the material world of the medieval peasantry as universally reflecting cohesion, the principles of patriarchy and so on, archaeologists should rather attend to the manifest variety and contrasts in this world and therefore to very real differences in the social lives thus produced and reflected. The evidence from deserted medieval villages has proved invaluable in these researches as in many others.

Acknowledgements

I am most grateful to the editors for inviting me to contribute to this volume and also for their valuable comments on a draft of this paper. I would also like to thank Ilhong Ko for her helpful remarks. The research for this work was undertaken while in receipt of an Irish Research Council for the Humanities and Social Sciences Post-Doctoral Fellowship.

6

Deserted medieval villages and the objects from them

DAVID A. HINTON

In the first serious archaeological examination of a rural settlement abandoned during the later part of the Middle Ages – Woodperry (Oxon.) in the 1830s or 1840s – 'the spade brought to light' several objects sufficiently complete and eye-catching to have been deemed worthy of illustration. A few were misidentified: bone points are now known not to have been arrowheads, for instance, although their precise functions as leather piercers or the like is still ill-defined. Not illustrated was one of the most interesting discoveries, a large complete pottery bowl, found inside the church where 'the altar may be supposed to have stood, and carefully covered with a piece of ashlar stone'.[1]

The early Victorian investigation of the Woodperry deserted village and the objects from it (Figure 6.1) was not followed up. Only in the 1930s were general studies of medieval artefacts pursued, by Ward Perkins, Dunning and others.[2] Excavation at Seacourt (Oxon., but then Berks.) could have renewed interest in an integrated consideration of deserted villages and material culture, but was frustrated by the Second World War and not resumed until the late 1950s.[3] By then, Hurst and Beresford had begun to widen the scope of their project at Wharram Percy (Yorks.) from the quest to date the site's desertion, for which pottery was a crucial indicator, to broader topics about its entire history and the occupants' lifestyles.[4] In the 1950s and 1960s Jope, who excavated the first abandoned rural

1. 'JW' [The Rev. John Wilson], 'Antiquities found at Woodperry, Oxon', Archaeological Journal, 3 (1846), pp. 117–28, at 119; see C. Gerrard, Medieval archaeology. Understanding traditions and contemporary approaches (London, 2003), pp. 49–50. The claim that this was the first deserted medieval village excavation rests on Wilson's reference on p. 117 to 'the search for a church, churchyard, and village', which implies something more than observations of what labourers turned up. Most of the objects are still in the Ashmolean Museum.
2. Gerrard, Medieval archaeology, pp. 43–51, 72–4.
3. R.L.S. Bruce-Mitford, 'The excavations at Seacourt, Berkshire. An interim report', Oxoniensia, 5 (1940), pp. 31–41.
4. Chronicled in M. Beresford and J. Hurst, Wharram Percy deserted medieval village (London, 1990), pp. 27–38.

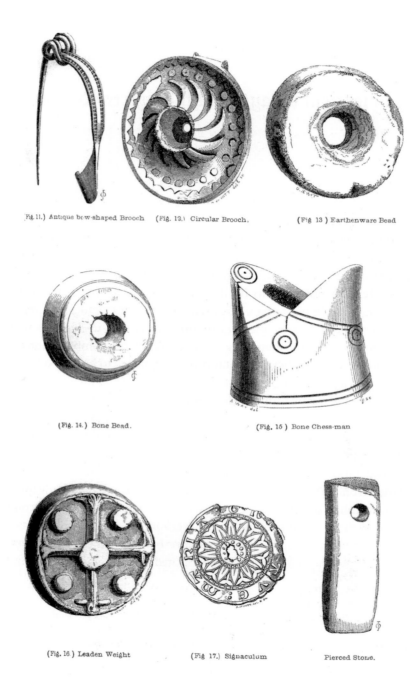

Fig. 11.) Antique bow-shaped Brooch   (Fig. 12.) Circular Brooch.   (Fig 13) Earthenware Bead

(Fig. 14.) Bone Bead.   (Fig. 15) Bone Chess-man

(Fig. 16.) Leaden Weight   (Fig 17.) Signaculum   Pierced Stone.

Figure 6.1 Miscellaneous objects found during excavations at Woodperry (Oxon.), as illustrated in the *Archaeological Journal*. The brooch is Roman, the 'beads' are probably spindle-whorls, and the 'pierced stone' a hone. The chess piece is correctly identified.

site, Beere (Devon), to be published in *Medieval Archaeology*, wrote a number of essays investigating the possibility of recognising different regional cultures through the distribution of artefacts, notably pottery.[5] Thirty-five years ago, in his masterly but brief summary of the importance of artefacts in rural studies, Hurst did not discuss regionalism, only dating problems, trade and craft activity; indeed, he touched on social significance only in reviewing the ratios and quality of glazed wares.[6] He and others had already noted the implications of such items as keys in suggesting that peasants had property that was worth protecting behind locked doors and in chests, and the possibly limited role of artificial lighting indicated by the paucity of cresset lamps or candle-holders; more excavations have added new examples, but have not affected his interpretations.[7]

New methods of using pottery on deserted sites were applied in the 1980s by both Moorhouse and Wrathmell, who used sherd scatters to reveal different activity areas, the latter showing at Wharram Percy how buildings needed to be reinterpreted in the light of such evidence.[8] In another summary statement some years later, Jope, as Wrathmell reminds us, had left open the door to the study of social groupings.[9] Recognition of the expression of identity by the different stratified ranks in medieval society has been pursued, but remains one reason for further work on artefacts to be undertaken.

Some issues with the data

One factor that may have caused some medieval rural sites to have been abandoned while others were maintained is their relative poverty; it is unlikely that this could ever be demonstrated in the material record, not least because large-scale excavation of the sites that remained functioning is rarely possible, except in

5. E.M. Jope and R.I. Threlfall, 'Excavation of a medieval settlement at Beere, North Tawton, Devon', *Med. Arch.*, 2 (1958), pp. 112–40; E.M. Jope, 'The regional cultures of medieval Britain', in I.L.L. Foster and L. Alcock (eds), *Culture and environment. Essays in honour of Cyril Fox* (London, 1963), pp. 327–50; the example of vernacular architecture was provided by S.E. Rigold in what was published rather derogatorily as an 'Appendix' to Jope's paper, pp. 351–4.
6. J.G. Hurst, 'A review of archaeological research (to 1968)', in DMVS, pp. 76–144, at 140–4.
7. The contrast in lamp numbers with the properties used by academics in Oxford has been made recently by A. Norton and G. Cockin, 'Excavations at the Classics Centre, 65–7 St Giles, Oxford', *Oxoniensia*, 73 (2008), pp. 161–94, at 168–73.
8. S. Wrathmell, *Wharram. A study of settlement on the Yorkshire Wolds, VI. Domestic settlements 2: Medieval peasant farmsteads*, York University Publications, 8 (1989), pp. 13–40; S. Moorhouse, 'The non-dating uses of medieval pottery', *Medieval Ceramics*, 10 (1986), pp. 85–124 (on Sandal Castle, Yorkshire).
9. S. Wrathmell, 'Rural settlements in medieval England: perspectives and perceptions', in B. Vyner (ed.), *Building on the past*, Royal Archaeological Institute (London, 1994), pp. 178–99.

certain areas.[10] Test- and shovel-pit sampling can be invaluable in revealing periods of occupation, and may produce occasional objects of individual interest, but has to be very comprehensive to produce material in sufficient, adequately stratified quantity to be fully representative and comparable with assemblages from sites in fields, where open-area excavation is possible.[11] Even 'rescue' work in existing villages tends to be too limited. In any case, a more meaningful overview of the importance of artefacts can be obtained from a consideration not only of excavations but also of material from fieldwalking and metal-detection.

Because medieval farmers knew full well the value of manure, most of the rubbish that accumulated in the middens outside their houses and barns ended up spread on the surrounding fields rather than deposited in pits. Once the early Anglo-Saxon period ended sunken-featured buildings all but disappeared, and with them another valuable source of accumulations, as their hollows were filled with sometimes copious quantities of animal bones, loomweights, broken pottery and spindlewhorls. Even then, of course, the record is biased; depending on soil conditions, animal bones make assessment of meat consumption possible in ways that tiny residues of charred grains will never allow for the cereal component of the diet. Similarly, organic materials other than bone – wood, textiles, horn, leather – are much less likely to be retrieved than pottery or stone tools. Metal objects were subject to recycling as well as to deterioration, and Egan has argued that soil conditions often make lead even more susceptible to decay than iron.[12] Nevertheless, something of the lives and ambitions of the medieval peasants, whether bond or free in status, ought to have been expressed at least in part by the goods on which they chose to spend some of their money, and ought to be at least in part recognisable in the surviving physical record.

10. West Whelpington, for instance, in the northern uplands, was used well beyond the Middle Ages: D.H. Evans and M.G. Jarrett, 'The deserted village of West Whelpington, Northumberland: third report, part one', *Archaeologia Aeliana*, 15 (1987), pp. 199–308; D.H. Evans, M.G. Jarrett and S. Wrathmell, 'The deserted village of West Whelpington, Northumberland: third interim report, part two', *Archaeologia Aeliana*, 16 (1988), pp. 139–92. Note also how Wrathmell argues for a later abandonment of Wharram Percy in the present volume; any argument based on its 'poverty' in the High Middle Ages would now be suspect. The potential of sites emparked in the eighteenth century is a possibility mooted but not yet much pursued: C. Gerrard, 'Not all archaeology is rubbish; the elusive life histories of three artefacts from Shapwick, Somerset', in M. Costen (ed.), *People and places. Essays in honour of Mick Aston* (Oxford, 2007), pp. 166–80, at 170–1.
11. C. Lewis, 'New avenues for the investigation of currently occupied medieval rural settlement: preliminary observations from the Higher Education Field Academy', *Med. Arch.*, 51 (2007), pp. 133–63. A. Gutiérrez, 'The pottery', in C. Gerrard with M. Aston, *The Shapwick project, Somerset. A rural landscape explored*, SMAMS, 25 (2007), pp. 601–700, at 602–8 for ratios from different collection methods less than 1 per cent came from back gardens and shovel pits.
12. G. Egan, 'Urban and rural finds: material culture of country and town, *c.* 1050–1200', in K. Giles and C. Dyer (eds), *Town and country in the Middle Ages*, SMAMS, 22 (2005), pp. 197–210, at 198–9.

Even terminology creates potential difficulties: the word 'peasants', for instance, may not be appropriate for the beginnings of the medieval period, since the immediate post-Roman systems of social exploitation are not really known. The sunken-featured buildings may have been used by people who were grouped in families within small-scale tribal groups rather than being controlled by a lord. Certainly it has been remarked that the quantities of seemingly valuable things found on these early sites vary from one site to another, but it has been suggested recently that this may be biased by some at least of the building hollows having had some special things deliberately placed in them.[13] It is also problematic to assume that the peasants, of whom it is probably true to speak from at least the later seventh century, had 'money' to spend, rather than to hoard for rent and tithe payments.[14] Even though for many the low wages and high rents of the thirteenth century became high wages and low rents in the second half of the fourteenth, subsistence needs must still have been a constraint.

The difference between the archaeological and the documentary databases is that the former is growing – which is not to deny that many documents, such as manorial court records, are still effectively as hidden while lying unpublished in various archives as are unexcavated deserted settlements. Publishing an excavation may be likened to publishing a lay subsidy roll. But what has changed in the archaeological record is the huge increase in finds resulting from the boom in metal-detecting. This is most graphically demonstrated by coins: even in urban excavations, few are found; churches often yield one or two, but it is not unusual for a rural site to have none at all. In the 1960s Rigold recognised that, despite the small numbers of single finds, an increasing quantity could be charted through the twelfth and thirteenth centuries, followed by a decline in the fourteenth and fifteenth. Of course, some of the rural sites from which coins were excavated had been deserted, so by definition they would not have yielded finds subsequent to their abandonment, but the overall pattern of loss was not different at towns or churches. Later analysis by Dyer showed the same trends.[15] Excavations of all sites yielded such small numbers, however, that they could be used to suggest little everyday handling of coins by medieval people generally, despite the records of mint output and the occasional large hoard.

The metal-detecting revolution has not significantly changed the overall

---

13. H. Hamerow, '"Special deposits" in Anglo-Saxon settlements', *Med. Arch.*, 50 (2006), pp. 1–30. The early and mid Anglo-Saxon settlements of which so many have been excavated should be seen as 'deserted', like later sites, but are not further considered in this paper.
14. By then, landlords can be identified in charters, and legal terminology of *thegns* and *ceorls* implies a land-holding class above farmer-producers.
15. C. Dyer, 'Peasants and coins: the uses of money in the Middle Ages', *British Numismatic Journal*, 67 (1997), pp. 30–47.

pattern of peaks and troughs in the numbers found, nor the ratios of finds from different types of site: practitioners can rarely work in towns, although the Thames Mudlarks have retrieved much of London's detritus by working on the foreshore and in wasteland where rubble from the city has been taken and dumped. Church sites are either unavailable because they are still in use or because they are Scheduled Ancient Monuments on which no-one will admit to having detected. Rather, it is the quantities that are remarkable, particularly since nearly all have been retrieved from fields rather than settlements. Reports to the Portable Antiquities Scheme are in the hundreds. Precise identification is often difficult, but, even allowing for uncertainty over some of the attributions to particular reigns, the totals when counted in 2005 were impressive. Metal detectors' finds dated to the thirty years at the end of the twelfth century average about nine coins for each year, compared with thirty coins found for each year in 1270–1300. There is then a marked downturn, to as few as three per annum by the end of the fourteenth century.

As Dyer pointed out, the metal-detected finds are casual losses; he thought that most of them were losses from settlements, be they now deserted or not, spread with manuring. It seems likely enough that it was not uncommon to set out for work with a penny or two on the person; court cases involving robbery suggest that people really did have valuables on them, such as the boy sent out with a gold ring round his neck to relieve his poor sight; unsurprisingly, it was stolen. Even a gold ring was not necessarily of great value, however; thefts put them at sums like 2s, or even as low as 6d – perhaps two days' wage for a man.[16] The Portable Antiquities Scheme is again confirming what these records indicated, that precious-metal finger rings were certainly not uncommon, and perhaps surprisingly were almost as often of gold as of silver – which was often gilded to gloss over its real nature. The *Treasure Annual Report* 2005/6 attributes forty-three gold rings to the twelfth to sixteenth centuries, against sixty-three silver and silver-gilt.[17] Finger rings cannot be closely dated in most cases: clasped hands, presumably to symbolise marriage, and stirrup shapes set with small stones can be twelfth century but still appear in hoards in the fifteenth. Iconographic and inscribed 'posy' rings seem unlikely to date from earlier than the late fourteenth century, however, and the *Report* includes twelve of the former and fifteen of the latter, as well as a number of other rings attributed to the fifteenth century. This suggests that the decline in coin loss after the mid fourteenth century is not directly mirrored in other precious-metal objects. Most base-metal finds, such as

16. D.A. Hinton, *Gold and gilt, pots and pins. Possessions and people in medieval Britain* (Oxford, 2005), p. 197.

17. Department for Culture, Media and Sport, *Treasure Annual Report* 2005/6 (London, 2008), pp. 114–25.

the large numbers of small buckle frames being recovered, are not datable even within the broad limits ascribed to finger rings, so cannot be usefully quantified. Later medieval seal-dies, however, seem to be found in increasing numbers, much as would be expected from the numbers of seals attached to thirteenth-century and later documents.[18]

An objection to the use of casual finds in research is of course that in no case can there be certainty about the owner at the time of loss – some items may have been owned by aristocrats exercising hunting rights over tenants' fields, for instance. Deserted village excavations are rarely on tenements whose occupiers are known by name, but at least the loser is likely to have been an immediately local inhabitant, not a traveller. The group of five silver coins found in a niche in a drystone wall at the excavated upland deserted village at West Whelpington (Northumberland) is especially interesting in this respect, as it is most unlikely to be anything other than a cache hidden by the building's occupant early in the fourteenth century, at that time and in that area very probably because of Scottish raids. So even someone in a fairly marginal settlement had a few coins to hide. The entire site yielded only three medieval coins as casual losses, none after 1327, evidence that is taken as a sign of the site's decline thereafter, although the national coin-loss pattern now shows that, on its own, that would not be considered sufficient evidence.[19] No other site has produced a hoard like that, the only other 'concentration' of wealth at a deserted site being a gold quarter-noble of c. 1370 found on the floor of a building at Gomeldon (Wilts.).[20] Neither West Whelpington nor Gomeldon seems to have had a manor house, so no problem arises of mislaid coins or discarded rubbish from a markedly superior household intermingling with that of toft-holders, which cannot be certain in many village contexts.

Evidence of beliefs and customs

A piece of thirteenth-century blue glass from a gilded bottle probably made in Corinth, found during the excavation of Seacourt in 1958, remains a unique discovery. Harden, its original publisher, speculated that it had contained 'some rich Arabic scent' brought back by a crusader for his 'lady-love'; putting to one side the gender implication – a man was at least as likely to have wanted the scent

18. P.D.A. Harvey and A. McGuinness, *A guide to British medieval seals* (London, 1996), pp. 77–81. It should be noted that there are geographical biases in the Portable Antiquities Scheme: J. Naylor and J.D. Richards, 'Detecting the past', MSRGAR, 20 (2005), pp. 19–24.
19. Evans and Jarrett, 'West Whelpington', pp. 254–5; Evans et al., 'West Whelpington', pp. 142, 190.
20. J. Musty and D.J. Algar, 'Excavations at the deserted medieval village of Gomeldon, near Salisbury', *Wiltshire Archaeological and Natural History Magazine*, 80 (1986), pp. 127–69 at 142.

for himself – this did not account for its arrival at a peasant site. Seacourt probably had a manor house, which was not excavated, and one possibility therefore could be that the glass, perhaps already broken, filtered down the social scale as a curiosity. In the twelfth and thirteenth centuries, however, the manor was held by a minor family, perhaps little more likely than their tenants to have owned such an exotic thing as a scent container. Tyson has suggested that it did not get to Seacourt as a whole bottle, but was already broken, having caught someone's eye on a rubbish dump elsewhere. As only one other fragment of glass of this type has been recorded in England, however, the chance that it had been casually discarded somewhere like a castle socially more likely to have occupiers using scent, and then seized upon, seems remote.[21]

The Seacourt glass fragment might have been treasured as an amulet, an interpretation less outrageous than it would have seemed fifty years ago when Harden was writing. The only other such bottle known in England is from a priory site, and a piece of Islamic gilded and enamelled glass from the Pyx Chamber at Westminster Abbey may have been finally used as a Christian reliquary, despite its origin.[22] Bruce-Mitford, reporting on the first year's work on Seacourt in 1939, noted that the site was associated with a pilgrims' route to the nearby St Margaret's well at Binsey.[23] The mid-twelfth-century writer John of Salisbury condemned all polished and bright things as they drew the gaze and could lead to contemplation not of God but of the devil – a sure sign that people were attracted to showy objects which might lead their thoughts astray. A little later in date, the two small mirror-cases found at the deserted sites at Westbury (Bucks.) and Thuxton (Norfolk) similarly cross the line between secular and religious – both have forms of the Cross on their lids.[24] Consideration of such objects shows how superstition can again be discussed by archaeologists.[25] Gilchrist has reviewed the evidence of objects placed, rather than accidentally incorporated, within graves, including some from abandoned sites such as Wharram Percy. The list includes

---

21. D.B. Harden, 'Objects of glass', in M. Biddle, 'The deserted medieval village of Seacourt, Berkshire', *Oxoniensia*, 26/27 (1961–2), pp. 70–201, at 185; R. Tyson, *Medieval glass vessels found in England c. AD 1200–1500*, CBA Research Report, 121 (2000), pp. 23, 139.

22. Tyson, *Medieval glass*, p. 138. It has the remains of an inscription that would have seemed very appropriate on a Christian object if only partly translated – 'Glory to our Lord'; but it would have been less acceptable if the full text with its two final words were also supplied – 'the Sultan'.

23. Bruce-Mitford, 'Seacourt', pp. 31–3.

24. R. Ivens, P. Busby and N. Shepherd, *Tattenhoe and Westbury. Two deserted medieval settlements in Milton Keynes*, Buckinghamshire Archaeological Society Monograph Series, 8 (1995), pp. 350, 355; L. Butler and P. Wade-Martins, *The deserted medieval village of Thuxton, Norfolk*, East Anglian Archaeology, 46 (1989), pp. 36–8.

25. Because its author was so highly respected, R. Merrifield's *The archaeology of magic and ritual* (London, 1987) gave the subject respectability.

coins, some folded as evidence of a vow taken and presumably fulfilled, spindlewhorls, which were symbolic of the home, and sea-urchin fossils, regarded as 'thunder-stones' brought down from the skies and able to ward off evil spirits.[26] The deterioration of lead may have deprived us of much evidence of other sorts of belief in rural contexts; the large numbers of badges – pilgrims', apotropaic, scatological and sexual – do not suggest a form of expression limited to urban culture.[27]

Fossils were not the only things regarded as rained down from above; prehistoric flint axes were as well. A remarkable chance find recently was of a copper-alloy strap-end quite clearly modelled on a flint arrowhead, presumably chosen for an amuletic reason.[28] That object would have proclaimed itself as something remarkable wherever found, but if a flint is excavated within a medieval house, how likely is it to be seen as other than an accidental, residual inclusion? Gilchrist noted that the infant buried in a house at another deserted site, Upton (Glos.), was found in the same context as a spindlewhorl, which suggests the same 'household' associations as those in churchyard graves.[29] How often is a spindlewhorl in a house floor going to occasion comment when it is not found with something that alerts suspicion? 'Foundation deposits' may have been underestimated. Merrifield's only suggested example, at Thuxton, does not convince, since it consisted of four horse skulls buried in a pit outside the corner of a yard building – that is, not necessarily directly associated with it. The excavators thought that the skulls were to protect the living horses inside a stable, but such deposits are more to be expected at entranceways, to stop spirits from entering. Merrifield knew of pots buried in doorways in houses in the late medieval Low Countries, but of none in England after the Norman Conquest.[30] Evidence of witch deterrence from the sixteenth century and later is fairly

26. R. Gilchrist, 'Magic for the dead? The archaeology of magic in later medieval burials', *Med. Arch.*, 52 (2008), pp. 119–60, especially at 128–44.
27. M. Jones, *The secret world of the Middle Ages. Discovering the real medieval world* (Stroud, 2002).
28. N. Griffiths, 'An unusual medieval strap-end from Market Lavington', *Wiltshire Archaeological and Natural History Magazine*, 91 (1998), p. 149. See also M.A. Hall, 'Burgh mentalities; a town-in-the-country case study of Perth, Scotland', in Giles and Dyer (eds), *Town and country*, pp. 211–28, at 213. The bizarre creation of what might have been used as a letter-opener by fitting a Bronze Age blade into a twelfth-century mount seems more likely to be an eighteenth-century than a medieval concoction: C.M. Gerrard and S.M. Youngs, 'A bronze socketed mount and blade from Shapwick House, Somerset', *Med. Arch.*, 41 (1997), pp. 210–14, republished by Gerrard with other Shapwick objects discussed below: 'Not all archaeology is rubbish', pp. 166–70.
29. Gilchrist, 'Magic?', p. 133. Another was found at Gomeldon, under – quite probably inserted under – the wall of a building of uncertain function; the gold quarter-noble was on the building's floor, so not necessarily in direct association: Musty and Algar, 'Gomeldon', pp. 142–3.
30. Merrifield, *Magic and ritual*, pp. 119–23; Butler and Wade-Martins, *Thuxton*, pp. 32–3.

Figure 6.2 The cistern found at Churchill (Oxon.). Height: 0.555m; capacity 70 litres (15 gallons or 2 bushels).

abundant, but earlier belief would have been in evil spirits rather than in the powers of the living and their familiars, so shoes, pins and the like may not have carried any associations of exclusion. A possible case of deliberate deposition of a pot is the complete and very large cistern at Churchill (Oxon.), unfortunately not excavated by archaeologists so that the precise context is not known (Figure 6.2). It was reported as having had two flat stones across its top, and inside were a length of iron chain and a rolled-up lead strip. A large iron key and a penny of Edward III were found nearby. Association with a building, let alone a doorway, could not definitely be made.[31] Another cistern, fifteenth- or sixteenth-century in date, seems to have been pressed upside down next to a hearth at Shapwick (Somers.); it was already broken at the rim and may have been put there for no deeper reason than to act as a convenient stand.[32]

Also to be considered is the possibility of 'closing events' being recognisable from the deliberate placing of objects on the floors of houses before their abandonment, as has been identified on South Uist, where foundation offerings have also been claimed.[33] Gerrard has discussed a pit at Shapwick, which contained four whole pots and a broken Roman antler rake, seemingly discovered by a medieval villager and deliberately broken. That pit, however, was not close to occupation or a building and may have been a quarry into a rock outcrop; furthermore, the reconstructable pot in the lowest level was early twelfth century in date, whereas three higher up were late twelfth–early thirteenth. More than one event seems to have been involved. Elsewhere at the site, two pierced fourth-century Roman coins also suggest at the least an interest in curiosities, more probably belief in their apotropaic powers, like the gold ring stolen from the boy's neck in the criminal record.[34]

In contrast to the situation with English houses, Merrifield found several examples of pots buried in English churches, although he did not refer to the large one at Woodperry; he suggested that some could have been heart-burials,[35] but earthenware seems unlikely to have had sufficient status for someone whose entrails merited burial in a prestigious position separate from their body. He noted that no pots resulting from the burning of sweet-smelling substances seemed to be found in English graves, although examples exist from France and Scotland; since then, one has been noted at the Dominican church in Oxford.[36] Pottery

31. D.A. Hinton, 'A medieval cistern from Churchill', *Oxoniensia*, 33 (1968), pp. 66–70. Another early engagement with superstitious practice may have come for me when demolishing a cruck house: idem, 'A cruck house at Lower Radley, Berkshire' *Oxoniensia*, 32 (1967), pp. 13–33. There, stuffed into the back of an auger-hole, were screwed-up strips of paper in a leather purse. My pragmatic mind allowed me to offer no interpretation; my older phenomenological self wonders if they had not had a curse written on them, cf. Merrifield, *Magic and ritual*, pp. 142–58.

32. C.J. Webster, 'Excavations within the village of Shapwick', *Proceedings of the Somerset Archaeological and Natural History Society*, 136 (1992), pp. 117–26 at 123; Gutiérrez, 'The pottery', pp. 649–53.

33. M. Parker Pearson, H. Smith, J. Mulville and M. Brennand, 'Cille Pheadair: the life and times of a Norse-period farmstead *c.* 1000–1300', in J. Hines, A. Lane and M. Redknap (eds), *Land, sea and home*, SMAMS, 20 (2003), pp. 235–54, at 246. Dating is still provisional, but the customs may have outlasted the eleventh century (the Seacourt glass fragment was not from a context that could be given this sort of significance).

34. Webster, 'Shapwick', p. 122; Gerrard, 'Not all archaeology is rubbish', pp. 166–70; Gutiérrez, 'The pottery', pp. 649–53.

35. Merrifield, *Magic and ritual*, p. 121; but I do not offer a better alternative.

36. Ibid.; R. Gilchrist and B. Sloane, *Requiem: the medieval monastic cemetery in Britain* (London, 2005), p. 165.

found in churches and churchyards may have had a range of uses, or be the residues of fairs: discussing the Wharram Percy material, Le Patourel noted that the differences between such assemblages and domestic ones could indicate activities near churches such as trading, bringing food to festivals or placing flowers in containers in the church or on graves. A church in Hampshire at Otterbourne, at some distance from any houses and therefore unlikely to have pottery thrown over the churchyard wall as rubbish, had not only a higher ratio of glazed to unglazed ware than is normal in the area, but also some imports, not uncommon in the large towns but very infrequently found outside them. As at one church on Humberside, one of the vessels was a bung-hole cistern, which reminds us that church-ales were held to raise funds.[37]

Pots in their domestic places

Not all whole pots found in domestic situations had superstitious associations. As Moorhouse has pointed out, there are good practical reasons for the burial of a pot close to a hearth, not to ward off evil spirits, but for distilling and particular types of cooking.[38] Some may have been to hold water for use while cooking on the open fire. An example from a sand-inundated house with a high degree of preservation on the Gower peninsula in south Wales at Pennard (Glamorgan) had the sunken pot next to a couple of flat stone slabs rather than immediately adjacent to the hearth. The vessel was heavily sooted inside but not outside, so might have had ashes put into it to keep food or water hot in a pot put above it; Brears has suggested that some pots may have been ash-pans used to keep embers warm overnight so that they could be used to restart a fire in the morning.[39] The Pennard pot seemed to have lost its rim and upper part before being buried, which may have been deliberate, to give a wider opening at the top into which to put ashes, or accidental, in which case the employment of this particular pot could have been simply a way of making use of a broken vessel. Such an explanation does not suffice for the inverted pots found at Westbury (Bucks.), however, as some had partly intact bases and some had been used as hearth bases.[40] Residue analyses are

---

37. H.E.J. Le Patourel, 'Medieval pottery', in R.D. Bell, M.W. Beresford *et al.* (eds), *Wharram. A study of settlement on the Yorkshire Wolds, III, Wharram Percy: the church of St Martin*, SMAMS, 11 (1987), pp. 154–65; D.A. Hinton, 'Excavations at Otterbourne old church, Hampshire', *Proceedings of the Hampshire Field Club and Archaeological Society*, 46 (1981), pp. 73–89, at 83–5; C. Hayfield, 'The pottery', in G. Coppack, 'St Lawrence Church, Burnham, South Humberside', *Lincolnshire Archaeology and History*, 21 (1986), pp. 39–60, at 51–6.
38. Moorhouse, 'Non-dating uses of medieval pottery', pp. 115–17.
39. P. Brears, *Cooking and dining in medieval England* (Totnes, 2008), p. 62.
40. Ivens *et al.*, *Tattenhoe and Westbury*, pp. 271–81. The cistern at Shapwick is another example: Gutiérrez, 'The pottery', p. 650 plausibly interprets it as a stand.

beginning to identify some of the contents of everyday vessels, from beeswax to animal fats, and will be another route into understanding the range of peasant commodities and activities. Presumably it will never be possible to reveal the quantities of pottage or dairy products put into the pots, nor how many different people consumed them.[41]

It seems odd that more pots buried in floors have not been recorded if they had so many possible uses. They have been found in deserted sites in various areas, so are not a reflection of specific regional practice, and are likely to have a better chance of survival than those used only at or above ground level.[42] On Dartmoor (Devon), a house excavated at Dinna Clerks had clearly burnt down (Figure 6.3). There was nothing unusual about that, but what made it stand out for archaeologists was that because the place was so isolated, the house had not been quarried for building materials, and the remains of its turf roof still covered the floor. As well as the *in situ* pot there were the remains of four other unglazed cooking and storage vessels, a green-glazed jug, some bits of iron and two wooden vessels in the same room, and in an inner room another cooking vessel, a cistern and two yellow-glazed pots. A Long Cross penny of *c.* 1253–60 was found in the attached byre, where a ritual deposition is perhaps unlikely.[43] As it was from an issue demonetised in 1279–80, it would probably have been out of circulation soon after that, so was taken as giving a reasonably close date for the building's destruction. Allen, however, subsequently argued that the cistern is a type of vessel unlikely to be earlier than *c.* 1340, which puts the site into a post-Black Death desertion category, with the coin lying unnoticed in the dark byre for some years before desertion.[44] Beresford thought that this range of material might indicate its ownership by someone of higher than usual status, but the quantities of pennies now known to have been circulating shows that a single one is likely enough to be found anywhere.

41. W.B. Stern, Y. Gerber and G. Helmig, 'Residues in medieval pottery from Basel', in G. Helmig, B. Scholkmann and M. Untermann (eds), *Centre, region, periphery: medieval Europe: Basel 2002*, Volume 3, Third International Conference of Medieval and Later Archaeology (Hertingen, 2002), pp. 197–200; R. Berstan, A.W. Stott, P. Minnitt, C. Bronk Ramsey, R.E.M. Hedges and R.P. Evershed, 'Direct dating of pottery from its organic residues', *Antiquity*, 82 (2008), pp. 702–13.

42. The only one I have noted other than at Westbury since Moorhouse's publication is M.J. Saunders, 'The excavation of a medieval site at Walsingham School, St Paul's Cray, Bromley, 1995', *Archaeologia Cantiana*, 117 (1997), pp. 199–225, at 207 and 209 and P.J. Fasham and G. Keevil, *Brighton Hill South (Hatch Warren): an Iron Age farmstead and deserted medieval village in Hampshire*, Wessex Archaeology Report, 7 (1995), p. 97. The two at West Whelpington takes them at least into the far north of England.

43. G. Beresford, 'Three deserted medieval settlements on Dartmoor: a report on the late E. Marie Minter's excavations', *Med. Arch.*, 23 (1979), pp. 98–158 at 135–6 and 147–50.

44. J. Allen, 'Medieval pottery and the dating of deserted settlements on Dartmoor', *Devon Archaeological Society Proceedings*, 52 (1994), pp. 141–7, at 145.

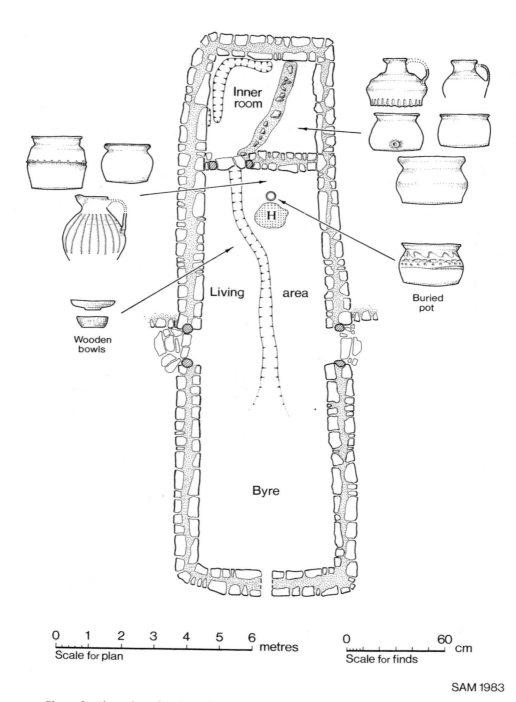

Inner room

Living   area

Byre

Wooden bowls

H

Buried pot

0 1 2 3 4 5 6 metres
Scale for plan

0   60 cm
Scale for finds

SAM 1983

Figure 6.3 Floor plan of the burnt building found at Dinna Clerks (Devon), showing position of hearth and pots (source: S. Moorhouse, 'The non-dating uses of medieval pottery', *Medieval Ceramics*, 10 (1986), pp. 85–124. (Reproduced with kind permission of the author).

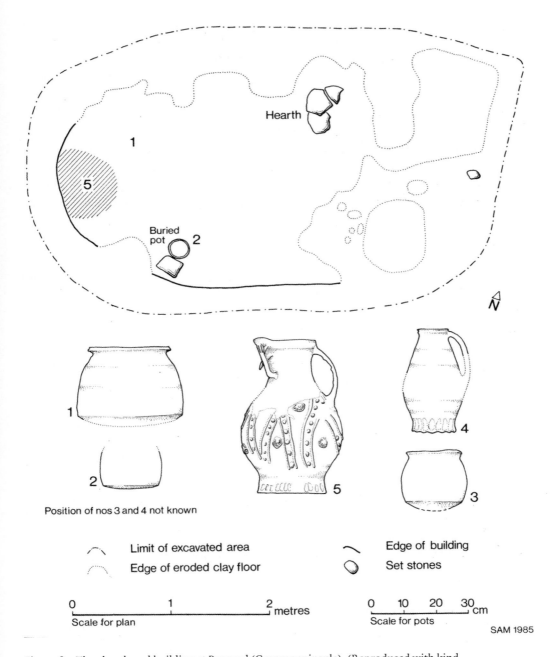

Figure 6.4 The abandoned building at Pennard (Gower peninsula). (Reproduced with kind permission of S. Moorhouse).

At Pennard, one of the unglazed pots had been repaired using, unusually, copper alloy; lead is more often found because it is easier to manipulate into shape. Repairs generally are not all that common, however, suggesting that replacements for breakages could usually be afforded. Perhaps this accounts for the four jars in the 'quarry pit' at Shapwick; they were not quite complete and may therefore have simply been discarded after domestic accidents. If we had just a few more rural pits we might have very many more nearly whole pots. One other unglazed vessel was found in reasonably complete condition at Pennard, as were two glazed jugs, although no coins; a thirteenth-/fourteenth-century date is probable (Figure 6.4).[45] Moorhouse and others have teased out a number of deductions from these two unusual survivals of houses which were abandoned and not damaged by subsequent dismantling and scavenging. The two wooden vessels at Dinna Clerks are a reminder of the under-representation of such treen – which probably mostly ended up in the fire when they could no longer be used – and also show that peasants used cups, vessels rarely made in pottery at the time.[46] In both places, jugs were found close to walls, suggesting that they had fallen from shelves or a piece of furniture: evidence of internal fittings – 'cup-boards' for display such as were to be found in higher-status households.[47] The ratios of the glazed pieces to the unglazed cooking and storage vessels was higher than at most sites,[48] but is quite likely to be more representative of what was in the houses at any one moment while they were in use – if jugs were kept off floors and away from cooking hearths, they were less likely to get kicked over, or dropped, and would have had longer lives.

45. S. Moorhouse, 'The ceramic contents of a thirteenth-century timber building destroyed by fire', *Medieval and later pottery in Wales*, 8 (1985), pp. 1–9; J. Draper, *Dorset country pottery. The kilns of the Verwood district* (Ramsbury, 2002), pp. 49 and 68, cites examples of pots built into the cob walls of eighteenth-/nineteenth-century houses and outbuildings; some were used as small cupboards, although not all are of appropriate shapes for that. It is just possible that that could account for the locations of the medieval jugs; but I have not come across any hint of such practice in medieval buildings, although acoustic jars were concealed in some church walls.

46. R. Wood, 'What did medieval people eat from?', *Medieval Ceramics*, 29 (2005), pp. 19–20, is a recent reminder of the large numbers of wooden cups recorded in some higher social level purchase accounts.

47. D.M. Hadley, 'Dining in disharmony in the later Middle Ages', in M. Carroll, D.M. Hadley and H. Willmott (eds), *Consuming passions. Dining from antiquity to the eighteenth century* (Stroud, 2005), pp. 101–20, at 112–13. Hurst pondered whether such vessels should be seen as the medieval equivalent of 'the plaster animals purchased or won at present-day fairs' despite the amount of work that went into them, *DMVS*, pp. 141–2, but his alternative that they should be seen as the equivalent of nineteenth-century Staffordshire figures on cottage mantlepieces is probably a closer analogy because those involved a degree of individual hand painting.

48. Estimates vary up to 1:10, or even more: Hurst, *DMVS*, p. 141. V. Bryant, 'Death and desire', *Medieval Ceramics*, 28 (2004), pp. 117–21, reports a house burnt in Worcester where the ratio was as high as 1:1.

Each of the two sites had one jug that was highly decorated; at Pennard, it was anthropomorphic, its bridge-spout decorated to look like a human beard held up by a man's arms, and elaborately decorated with applied trails and rosettes. One of the Dinna Clerks jugs was also bridge-spouted and decorated with applied trails. This shows that pots as good as any to be found in urban houses were getting into farms and hamlets, and were not even confined to the highest consumer level among the peasantry, since there seems to have been nothing very special about the Dartmoor and Gower sites before their abandonments. Another example is the knight-jug, modelled with mounted riders processing around the pot, excavated at the deserted site at Hatterborough (Yorks.).[49] This was an easily damaged piece that had almost certainly been made at Scarborough, admittedly close by, but nonetheless a fragile object to transport, and with an iconography that clearly was not only of interest to those who could afford to see themselves as knights. Allen did not discuss the glazed bridge-spouted jug in his reconsideration of the dating of the Dinna Clerks site, but manufacture in the late thirteenth or early fourteenth century seems more likely than after *c.* 1340, so that it may have been of some age and carefully looked after until it succumbed to the house's fire.

Something of the same sort of acquisition of fancy goods has been claimed from the assemblage at West Cotton (Northants.), a site exceptional because the waste from the thirteenth-/early-fourteenth-century houses appears to have been allowed to accumulate in the yards rather than being carefully spread on to gardens and fields. Over 100,000 sherds were collected and, although over 80 per cent were unglazed shelly wares, there was a range of glazed wares as well. The less eye-catching were from fairly local kilns at Lyveden/Stanion and Potterspury, but there was also a proportion of baluster and three-decker jugs, less capacious but more highly coloured and finished, made at Brill/Boarstall forty-four miles (70km) away. Some of the rubbish can be attributed, it is said, to particular rooms; the Brill/Boarstall vessels were mostly from the peasants' halls. Blinkhorn took this to indicate that drink was brought from storage to be decanted into the smarter-looking smaller jugs for serving, which is consistent with their being kept on 'cup-boards' in halls.[50] This insight into peasant behaviour can be developed by consideration of the two wooden vessels at Dinna Clerks; both were of the bowl-like shape that is shown as used for drinking in manuscript illustrations, so it seems likely that even in an isolated peasant household on Dartmoor the family

49. F.C. Rimington, *The deserted medieval village of Hatterboard, near Scarborough*, Scarborough and District Archaeological Society Research Report, 2 (1961), p. 31.
50. P. Blinkhorn, 'The trials of being a pot: pottery functions at the medieval hamlet of West Cotton, Northamptonshire', *Medieval Ceramics*, 22/3 (1998–9), pp. 37–46. At the time of writing (May 2009), the report on this site was still awaited.

used some ceremony in pouring from glazed jug to drinking vessel.[51] Whether that could also mean that meals were already in the first half of the fourteenth century served formally at a table, rather than eaten squatting around the open hearth on which a stew-pot simmered, is perhaps not deducible from this evidence. It does, however, show that changing fourteenth- and fifteenth-century habits in towns, such as drinking beer rather than ale and using earthenware cups, could have spread quickly to the countryside, as would late medieval white, black, red and stone wares, so that absence of the last is good evidence of the date of the end of occupation. Declining quantities of unglazed pottery are less reliable, as they can be put down to increasing use of metal; this point was made in the Seacourt publication, and remains valid.[52]

There are some differences between the pottery found on rural and on urban sites, but they are at least as much for functional reasons as because occupants of deserted villages lacked purchasing power or social aspirations. Brown has shown how larger quantities of vessels probably used in dairies can be expected on village sites, for instance.[53] Imports from the Continent are few until very late in the Middle Ages, but they are never frequent except in ports, so may never have reached the open market and thus did not get into deserted villages. That would explain the absence of the very fine whiteware from Saintonge in the south-west of France, painted with polychrome shields, birds, scrolls and faces – but that is only very occasionally found in most towns, and was probably associated with the wine

51. Brears, *Cooking and dining*, p. 391, is rather fierce about archaeologists who refer to these vessels as 'bowls' rather than using the medieval term 'cups'; unfortunately the words now imply specific shapes, and it seems not inappropriate to follow modern usage when it is more explanatory.

52. Biddle, 'Seacourt', p. 135. 'Brass' pots figure as occasional fragments in archaeology but much more frequently in inventories, as they were worth valuing. A range of values from 6d to 6s 8d were attributed to them in the Lay Subsidy of 1312 for Minety, Wiltshire — a little ironically, as clay potting was an important activity there. Only William the Crockar can be identified by name as having an association: E.H. Fuller, 'The tallage of 6 Edward II (Dec. 16, 1312) and the Bristol rebellion', *Transactions of the Bristol and Gloucestershire Archaeological Society*, 19 (1894–5), pp. 171–278, at 196–8.

53. D.H. Brown, 'Pots from houses', *Medieval Ceramics*, 21 (1997), pp. 83–94, amplified as 'Pottery and manors', in M. Carroll, D.M. Hadley and H. Willmott (eds), *Consuming passions. Dining from antiquity to the eighteenth century* (Stroud, 2005), pp. 87–100. M. Mellor, 'Early Saxon, medieval and post-medieval pottery', in T. Allen, 'A medieval grange of Abingdon Abbey at Dean Court Farm, Cumnor, Oxon.', *Oxoniensia*, 59 (1994), pp. 219–447, pp. 325–54, at 339–41, found less contrast in the quality of the pottery at a fourteenth-century toft compared to nearby Oxford, but with a high ratio of bowls to other vessel types. The toft was attached to a monastic grange, where dairying was also implied by the pottery range: *eadem*, at 325 and 353. Bowls could also be used as meal and flour measures in bakehouses, and, until beer became popular and increasingly a specialised product, brewing pans and storage cisterns, although these would have been needed as much in towns as in the countryside; A. Woodward and P. Blinkhorn, 'Size matters: Iron Age vessel capacities in central and southern England', in C.G. Cumberpatch and P.W. Blinkhorn (eds), *Not so much a pot, more a way of life*, Oxbow Monograph, 83 (1997), pp. 153–62, at 154.

trade.[54] Also apparently absent are any examples of aquamaniles;[55] cast in bronze, these were certainly used in great households for washing, water from them being poured by a servant over a lord's or honoured guest's hands and into basins. They were imitated in pottery, although noble beasts like lions were adapted into more familiar creatures such as rams. There do not seem to have been any ceramic basins obviously made to accompany them, however, so they might have been used as rather inconvenient serving jugs, not for fastidious cleanliness; their absence from excavated rural sites suggests that the elegant behaviour involving the metal ones was not observed or emulated by the peasantry.[56]

The 100,000 sherds from West Cotton is a remarkable record of the sheer amount of pottery, and by implication organic goods, that peasants owned.[57] It was a large site, and of course the number of households represented, and the time-span covered, will affect the impression that such an assemblage represents. Yet even a smaller group can be indicative, if closely dated: 525 sherds excavated at West Mead in central Dorset were attributed to midden material brought there in the early–mid thirteenth century that for some reason had never been spread on to fields; no less than fourteen different fabrics were represented, from sources east, west and south of the site.[58] The peasants who had broken these pots clearly had access to a wide range of products although they may never have travelled further

54. Assuming that the six sherds at Hatch Warren (Hants.) were from a manorial complex: Fasham and Keevil, *Brighton Hill South*, pp. 119, 132 and 150.
55. Some have been reported from places like Mere (Wilts.) and Rushey Platt, Swindon (Wilts.), which suggests a rural not an urban provenance, but that does not mean that they came from a peasant household. They were claimed at West Whelpington, but the sherd illustrated looks simply like a small jug handle: Evans and Jarrett, 'West Whelpington', p. 255 and sherd no. 366.
56. Hadley, 'Dining in disharmony', pp. 112–13, discusses them, and there is a splendid catalogue of metal examples published by the Bard Graduate Center: P. Barnet and P. Dandridge, *Lions, dragons and other beasts: aquamanilia of the Middle Ages, vessels for church and table* (New Haven/London, 2006). I wonder if the pottery ones were not 'subversive', making a mockery of knights and turning noble beasts into farmyard stock.
57. Another large Midlands site, Great Linford, Buckinghamshire, had some 50,000, but in that case some were from a manor house: D.C. Mynard, R.J. Zeepvat and R.J. Williams, *Excavations at Great Linford, 1974–80*, Buckinghamshire Archaeological Society Monograph, 3 (1991). Intensive fieldwalking of twelve parishes in the Whittlewood project led to 16,000 sherds being collected, with 20,000 excavated in test-pits. Although fewer than from the Northamptonshire sites, these overall totals are high given that they mostly came from dispersed settlements: R. Jones, 'Signatures in the soil: the use of pottery in manure scatters in the identification of medieval arable farming regimes', *Archaeological Journal*, 161 (2004), pp. 159–88. West Whelpington had a longer time-span than some sites, but an estimated minimum of *c.* 1300 medieval vessels is comparable: Evans and Jarrett, 'West Whelpington', p. 255.
58. L. Mepham, 'Medieval pottery from West Mead', in C.M. Hearne and V. Birbeck, *A35 Tolpuddle to Puddletown Bypass DBFO, Dorset, 1996–8*, Wessex Archaeology Report, 15 (1999), pp. 127–32 (the author notes the possibility of some late twelfth-century material, but it would not affect the argument).

than the market at Dorchester to acquire them. Brown found something of the sort at the deserted farmstead at Wroughton Copse, probably supplied by Marlborough; he saw this range as rather limited compared to households in Winchester and Southampton, but a wine merchant was in a different league from a peasant living at a very isolated site, so that the latter had any choice at all seems important.[59] A group like that at West Mead, not directly associated with an occupation site, is unusual, although it does typify another problem within modern studies – the number of sites excavated to an exemplary standard but which are only partially complete, as they are from linear pipe-line and road construction sites, which preclude wholesale excavation.[60] Tattenhoe and Westbury are increasingly rare examples of total excavation, or at least of a substantial proportion of a site.

Peasants might visit markets like Marlborough or Dorchester where a wide range of goods was available to them, and even smaller towns probably enjoyed a few extra stalls during annual fairs. Another commercial system was probably the occasional visit to a village by middlemen/pedlars – a system still used to distribute pots from rural kilns in Dorset during the first part of the twentieth century, maintained even when motor vans replaced horses and carts.[61] The 'feudal' economy meant, however, that many peasants had carting duties to perform, which may have directed them to markets further away from their homes, but to which they were bound to go. Mellor has shown that more of the pottery at Seacourt had arrived there from the south than would be expected if the villagers had used their nearest market, Oxford, to the east.[62] Perhaps they were more often going south to Abingdon, as the village had been owned by the abbey there before being sub-infeudated; the service ties might have been broken, but family links could have become established, and the payment of tolls to access the Oxford market might have been a disincentive, as it seems to have been in Bedford.[63]

---

59. Brown, 'Pots from houses', pp. 85–6.
60. This is not meant to decry the work that goes into this type of report, which can add usefully to discussion of, for instance, local marketing systems: e.g. J. Hurst, 'Medieval period discussion', in A.B. Powell, P. Booth, A.P. Fitzpatrick and A.D. Crockett, *The archaeology of the M6 Toll 2000–2003*, Oxford Wessex Archaeology Monograph, 2 (2008), pp. 542–56. Book titles like that may not be inspiring, but attempting to disguise their nature — e.g. T. Oliver, C. Howard-Davis and R. Newman, *Transect through time* — is given away by informative subtitling — *The archaeological landscape of the Shell north-western ethylene pipe-line (English section)* (Lancaster, 1996). That example has a useful report on a sunken-featured building — and one on a shieling that by yielding no artefacts could be of any date.
61. Draper, *Dorset country pottery*, pp. 101–2. The Verwood hawkers usually also carted besom brooms, another local handicraft item in everyday household demand.
62. Mellor, 'Early Saxon', p. 352.
63. D. Baker, E. Baker, J. Hassall and A. Simco, 'Excavations in Bedford 1967–1977', *Bedfordshire Archaeological Journal*, 13 (1979), pp. 1–309, at 294.

Other objects at deserted villages

Pottery gives the best idea of the volume of consumption of cheap goods by the peasantry. Other almost indestructible items include honestones and stone querns, mortars and grinding stones, Devon and other slates and occasional clay tiles, none found in such numbers as to be used with confidence quantitatively, but providing another means by which distant trading networks can be judged – the hones often from Norway, the querns from the Rhineland and the mortars sometimes from Caen as well as from various inland sources. Everyone needed the means to sharpen a knife, but the acquisition of a stone that had travelled across the North Sea must have been sought either because it was viewed as more effective, or because it lent a little status to someone who could show that they could afford it. Hones are not likely to have been 'trickle-down' items from the local manor house, unlike mortars which broke easily and were then useful as rubble.[64] As the latter were used for food preparation, they are evidence of the pounding of ingredients, but precisely what is another matter; herbs may have been used by peasants, but were spices, or even pepper? Anyway, for the last, querns seem to have been more often used. Presumably no reeve could object to a stone used for that sort of grinding, even if the number of quernstones identified is not great, and gives some credence to the ban on their use by bond tenants – and that the free tenants found it worthwhile to take grain to the lord's mill and pay a fee rather than prepare their own flour.[65] Another sort of stone item, identified at Wharram Percy as a bake-stone, is also mentioned in northern documents; that none has been identified in the Midlands or south, nor noticed in an inventory, could be an indication of a cultural difference – oat-cakes and parkin are still not much sold south of Staffordshire.[66]

Less durable than stone, apart from gold, are metals, and as all of them were subject to recycling, relative quantities excavated at deserted sites are even less likely to be a useful guide to what peasants owned in total. Nevertheless, the impression gained early at Seacourt that a wide range of small items was available

64. One that had lost its base even had reuse as a drain: *Oxoniensia*, 71 (2006), p. 353 (not a rural site).
65. Neither hones nor mortars/querns from medieval sites have been systematically assessed recently, and would make a student project. R. Holt, *The mills of medieval England* (Oxford, 1988), pp. 39–53, for documentary evidence about hand-querns, mills, and their willing and unwilling usage.
66. Brears, *Cooking and dining*, p. 110, is convinced that effete southern archaeologists have failed to notice them, except for Jope identifying one of iron on an upland Devon site: Jope and Threlfall, 'Great Beere, North Tawton', pp. 138–9. Early medieval ceramic examples in the south-west have been claimed also by C. O'Mahoney, 'Pottery', in G. Beresford, 'Old Lanyon, Madron', *Cornish Archaeology*, 33 (1994), pp. 130–69, pp. 152–66, at 154; D. Allen, 'Excavations at Hafod Y Nant Criafolen, Brenig Valley, Clwyd, 1973–4', *Post-Med. Arch.*, 13 (1979), pp. 1–50, reports a probable one at p. 45.

to them has been confirmed at other large sites, such as Tattenhoe and Westbury, where examples of just about anything that might be expected in an urban rubbish-pit were found, showing that the villagers had full access to the things that their town cousins could acquire.[67] Their visitors included itinerant tinkers; the man with a bellows on his back was a familiar image, and the recent report of the stack of thirteenth-century copper-alloy brooches found at Hambleden (Bucks.), nearly all of which had not yet had pins fitted, strongly suggests that peasants did not always have to rely on going themselves to an urban market for such items.[68]

Village blacksmiths – and documents such as the newly published Shaftesbury cartulary show how many of them there were by the early twelfth century – were presumably able to make and mend the estate tools, basic knives and structural ironwork, but not perhaps to make complicated padlocks or spurs.[69] Their ability must have varied, but whether they could have obtained and used the steel-like ores needed for a good sharp knife point may be doubted, and makers' marks show that at least in the later Middle Ages knives would normally have been another urban product.[70] Brazing other metals on to iron keys and the like might also have been beyond a village artisan, although the only smithy excavated at a deserted village, Goltho (Lincs.), had 'associated' with it four padlock bolts, which suggests that they were not beyond that occupant's ability.[71] The range of tools, at Goltho as elsewhere, is not great, but the evidence does not suggest that demesnes had better types of equipment than the peasants.[72] The peasants may also have been as well-equipped with bows and arrows as their manorial lords; those from Seacourt have recently been discussed by Wadge in relation to hunting and poaching, which as he points out was an issue at several deserted villages.[73]

67. J.M. Mills, 'The finds catalogue', in Ivens *et al.*, *Tattenhoe and Westbury*, pp. 335–96.

68. L. Babb, 'A thirteenth-century brooch hoard from Hambleden, Buckinghamshire', *Med. Arch.*, 41 (1997), pp. 233–6. For vignettes, D. Hartley and M.M. Elliot, *Life and work of the people of England. Volume one: the Middle Ages, A.D. 1000–1490* (London; n.d. *c.* 1931), fourteenth-century section, plate 33.

69. N.E. Stacey (ed.), *Charters and custumals of Shaftesbury Abbey 1089–1216* (Oxford, 2006), *s.v.*; smiths are recorded on several estates, but not all. Recycling is shown by Sixpenny Handley's *Ricardus faber* who was to receive the old iron (*recipere vetera ferra*).

70. I am grateful to the editors for reminding me of the evidence about knives from the deserted village at Goltho, Lincolnshire: R.F. Tylecote, 'Metallurgical report', in G. Beresford, *The medieval clay-land village: excavations at Goltho and Barton Blount*, SMAMS, 6 (1975), pp. 81–2.

71. Beresford, *Medieval clay-land village*, 46.

72. This deserves more consideration; it has implications for peasant innovation and drive: J. Langdon, 'Agricultural equipment', in G. Astill and A. Grant (eds), *The countryside of medieval England* (Oxford, 1988), pp. 86–107.

73. R. Wadge, 'Medieval arrowheads from Oxfordshire', *Oxoniensia*, 73 (2008), pp. 1–16; Seacourt had four – which by chance is also the number of iron ones illustrated from Woodperry: 'JW', 'Woodperry', p. 120.

Sometimes absences are as important as discoveries for revealing the material culture of inhabitants of deserted villages. In particular, loomweights do not continue to be found at rural sites after they cease to be found in urban ones. The implication is that rural peasants did not continue to use traditional vertical looms; a few may have had the new horizontal type, as the 'webber' surname is not confined to towns, but the implication is that most peasants were buying their cloth, not producing for their own use or as a by-employment. Spindlewhorls do continue to be found, although here some quantification really would be useful; are there fewer of them over time, and in particular after the introduction of the spinning wheel? Another near-absentee is vessel glass, partly because potash causes deterioration, but also because glass was little used for drinking except at the very highest levels until the late sixteenth century.[74]

Conclusion

One consequence of the outburst of metal-detecting has been a confirmation of what excavations of rural sites had already suggested; whatever regional differences in material culture may have existed, they were not caused by non-availability of consumer goods, at least after the mid twelfth century. Even the western islands of Scotland were receiving Minety ware from north Wiltshire – shipped through Bristol? – in the thirteenth century.[75] In Wales we see the penetration of English modes whatever the political situation.[76] Even the sixteenth-century pistol found at the upland shieling Hafod Y Nant Criafolen (Clwyd) may have been a status assertion rather than a weapon essential for defence.[77]

Jope's work showed that although regional differences did indeed exist, they are not the result of fundamental racial, political or religious traditions, but exist within a relative uniformity; baluster jugs in Oxford were not very different in shape from those in York, and the area in which vertical-sided cooking pots were found bore no relation to, for instance, the distribution of 'wealden' or cruck houses. Uniformity has since been shown even more emphatically by small objects

74. Tyson, *Medieval glass*, pp. 6–8 and 23.
75. Parker Pearson *et al.*, 'Cille Pheadair', p. 247. Unlike England, Scotland occasionally followed the French custom of placing pots in graves. Urban modes may have differed from rural — Hall has worked on the various influences shaping the culture of Perth: see 'Burgh mentalities'.
76. Perhaps that is why there is no section on artefacts in K. Roberts (ed.), *Lost farmsteads. Deserted rural settlements in Wales*, CBA Research Report, 148 (2006), and D. Austin does not see a role for them in 'The future', in Roberts (ed.), *Lost farmsteads*, pp. 193–205!
77. P. Courtney, 'The tyranny of constructs: some thoughts on periodisation and culture change', in D. Gaimster and P. Stamper (eds), *The age of transition. The archaeology of English culture 1400–1600*, SMAMS, 15 (1997), pp. 9–24, at p. 18; Allen, 'Hafod Y Nant Criafolen', pp. 39, 41 and 56.

such as brooches. But although deeply meaningful regionalism in cultural material seems now unlikely to be recognised, it is certainly possible to look for peasant marketing regions, as Mellor has done for the Oxford region.[78] The opportunities for this sort of study have been reduced by funding reductions and changes, and with fewer large-scale sites being investigated the sort of study undertaken by Wrathmell in reinterpreting Wharram Percy will not be possible for 1990s and 2000s work. Nevertheless, even from small-scale work, such as that at West Mead, or from test-pit investigation as in the Whittlewood project, both cited above, additional evidence brings new ideas and checks on old ones.

Post-processualism encourages students to view peasants as individuals whose thoughts, aspirations and unwritten customs are not beyond recapture; the notion of the sound common sense and the precociously Protestant work-ethic of the English peasants, once tacitly assumed, was caused by the bias in medieval tax lists and manorial accounts that were only interested in them as economic units. At the same time, the spread of wealth highlighted by the metal-detecting discoveries has become a major issue, so economic questions still remain. There are few metal artefacts, not much glazed pottery and not all that many single coin finds from the later eleventh and the first half of the twelfth centuries; was this because of a hundred years of Norman taxation? Thereafter, an increase in coins, artefacts and decorated pottery all coincide – how does that square with documentary evidence of low wages?[79] An agenda exists for the future.

---

78. Mellor, 'Early Saxon'; also work such as that by P. Spoerry, *Ely wares*, East Anglian Archaeology, 122 (2008).
79. Hinton, *Gold and gilt*, pp. 172–9, argues for the former but fails to explain the latter.

7

The desertion of Wharram Percy village and its wider context

STUART WRATHMELL

Wharram Percy, undoubtedly the best-known deserted medieval village site in England, lies on the Yorkshire Wolds about six miles (10km) south-east of the town of Malton. Its well-preserved earthworks indicate that it once comprised three rows of homesteads set along the sides of a triangular village green, two of the rows occupying the edges of the chalk plateau, the third located in the narrow, steep-sided valley below. The medieval parish church stands, roofless, in the valley at the southern end of the village site, while the location of the thirteenth- and fourteenth-century manor house and its outbuildings is still clearly marked by earthworks at the northern end of the former settlement.

Archaeological investigation of the site began in 1950, and excavations took place each summer from then until 1990. Over these four decades a wide range of research questions was framed, and in some cases these questions were at least partially answered: questions relating to the date of the village's desertion; to the origins and chronological development of the settlement as a whole; to the character of its farmsteads and the standard of living of their occupants; to the origins and chronology of the church, its graveyard and vicarage; and to the development of the adjacent former millpond. This present contribution will explore afresh the very first of these research questions, the one that motivated the initial trenching in 1950.

Depopulation and sheep farming at Wharram

The year 1979 saw the publication of the first in the series of monographs on the excavations at Wharram. As Beresford noted in that volume, 'The archaeological investigation ... was initially intended to check the known documentary evidence for a peasant community and for the death of that community early in the 16th century.'[1]

---

1. M.W. Beresford, 'Documentary evidence for the history of Wharram Percy', in D.D. Andrews and G. Milne (eds), *Wharram. A study of settlement on the Yorkshire Wolds, I, domestic settlement, 1: areas 10 and 6*, SMAMS, 8 (1979), p. 5.

The documentary evidence to which Beresford alluded is neither comprehensive nor unambiguous, but there are indications of a significant decline in the size of the village during the late fourteenth and early fifteenth centuries. A detailed record of the demesne and tenant holdings, made in 1368 for the purposes of assigning a dower interest, indicates a total of about thirty farmhouses (or messuages) and cottages in the village, although by that date a few of them were already apparently untenanted.[2] This number conforms to the evidence of the earthworks themselves, which indicate a total of between thirty and forty homesteads – assuming that all the house sites were at some point occupied simultaneously.[3]

Some seventy years later, however, Wharram seems to have contained only about half that number of holdings. An extent made in 1435 records only sixteen messuages and sixteen bovates, presumably one bovate for each messuage.[4] This information is repeated in a further extent of 1458.[5] While we may doubt whether these records constitute an accurate reflection of fifteenth-century agricultural organisation and practice at Wharram, they are *prima facie* evidence of a substantial shrinkage in the size of the farming community.

A further reduction is noted in an abstract of returns to the commission of enquiry set up in May 1517 in the wake of renewed government anxiety over the enclosure of arable land for pasture and consequent rural depopulation and impoverishment. For Wharram Percy, it records that 'after the said Michaelmas [1488] four messuages and four ploughs were thrown down', although Beresford suggested that the wording of the entry might narrow down this date range to the period 1488–1506.[6] We have no way of knowing whether the four events took place all at the same time, or whether they resulted from distinct actions perpetrated at different times and perhaps even by different people. Whatever the case, it is clear that Beresford regarded this abstract as the record of what was effectively the final phase of depopulation at Wharram:

> This shrinking community was reduced further, probably as a result of the general substitution of grass for arable characteristic of that period. If so, most of the depopulation occurred before 1488, since only four houses were pulled down between 1488 and 1517. In [the Hearth Tax returns of] 1672, and probably for a

---

2. Ibid., p.13.
3. A. Oswald, *Wharram Percy deserted medieval village, North Yorkshire: archaeological investigation and survey*, English Heritage Archaeological Investigation Report Series, A1/19/2004 (2004), p. 49.
4. In northern England the bovate or oxgang was a standard measure of landholding, notionally amounting to 15 acres: see B.K. Roberts, *Landscapes, documents and maps: villages in northern England and beyond AD 900–1250* (Oxford, 2008), p. 82.
5. Beresford, 'Documentary evidence' (1979), p. 13.
6. Ibid., pp. 6–7.

century before, the farm at Wharram Grange was the only one in the township, although for a while the glebe may have been farmed from the vicarage.[7]

These initial conclusions were, of course, refined in later years as new documentary sources came to light, and as those already discovered were explored more extensively. It was acknowledged that the vicarage continued to be occupied at least intermittently during the sixteenth to eighteenth centuries, the vicar serving the needs of the inhabitants of other townships in the parish.[8] It was also recognised that Wharram Grange farm, located over a kilometre north of the village site, had been part of Wharram le Street township, not Wharram Percy. Consequently the house recorded along with the vicarage in the 1672 Hearth Tax returns for Wharram Percy was probably situated on the former village site. Evidence was also found of some land being returned to arable before the 'improvement' of Wharram in the 1770s.[9]

The end of the excavations in 1990 did not mark a cessation of documentary research; rather, the programme of post-excavation analysis funded by English Heritage provided an opportunity for more systematic examination of the sources that Beresford had identified. Among these, the most productive were groups of documents surviving from two legal cases, or causes, brought in the court of the archbishops of York during the mid sixteenth century.[10]

It is the later of these cases, a dilapidations cause, that gives us, retrospectively, the key information about the final extinction of Wharram's open-field farming community.[11] It was brought in 1555 by William Firby, then vicar of Wharram Percy, against Marmaduke Atkinson, his predecessor. Firby's case was that in 1553, during Atkinson's incumbency, both the vicarage house and its attached grain barn had been destroyed by fire and that, although Atkinson had rebuilt the house (albeit inadequately), he had not replaced the barn. Atkinson's response was that the two bovates of glebe land no longer provided sufficient crops to justify rebuilding the barn.

Each side called witnesses who deposed as to the amount of crops that could be harvested from the glebe bovates. Firby's witnesses focused on the number of

7. Ibid., p. 16.
8. M.W. Beresford, 'The documentary evidence', in R.D. Bell, M.W. Beresford et al., Wharram. A study of settlement on the Yorkshire Wolds, III, Wharram Percy: the church of St Martin, SMAMS, 11 (1987), pp. 30–1.
9. M.W. Beresford and J.G. Hurst, Wharram Percy deserted medieval village (London, 1990), pp. 101, 110–12.
10. S. Wrathmell, 'The rectory, chantry house and vicarage from the 14th to 19th centuries', in C. Harding and S. Wrathmell (eds), Wharram: a study of settlement on the Yorkshire Wolds, XII, The post-medieval farm and vicarage, York University Archaeological Publications, 14 (2009), pp. 17–22.
11. Borthwick Institute, University of York (hereafter Borthwick), Cause Papers, CP G.917, G.3537.

loads that two bovates *should* provide – around sixteen or more; whereas Atkinson's deponents reported what *used to be* harvested from the Wharram vicar's two bovates – six or fewer. The context of this poor return was outlined by Robert Pickering of Raisthorpe, a husbandman aged about seventy: he deposed that the glebe bovates had not supplied more than three loads 'since the town was laid to grass which is 28 years since'.[12]

The inference of Pickering's statement is that the open fields had continued to be cultivated until 1527, presumably by a number of remaining tenant farmers, although perhaps on a more restricted basis than in earlier centuries. The conversion of the arable fields to grass in that year was presumably carried out either by the lord of the manor, Baron Hilton, or with his acquiescence.

We can infer from the other ecclesiastical cause that the beneficiary of this conversion may have been John Thorpe, a sheep master from Appleton-le-Street, just under ten miles (16km) north-west of Wharram. It was a tithe cause, brought in 1542–3 by Marmaduke Atkinson, the respondent in Vicar Firby's cause a dozen years later. Atkinson, who had been vicar of Wharram Percy since 1540, was also at this time farming the rectory's tithes from the Crown. He claimed that John Thorpe had failed to provide the full tithe of fleeces from over 1,200 sheep he had pastured in the parish.[13] There are good circumstantial grounds for concluding that these sheep were pastured in Wharram Percy township, rather than in any of the other townships within the ecclesiastical parish.

In terms of the broad history of Wharram's depopulation and subsequent exploitation as sheep pasture, therefore, the further investigation of documentary sources since 1990 has largely corroborated the conclusions reached by Beresford in 1979. There are, however, some differences in detail and emphasis; and these are discussed here not because they are themselves particularly dramatic or unexpected on such an investigative timescale, but because they provide useful insights into the approach that structured decades of research into village shrinkage and desertion.

In the first Wharram volume the documentary chapter focused on the apparent economic difficulties of Wharram Percy in the fourteenth and fifteenth centuries, and the township's relative poverty as evidenced in tax assessments.[14] It would be easy enough to form a view that the abolition of open-field farming at Wharram, and the township's conversion to sheep pasture, was the result of soil exhaustion and general impoverishment – the land was fit for a sheepwalk and for little else. This could be the correct reading of the evidence, but it is not the only one possible.

---

12. Borthwick, CP G.917.
13. Borthwick, CP G.314.
14. Beresford, 'Documentary evidence' (1979), pp. 10–13.

In the first place, although the number of farming units at Wharram Percy was substantially reduced in the fifteenth century from its earlier peak, this is not inevitably a sign of a community in decline and suffering economic hardship. The reduction could have been caused by a few prospering tenants engrossing the holdings of less successful neighbours; they would have been able, with larger holdings, to rest individual open-field furlongs for longer periods between crops, or to introduce some form of infield–outfield system. The lord of Wharram may have been a passive partner in this: it was not always a story of grasping landlords and downtrodden tenantry, as Katherine Heppell of Bilton in Northumberland could have testified in 1609, after she had been, allegedly, duped by a fellow copyhold tenant and lost her farm to him.[15]

Secondly, although Wharram Percy may have been relatively small and poor compared to some neighbouring townships, it is worth remembering that it was well provided with water, and this may be one reason why it was put down to sheep pasture. With access to a continuously running stream it contrasts with a number of neighbouring townships further south, on the High Wolds, which had to make do with ponds fed by rainfall alone.[16] Although we have no local sources on sheep management surviving from John Thorpe's time, the instructions provided a century later by Henry Best of Elmswell, about ten miles (16km) south-east of Wharram, emphasise the importance of having a clean, unimpeded watercourse of sufficient depth for washing the sheep before clipping.[17]

The papers in Atkinson's tithe cause indicate quite clearly that Thorpe pastured hundreds of sheep at Wharram for a whole year, including the washing and clipping months of May and June. The combination of good wolds sheep pastures and an adequate supply of water may have made Wharram particularly attractive to a sheep master who could perhaps offer the lord a better return even than successful tenants of mixed farms still based in the village site: the conversion of Wharram to a sheepwalk was not necessarily a last-ditch attempt to get some kind of return from an otherwise valueless piece of land.

Thirdly, after its pastoral conversion the township was not bereft of inhabitants. One of the deponents in the 1543–4 tithe cause, Thomas Carter, had recently lived in Wharram Percy for a few years and had kept ten sheep in the same pasture as Thorpe's large flocks. Another witness, John Wilson, was a current

15. S. Wrathmell, 'Deserted and shrunken villages in southern Northumberland' (PhD thesis, University of Wales, 1975), p. 175.
16. S. Wrathmell, 'The documentary evidence', in C. Treen and M. Atkin (eds), *Wharram: a study of settlement on the Yorkshire Wolds, X, water resources and their management*, York University Archaeological Publications, 12 (2005), p. 1.
17. D. Woodward, *The farming and memorandum books of Henry Best of Elmswell*, Records of Social and Economic History, new series, 8 (Oxford, 1984), pp. 19–20.

inhabitant of the township, and probably so, too, were Thorpe's shepherds George Alan and George Gurwell.[18] The likelihood is that, even discounting the vicar and his family, Wharram Percy was never entirely uninhabited.

Finally, although there were probably several decades in the sixteenth century when there was no cultivation at all at Wharram, it had become before the end of that century a single farmhold rented by at least one prosperous farming family who occupied a 'chief messuage' and cultivated the township on an infield–outfield system.[19] The infield was the heavily manured land that was cropped on a regular basis (although not, apparently, continuously: Harris notes that on the Wolds an intervening fallow between crops seems to have been universal). Parts of the outfield were cropped on a far less frequent basis, perhaps every ten years or so.[20]

The components of the farm, shown in Figure 7.1, can be reconstructed from later documents, principally a mid-eighteenth-century rental[21] and an 1836 estate map.[22] They included enclosed cattle pastures in the valleys, the cultivated infield, and a far more extensive outfield. A lease of 1636 implies that the infield was about 200 acres (assuming half under crop at any one time), and that this was supplemented by the cultivation of up to 400 acres of outfield at any one time.[23] Wharram Percy was not for long devoid of cultivated grounds.

Depopulation and desertion on the northern Yorkshire Wolds

To what extent was Wharram's experience mirrored in other townships in this part of the Wolds? In 1979 Beresford noted that, in Wharram Percy parish, the township of Towthorpe contained a shrunken village, and Burdale and Raisthorpe had been reduced to single farms. He also referred to depopulation in Hanging Grimston, in the adjoining parish of Kirby Underdale, which, like Wharram, featured in the records of the 1517 commission of enquiry.[24]

What is striking about the records of the 1517 commission, however, is the paucity of local evidence for the decay of houses and conversion of arable lands to pasture. In the wapentake of Buckrose, which encompassed this part of the Wolds,

---

18. Borthwick, CP G.314; S. Wrathmell, 'Farming, farmers and farmsteads from the 16th to 19th centuries', in C. Harding and S. Wrathmell (eds), *Wharram: a study of settlement on the Yorkshire Wolds, XII, The post-medieval farm and vicarage*, York University Archaeological Publications, 14 (2009), pp. 2–3.

19. NYRO, ZAZ 10; RUL, MS EN 1/2/296; Wrathmell, 'Farming, farmers and farmsteads', pp. 3–8.

20. A. Harris, *The rural landscape of the East Riding of Yorkshire, 1700–1850* (Oxford, 1961), pp. 24–5.

21. Beresford and Hurst, *Wharram Percy*, p. 113.

22. Wrathmell, 'Farming, farmers and farmsteads', pp. 6–9.

23. RUL, MS EN 1/2/296.

24. Beresford, 'Documentary evidence' (1979), pp. 7–9.

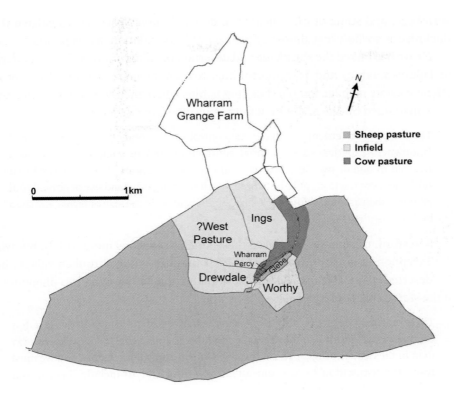

Figure 7.1 Reconstruction of the seventeenth- and eighteenth-century infield and outfield at Wharram Percy.

Wharram Percy and Hanging Grimston are the only two townships to make an appearance in these records, with a combined total of only six decayed messuages.[25] Did most of the northern Wolds desertions take place before 1488, as Beresford implied for Wharram itself?

Thanks to a detailed study by Susan Neave,[26] we are now in a position to answer that question. The vast majority of farmers in this region continued to inhabit villages and to participate in open-field cultivation for another century or two after Wharram's conversion to a sheepwalk. In the late seventeenth and early eighteenth centuries, however, many Wolds villages experienced significant

25. I.S. Leadam, 'The Inquisition of 1517. Inclosures and evictions, part II', *Transactions of the Royal Historical Society*, new series, 7 (1893), p. 248.
26. S. Neave, 'Rural settlement contraction in the East Riding of Yorkshire, c. 1660–1760' (PhD thesis, Hull, 1990); S. Neave, 'Rural settlement contraction in the East Riding of Yorkshire between the mid-seventeenth and mid-eighteenth centuries', *Agricultural History Review*, 41 (1993), pp. 124–36.

shrinkage, and some of them near total depopulation: Neave has calculated that Buckrose as a whole lost almost 27 per cent of its population in this period.[27]

Neave has linked the shrinkage and desertion of villages at this time to patterns of landownership, and to opportunities for landowners to profit from more efficient estate management in those townships where their freedom of action was not constrained by the existence of numerous other freeholders:

> The majority of settlements under the control of only one or a small number of landowners experienced substantial contraction, and in some cases had been reduced to one or two farms by the mid-eighteenth century. This suggested that settlement contraction could be a direct result of changes in land use or agricultural practice, such as emparking, enclosure, or an increase in the size of farms, initiated by major landowners.[28]

Beresford, of course, recognised these kinds of changes more widely, but with the exception of emparking identified their product as the shrunken village, not the deserted village. He made a very clear distinction between the two phenomena at the start of his book *Lost villages*:

> There are many villages still alive whose changes of fortunes in the last few centuries have meant that more people might be found in the Poll Tax lists of 1377 than in the Census of 1951. These shrunken villages are another story, and we must resist the temptation to turn our attention to them or to include them in our definition of depopulation.[29]

In *Deserted medieval villages: studies* he gave his reasons for drawing such a sharp distinction between complete desertion and shrinkage:

> The encloser after *c.* 1550 ... certainly shared one aim with the depopulating grazier of earlier times: that is, the elimination of the open fields and the complete transformation of the landscape to hedged fields. But no more... Both grain and meat could most profitably be produced in enclosed fields ... [Enclosure] was still the enemy of Habitation, in the sense that some reduction in the village labour-force was part of the cost of greater efficiency, but [it] did not produce total depopulation ... If these later enclosures have an archaeological product, it is not the depopulated but the shrunken village.[30]

So how should we explain the experience of Eastburn, in Kirkburn parish, just over eleven miles (18km) south-east of Wharram Percy? As at Wharram, the entire township was converted to a sheepwalk and the settlement depopulated. But here

27. Neave, 'Rural settlement contraction', p. 128.
28. Ibid., p. 130.
29. LVE, p. 21.
30. DMVS, pp. 18–19.

the depopulator was John Heron of Beverley, who had bought up the whole of Eastburn between 1664 and 1666, and who had pulled down most of the houses, according to deponents in a 1682 tithe cause.[31] It is a classic case of desertion and conversion to sheep pasture, but it took place over a century later than it should have in the context of Beresford's distinction between depopulation and shrinkage.

Or how should we explain the experience of Towthorpe and Raisthorpe, two of the five townships of Wharram Percy parish? At the former the resident yeomen farmers, William Taylor and his son Thomas, purchased various freeholds between 1660 and 1709, depopulating a village which had contained eleven households in 1672.[32] It became a single farm. Raisthorpe, too, was reduced to a single farm in the same period, in about 1680.[33] The depopulation histories of these settlements on the Yorkshire Wolds do not, therefore, appear to slot easily into the categories defined by Beresford. To what extent are they anomalous in terms of the broader patterns of depopulation, desertion and shrinkage?

Depopulation, desertion and shrinkage: the wider picture

My own study of deserted and shrunken medieval villages in Northumberland revealed chronologies of desertion and shrinkage very similar to those described by Neave, resulting from the same kinds of actions by landlords or dominant tenant families intent on agrarian reorganisation.[34] As we have seen, Beresford viewed the deserted village as a late medieval phenomenon (except for emparked villages), and the shrunken village as a manifestation of later improvement. The broad pattern identified in southern Northumberland was, in contrast, of villages that survived, although often reduced in size, until the late seventeenth and early eighteenth centuries, when they were either reduced to a single farm or completely depopulated.

Village depopulation was not necessarily accompanied by township depopulation. As open fields were enclosed and converted to ring-fence farms designed to be managed in severalty, it was sometimes appropriate to move the farmsteads to new locations in the centre of their holdings, rather than leaving them in the village which had been the focus of open-field farming. Figure 7.2 shows this kind of development at East Matfen, near Corbridge, where township enclosure in 1686 was followed by the dispersal of steadings from the village to

---

31. Neave, 'Rural settlement contraction', p. 133.
32. Ibid., p. 172.
33. Beresford, 'The documentary evidence' (1987), pp. 13, 221.
34. Wrathmell, 'Deserted and shrunken villages', chapter 6.

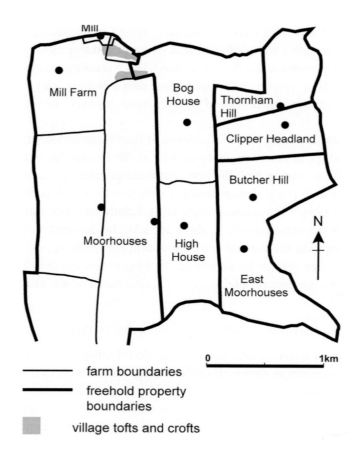

Figure 7.2 The late-seventeenth-century dispersal of farmsteads at East Matfen (Northumberland).

new locations, leaving the medieval settlement site entirely devoid of buildings.[35] A village could be abandoned entirely, and replaced by wholly dispersed farmsteads, without there having been any apparent reduction in the township's population. It would be easy enough to suppose that the experience of Northumberland was very different from that of counties further south, but similar farmstead dispersal (although not necessarily leading to village desertion) has been recorded by John Broad in seventeenth-century Buckinghamshire, at Middle Claydon and Boarstall (see below, pp. 127–34).[36]

These haphazardly accumulated case studies are perhaps sufficient to suggest

35. S. Wrathmell, 'Village depopulation in the 17th and 18th centuries: examples from Northumberland', *Post-Med. Arch.*, 14 (1980), pp. 119–23.

36. J. Broad, *Transforming English rural society: the Verneys and the Claydons 1600–1820* (Cambridge, 2004), pp. 59–60, 243.

that some counties outside Beresford's core midland region had different experiences from those he chose to emphasise; but are they sufficient to warrant a fresh look at the midland counties themselves? By 1968 Warwickshire had one of the highest frequencies of known deserted villages per 10,000 acres.[37] It was also the county that generated one of the key documents deployed by Beresford in his discussions of village desertion: John Rous's list of depopulated villages, written in about 1486. Beresford used the Rous list to emphasise the impact of conversions to sheep pasture at that period: 'This list is, I think, unique. No other county, even others as badly hit by the conversion to sheep pasture, can boast such first-hand, incontrovertible evidence.'[38]

Even this source, however, is not as unambiguous as Beresford's comment might lead us to suppose. Nearly thirty years after the appearance of *Lost villages*, James Bond published a study of the Rous list, and concluded that it needed to be 'treated with rather greater caution than hitherto'. Four of the sixty places listed had probably never been villages at all, and the evidence for nucleated settlements at four others was flimsy. Almost 20 per cent of the places listed had not been fully depopulated at the time he wrote; and of those that were, some seem to have been wholly or substantially depopulated before the fifteenth century.[39]

What emerges from these various local and regional studies is a far greater diversity in village depopulation histories than Beresford's simple categorisation would lead us to suppose. This is hardly surprising: his studies created a new intellectual landscape; ours are more detailed and intricate explorations of the landscape he created. It is, though, intriguing that he felt the need to construct such clear, precisely defined distinctions between fully deserted and shrunken villages – distinctions which shaped the settlement classifications that are still in use today.

The reason is probably to be found in the sharpness of the debates over Tudor depopulation – fact or fantasy – and over the numbers of deserted villages – few or many.[40] The depth of feeling generated in these disputes is evident from Beresford's anecdote, published in 1971, where he quotes a fellow historian who had advised him not to publish *Lost villages*.[41] In such circumstances it is easy to appreciate how positions became polarised and why categorical distinctions were over-emphasised, why there was such a determined attempt to force diverse and

37. DMVS, p. 39, table IX.
38. LVE, p. 82.
39. C.J. Bond, 'Deserted medieval villages in Warwickshire and Worcestershire', in T.R. Slater and P.J. Jarvis (eds), *Field and forest: an historical geography of Warwickshire and Worcestershire* (Norwich, 1982), pp. 150–2.
40. LVE, pp. 22, 79–80; DMVS, pp. 18–19.
41. DMVS, p. 3.

messy reality into a couple of neatly constructed boxes labelled 'deserted medieval villages' and 'shrunken medieval villages'. It may now be time, though, to attempt a more sophisticated analysis of these issues, and to employ databases and geographical information systems to achieve a new understanding of the regional and national patterns of desertion, shrinkage and depopulation.

8

Understanding village desertion in the seventeenth and eighteenth centuries

JOHN BROAD

The sense of excitement engendered by the discovery of deserted medieval settlements and the insights that research has given us into the medieval village community have all the fascination of uncovering the hidden and resurrecting forgotten landscapes. The pattern of development of English rural society in the seventeenth and eighteenth centuries, in contrast, rarely provides us with an equivalent sense of separateness and remoteness from the past. This chapter looks at two aspects of village desertion and disappearance in the seventeenth and eighteenth centuries. It ignores the most obvious and dramatic aspect of the process – the transplantation of whole villages, for example at Nuneham Courtenay in Oxfordshire and Milton Abbas in Dorset – which is covered elsewhere in this book (see Williamson, this volume). My primary concern is with the insidious processes of village shrinkage more characteristic of the period. How were the parishes containing what modern historians have designated as deserted or shrunken villages faring around 1700? In particular, to what extent did they survive as distinguishable entities and viable communities? Early-eighteenth-century perceptions of some sites can be seen through the prism of the information provided by the Anglican clergy to Bishop Wake of Lincoln. Lincoln diocese then included about 1,200 parishes in a vast swathe of eastern England running from the Thames, where it formed Buckinghamshire's southern border, to the Humber, the northernmost extremity of Lincolnshire (Figure 8.1). It included the whole of Bedfordshire, Buckinghamshire, Huntingdonshire, Leicestershire and Lincolnshire, as well as substantial parts of northern Hertfordshire.[1]

The period between 1600 and 1800 surveyed here started with the last

---

1. This data comes from J. Broad (ed.), *Bishop Wake's visitation returns 1706–15* (forthcoming), based on the Wake MSS at Christ Church, Oxford. This edition uses Wake's own collation of the material from the parish returns of 1706, 1709, and 1712 made soon after 1712, together with additional material from the parish returns of 1715. Evidence from the Wake MSS will be cited as *c.* 1710 and will not identify the individual return.

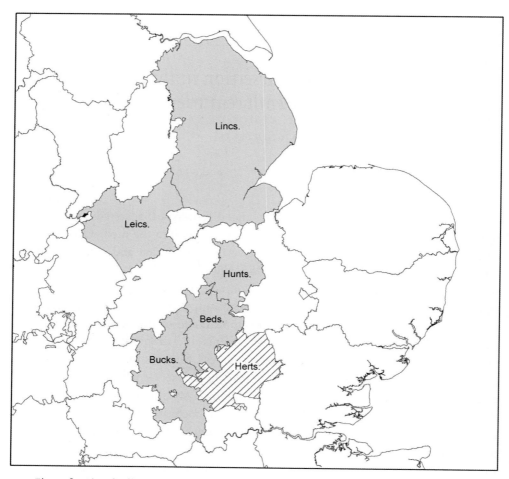

Figure 8.1 Lincoln diocese, *c.* 1710.

significant popular uprising against depopulating landlords – the Midland Revolt of 1607 – which culminated in the mass assembly of protestors at Newton near Kettering and the destruction of the Tresham family enclosures. Beginning in Northamptonshire, the revolt quickly spread to villages in Warwickshire and Leicestershire before being put down with some ferocity and exemplary executions.[2] The revolt came at the tail end of the period of depopulating

2.   E. Gay, 'The midland revolt and the inquisitions of depopulation of 1607', *Transactions of the Royal Historical Society*, new series, 18 (1904); L. Parker, 'The agrarian revolution at Cotesbach, 1501–1612', *Transactions of the Leicestershire Archaeological Society*, 24 (1948), pp. 41–75; WRO, MS CR136/C2623 for Sir Roger Newdigate's contemporary notes on the rebellion at Chilvers Coton, Warwickshire.

enclosure that turned open fields into vast sheep runs, employing a few shepherds at the expense of copyholders with their small farms. The revolt also triggered the setting-up of the last of the Crown's Depopulation Commissions, first used in 1517. In 1607 the Commission, significantly, only examined a small selection of Midland counties pinpointed as most vulnerable to enclosure.[3] The second quarter of the seventeenth century marked the twilight of the great demesne sheep farm as wool became less profitable and the rising population needed more grain for bread and beer. Bowden long ago provided numerous examples of the breaking-up of great demesne sheep runs, which were often subdivided and let out to tenants. They on occasion ploughed them up to take advantage of high grain prices, or turned to mixed farming in which cattle were more important, and sheep were kept for their manure and mutton as much as for their wool.[4] Legal agreements between lords and their village copyholders, such as that at Harlaxton in Lincolnshire, made a point of stressing in the preamble the 'improvement of the said lands, and yet to avoid all depopulation and decay of farms'.[5]

By 1800 the dynamics of enclosure and rural change were very different. Parliamentary enclosure was at its height, and the process of enclosure was in its final phase. The title of Goldsmith's poem 'The Deserted Village', written in 1770, may seem to echo the world of depopulating late medieval enclosure. Some, including Beresford, have wanted to link the poem's dedication to Sir Joshua Reynolds with the clearance of the village of Nuneham Courtenay in Oxfordshire.[6] This allowed the building of a fine residence and landscaped park, and the rebuilding of labourers' houses along the newly straightened main road. However, if the poem is based on a specific depopulation, modern scholarship has found other candidates for the real place, and, like my own reading of the text, prefers a far more generalised interpretation. It centres on the death of village community and an imagined peasant world ignorant of the cash nexus, and alludes in the final

3. J. Martin, 'Enclosure and the Inquisitions of 1607: an examination of Dr Kerridge's article "The returns of the Inquisitions of Depopulation"', *Agricultural History Review*, 30 (1982), pp. 41–8.

4. P. Bowden, 'Agricultural prices, profits and rents', in J. Thirsk (ed.), *Agrarian History of England and Wales*, 4, 1500–1640 (Cambridge, 1967), pp. 641–3; more examples are to be found among Eric Kerridge's work and his citations of these changes as a putative move to 'up and down husbandry'. See E. Kerridge, *The agricultural revolution* (London, 1967), chapter 3; see also J. Thirsk, 'Agrarian history, 1540–1950', in *VCH, Leicestershire*, 2, p. 219.

5. Lincolnshire Archives, 1PG/2/1/2/1 – one of a series of deeds and agreements 1622–7 at Harlaxton. Cited from the calendar available online Access to Archives at http://www.nationalarchives. gov.uk/a2a/ (retrieved 28 January 2009).

6. M.W. Beresford, 'The earliest pre-desertion plan of an English village', *Medieval Village Research Group Annual Report*, 33 (1985), p. 36. Beresford took as conclusive a statement by Lord Harcourt that this was the case.

stanzas both to the parliamentary enclosure of commons that took the last sources of free sustenance away from the poor, and to the migration to exotic foreign parts of many of the inhabitants:[7]

> But a bold peasantry, their country's pride,
> When once destroy'd, can never be supplied.
> A time there was, ere England's griefs began,
> When every rood of ground maintain'd its man;
> For him light Labour spread her wholesome store,
> Just gave what life requir'd, but gave no more:
> His best companions, Innocence and Health;
> And his best riches, ignorance of wealth.
>
> Where then, ah! where, shall poverty reside,
> To 'scape the pressure of continuous pride?
> If to some common's fenceless limits stray'd,
> He drives his flock to pick the scanty blade,
> Those fenceless fields the sons of wealth divide,
> And even the bare-worn common is denied.[8]

The poem harks back to a 'golden age' of hospitality, harmony and social ease centred on parsonage, schoolroom and alehouse, but it also reflects a wider concern among political economists and social thinkers in the 1750s and 1760s that Britain's population might be declining.[9] They were wrong about the nation's population as a whole, but some rural areas certainly saw significant falls. Recent figures produced by Wrigley and the Cambridge Group indicate that something like 10 per cent of English hundreds suffered population decline during the third quarter of the eighteenth century.[10] However, changes in rural population were evident at the level of the parish and groups of parishes, where growing landownership concentrations and changing management patterns were at the heart of a process of differentiation in population and social structure. Single landowners, or a very few large absentees, could pursue policies that eliminated small 'peasant' farms, increased the numbers of larger farms, reduced the

---

7. For example, P. Baines, 'The deserted village', *The Literary Encyclopedia* (2003), at http://www.litencyc.com/php/sworks.php?rec=true&UID=1100 (accessed 10 September 2009).
8. O. Goldsmith, *The deserted village*, lines 55–62, 303–8; cited from Electronic Text Center, University of Virginia Library: http://etext.virginia.edu (retrieved 10 September 2009).
9. See most recently S. Thompson, 'Parliamentary enclosure, property, population, and the decline of classical republicanism in eighteenth-century Britain', *The Historical Journal*, 51 (2008), pp. 621–42, especially pp. 628ff.
10. E. Wrigley, paper to Economic History Conference, Nottingham, March 2008; see also S. Neave, 'Rural settlement contraction in the East Riding of Yorkshire between the mid-seventeenth and mid-eighteenth centuries', *Agricultural History Review*, 41 (1993), pp. 123–37.

labouring population and caused village shrinkage in many communities. This was most apparent before the rural population explosion after 1780. However, these changes rarely went beyond shrinkage, simply because the newly enlarged farms tended to be mixed or dairy farms, which needed substantially more labour to work them than the earlier sheep runs.

The transition from a society that felt threatened by a depopulating enclosure that erased settlements from the map to one that acknowledged the inevitable destruction of a 'peasant' way of life took place during the first half the seventeenth century. Archbishop Laud raised over £40,000 for the Crown in the 1630s by fining depopulating landowners – most notoriously in 1634, when the shock waves around a £4,000 fine imposed on Sir Anthony Roper reverberated through the landed gentry and aristocracy.[11] However, those who understood the working of government were aware of the nuanced way in which Laud's agents applied the policy. Sir Edmund Verney, for instance, heard that the constable of Middle Claydon in Buckinghamshire had drawn up a response in the following terms in 1635:

> We do certify that there is of the lands of Sir Edmund Verney Knight between 30 and 40 acres by estimation now in the occupation of William Lea; Thomas Miller; John Aris, Clerk; Widow Simmons; John Cox; John Faulkner; Edward Henton; Will [blank] and Will Geech which was tillage within the space of 30 years and now is enclosed {signed} Roger Deely, Constable

This was an accurate representation of Verney's small-scale enclosure in the village, but Sir Edmund wrote to Deely urgently requiring him to amend the wording of his return of enclosures to show that farmers had not been evicted from the land. He wrote an alternative wording that he required the constable to use instead:

> I do certify that about thirteen years since Sir Edmund Verney Kt. Lord of the Manor converted to pasture between thirty and forty acres of land by estimation which had until then always been used in tillage, and that he is the owner and user of that land, but there is no decay of houses in the parish.[12]

Close analysis of the pattern of farming development in Middle Claydon does not suggest that farms were being amalgamated and enlarged at that time, but as new enclosed farms were put down to grass farmers from outside the parish were brought in as tenants. There was a sense in which the old village families and their farms were being undermined by new policies.[13]

11. K. Sharpe, *The personal rule of Charles I* (Newhaven/London, 1992), p. 472.
12. Verney MSS, Claydon House, Microfilm reel 2, Warrant and returns, dated 13 March 1634/5.
13. See J. Broad, *Transforming English rural society: the Verneys and the Claydons 1600–1820* (Cambridge, 2004), chapters 4 and 6 passim.

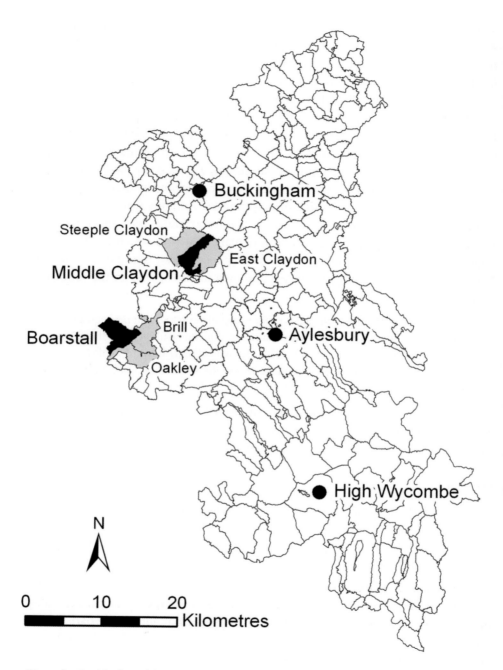

Figure 8.2 Buckinghamshire case studies, showing locations of Boarstall and Middle Claydon.

The turbulence of the years immediately preceding the English Civil War undoubtedly saw some 'levelling' attempts to reverse unpopular enclosures, and the intellectual ferment and local power vacuums during the period of the war accentuated the process. Direct agrarian action by groups of radicals such as the Diggers complemented the more mundane examples of hedge-breaking and resumption of common rights. Most dramatically, much of the drainage of the fens undertaken under patents from the early Stuart Crown was reversed by communities whose way of life had been destroyed by the process.[14] Yet the Commonwealth and Protectorate governments had no radical agrarian agenda. The substantial resumption of enclosure in the Midlands during the 1650s by landowners ruined by the war, or excluded from political power by their royalism, is particularly well documented for Leicestershire.[15] The era produced a pamphlet literature and debate on enclosure, some of which echoed traditional cries of depopulation. There was also a strongly articulated case made by men such as Samuel Hartlib and Walter Blith that prioritised 'improvement' and the more productive use of commons and parish 'waste' to feed an English population that was peaking just at that time. Perhaps the debate was also in reaction to the high prices produced from 1646–8 both by the poor growing conditions for grain and the raging epidemics among flocks and herds.[16] After the Restoration, the cry against village depopulation and enclosure faded away. Yet why should this happen when we know that processes that shrank village communities actively continued?

Examples from Buckinghamshire

Two case studies from Buckinghamshire (Figure 8.2) show how changing techniques of estate management affected communities and the landscape in different ways, tending to shrink villages rather than reduce them to next to nothing.

A dramatic example of village destruction is the disappearance of the village of Boarstall during the seventeenth century. Boarstall is famed for being mapped in a cartulary, village houses being thus depicted at the early date of c. 1440.[17] The village lay in the heart of the forest of Bernwood and, in the 1580s, a series of disputes over forest rights led to a further mapping of the area (Figure 8.3).[18] It

---

14. K. Lindley, *Fenland riots and the English Revolution* (London, 1982).
15. Thirsk, 'Agrarian history', p. 218.
16. S. Hindle, 'Dearth and the English Revolution: the harvest crisis of 1647–50', *Economic History Review*, 61, supplement 1 (2008), pp. 64–98.
17. R. Skelton and P. Harvey (eds), *Local maps and plans from medieval England* (Oxford, 1986).
18. J. Broad and R. Hoyle (eds), *Bernwood: life and death of a royal forest* (Preston, 1997).

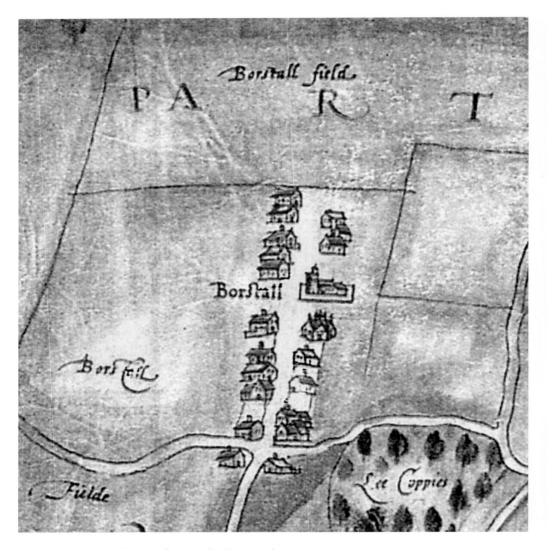

Figure 8.3 The site of Boarstall village *c.* 1580.

was the seat of the Dynhams, the principal landowning family in the parish in the early seventeenth century, and their residence, Boarstall Tower, became the eastern front-line strong point of the king's forces in the first civil war. The maps from the 1580s show that the village site was close to the tower; it was relatively small in size, but was certainly distinguishable as a nucleated settlement. However, the Royalists decided to raze all the houses to the ground to strengthen the tower's defences. After the war, the village was never rebuilt: instead the gardens of an

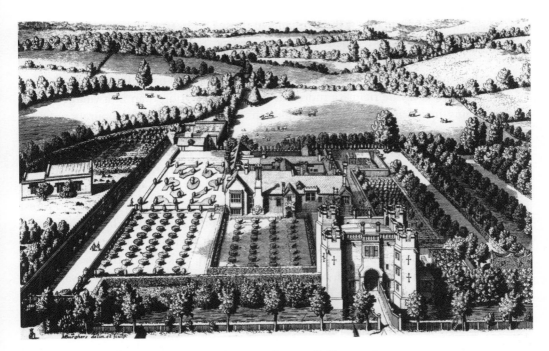

Figure 8.4 Michael Burghers' engraving of the site of Boarstall village *c.* 1690.

extended residence at Boarstall Tower covered much of the site, and the road was displaced.[19]

Yet it is most misleading to see this as a disappearing village community. It merely metamorphosed. Boarstall had not been a large village, for the Dynhams had prevented the spread in the forest of numerous squatter dwellings of the type that was particularly notable in the neighbouring parish of Brill. There were already large enclosed sheep pastures in various parts of the parish by 1610. The survey made by the Royal Purveyance authorities for Buckinghamshire in 1619 and 1620 show that land worth some £710 a year had become enclosed pasture.[20] These pastures had been enclosed from the forest by the Dynhams or their predecessors and represented roughly one-third of the total area of the parish. During the 1620s and 1630s the forest of Bernwood was disafforested and, after local people had been compensated with nearly 300 acres (121ha) for common pasture, the remainder was enclosed, and was either shared among the existing landholders or sold off to speculators. The medieval village of Boarstall did not disappear then, and even after the Civil War destruction the slightly reduced population moved elsewhere in the parish to be employed on the substantial ring-

19. S. Porter, 'The Civil War destruction of Boarstall', *Records of Buckinghamshire*, 26 (1984), pp. 86–91.
20. Bodleian Library, MS Willis 30.

fenced farms laid out by the Dynhams or those London merchants who invested in the forest lands to let them at economic rents. The resulting pasture farms were grazed by a mixture of cattle and sheep, and by the end of the seventeenth century dairying had become important.[21] The farmhouses and barns for such farms were placed out in the fields, a more advantageous position than in a village centre. Living-in servants rather than neighbours or cottage-dwelling labourers provided the continuous labour supply and there was much less seasonal labour and equipment sharing than on small mixed and arable farms.

The dispersion of farmsteads across the parish area provided better protection of stock and fencing. A good example of this can be seen in the story of the substantial amount of Boarstall land – some 231 acres (94ha) – assigned to forest cottagers from the adjoining villages of Brill and Oakley, who had only pasture rights. This land became known as the poor folk's pasture and lay on the border with the common pasture of the adjoining parish, Oakley. For fifty years eligible inhabitants used this land, but it was poorly managed and from 1685 it was let out to a single farmer and the rent used to provide charity payments to poor villagers. As in many such decisions, there were strident opponents prepared to challenge the change by asserting their pasture rights. The only way that the tenant could protect his property and manage his farm profitably was to build a farmstead on site. The trustees allowed him to build a brick farmhouse, and deduct the cost from his rent.[22]

Boarstall parish did not, therefore, become depopulated. Never a large village, it shrank from about 168 people in 1603 to fewer than 100 after the Civil War, only to recover to a figure slightly above that for 1603 by 1800. It retained its church and parson (Figure 8.4).[23]

Ten miles (16km) from Boarstall lay Middle Claydon, which appeared on the 1968 list of deserted villages.[24] It was one of three Claydon parishes, which *c.* 1600 all had populations of 200–300. After 1620, the Verney family decided to make it their country seat, buying out the gentry tenants of the demesne and proceeding to shape the village over the next 200 years.[25] It was an open-field parish working a three-field rotation, but in a wood-pasture area with plentiful common woodland and waste, which in 1600 had been intercommoned with adjoining parishes. Within forty years the Verneys had completely changed the economy of the parish,

21. Broad and Hoyle, *Bernwood*, pp. 78–80.
22. M. Airs and J. Broad, 'The management of rural building in seventeenth-century Buckinghamshire', *Vernacular Architecture*, 29 (1998), pp. 43–56.
23. For population estimates see Broad and Hoyle, *Bernwood*, p. 82.
24. DMVS, Appendix, pp. 193–5.
25. For a detailed study of this village and the processes described see Broad, *Transforming English rural society*, especially chapters 4 and 6.

Table 8.1 Middle Claydon: numbers of tenants by farm group size 1648–1787

Farm size	1648	1688	1722	1787
0–4 acres	6	15	7	9
5–19 acres	18	6	1	5
20–49 acres	18	6	1	5
50–74 acres	5	5	5	5
75–150 acres	4	9	12	2
150+ acres	2	2	1	8
No. farms >5 acres	47	28	20	25
Total nos	53	43	27	34

For a more detailed discussion of these changes see Broad, *Transforming English rural society*, pp.139–40

social relationships and the landscape. However, there was no sudden and massive depopulation. A process of defining previously fluid parish boundaries, excluding copyholders from their pasturing rights on the woods and common waste, and then a piecemeal enclosure in three stages took place between 1611 and the mid 1630s, leaving an attenuated two-field system. A combination of active estate involvement and cash inducements enabled the family to buy out the copyholders. When ring-fenced farms were carved from the wood-pasture waste new tenants were brought in from outside and expected to build their own houses. The old sheep run on the manorial demesne was split into three farms, and farm buildings erected on each. During the Civil War the parish suffered depredations from soldiers on both sides and the family fell into serious financial straits, but by 1653 they had more or less set their affairs in order. Sir Ralph Verney planned to continue the piecemeal enclosure, but the remaining open-field farmers persuaded him to complete the enclosure since the truncated farming system no longer worked effectively, having insufficient common pasture. Middle Claydon was finally enclosed by agreement. Such agreements were the most common means of enclosure in the seventeenth century, and accounted for the enclosure during that century of almost a quarter of England's land area.[26]

Middle Claydon was almost certainly added to the list of deserted medieval villages because at the same time as the enclosure Sir Ralph expanded his park, built new almshouses by the church and demolished the two or three village houses close to Claydon House and church. However, he left untouched the old village farmsteads at the edge of the park. Because these were again rebuilt in the eighteenth and nineteenth centuries, it would be easy to categorise them as an

26. J.R. Wordie, 'The chronology of English enclosure, 1500–1914', *Economic History Review*, 2nd series, 36 (1983), pp. 483–505.

Table 8.2 Middle Claydon: percentage of farm acreage by farm size group

Farm size	1648	1688	1722	1787
0–4 acres	1	1	2	0
5–19 acres	13	4	1	2
20–49 acres	30	17	8	5
50–74 acres	16	16	17	6
75–150 acres	21	46	65	9
150+ acres	19	16	8	78
Total	100	100	101	100

For more information see Broad, *Transforming English rural society*, p. 140.

apparently transplanted village – which, if this were the case, must have been transplanted at a much earlier stage, perhaps in the fifteenth or early sixteenth centuries when the great manor house was built and substantial sheep runs created on the demesne. Although seventeenth-century enclosure was accompanied by conversion to pasture, and new farmers came in from other parishes to take over several of the ring-fenced farms, this was not a case of depopulation. We know that a small number of families left the village but, overall, the population fell very little in the next fifty years. What we can see is gradual restructuring of the village's society and economy. One indicator of change is farm size, and Table 8.1 shows this over 140 years.

The numbers of small farmers was drastically cut in the years after enclosure, but the shift to really large farms did not come until the mid eighteenth century (Table 8.2). Only then did farms over 150 acres or more account for over three-quarters of the parish area, with eight farmers sharing an enormous proportion of the land. The population of Middle Claydon stood near to 215 around the time of enclosure, but fell only slowly to 206 fifty years later in 1709. A much more dramatic fall occurred during the eighteenth century, with only 103 inhabitants recorded in the census of 1801.

The management of farm size by incremental change rather than dramatic reorganisation meant that the size of the village dwindled in the long term. The smaller number of farms was linked to a polarisation of the rural population. In the sixteenth and seventeenth centuries yeomen, husbandmen and cottagers all held some stake in the land or pasture rights. By 1700 farmers and labourers were beginning to replace the earlier terms. Labourers were increasingly confined to garden plots rather than smallholdings, and their houses were described as cottages. Villages lost their middle ground of small farmers. Morton's *Northamptonshire History*, published in 1712, points up this divergence by providing numbers of farmers and cottages for each parish.[27] Wake's visitation returns for a number of villages in Lincolnshire, both shrunken and flourishing, describe the inhabitants as being all cottagers.[28]

The growing number of landless cottagers either depended on farmers in the neighbourhood for work or took up work in industry or services. Employment did not depend on inhabiting a particular village, but if labourers were unemployed or ill they needed parish charity or, ultimately, poor relief. The rising cost of poor relief in the late seventeenth century, combined with the coming of more precise settlement laws after 1662, meant that parishes with a few large farmers were able to use both carrot and stick to limit population growth and even bring about population shrinkage. The carrot might be a promise of a job elsewhere or an apprenticeship for teenage children.[29] The stick could be (as at Middle Claydon) pressure on those without good economic prospects not to marry, and the pulling down of houses to prevent squatters taking up residence. By the nineteenth century 'open' and 'close' villages had evolved from these social policies,[30] as can be seen in our Buckinghamshire examples of the Bernwood villages and the Claydons. In both areas there was one village which shrank and another where population rose rapidly as the population eased out of 'close' villages found refuge in a parish with fragmented landholding and no population control strategies (Table 8.3). In both, the most significant divergence came in the eighteenth century.

The kind of attenuation that occurred at Boarstall and Middle Claydon can be found widely. MacDonagh has recently described the equivalent process in neighbouring Northamptonshire villages.[31] Did the shrinking of the close villages destroy their sense of community? It certainly changed village composition and social structure, but were these dying communities? It is easy to assume that they were. To take a recent instance, the Whittlewood project looked at a number of shrunken villages in north Buckinghamshire; of these, two, Stowe and Lillingstone Dayrell, had resident elite families who actively managed the estates

27. J. Morton, *The natural history of Northamptonshire: with some account of the antiquities* (1712). I would like to thank Leigh Shaw Taylor for suggesting I examine this source.
28. Broad, *Bishop Wake's visitation returns*.
29. For examination of these mechanisms see in particular S. Hindle, *On the parish?* (Oxford, 2004), pp. 391–3, and J. Broad, 'Housing the rural poor in southern England, 1650–1850', *Agricultural History Review*, 48 (2000), pp. 151–70.
30. B. A. Holderness, '"Open" and "close" parishes in England in the eighteenth and nineteenth centuries', *Agricultural History Review*, 20 (1972), pp. 126–39.
31. B. MacDonagh, *Society for Landscape Studies Newsletter* (Winter 2008), at http://www.landscapeandenclosure.com/B.%20McDonagh%20SLS%20newsletter.pdf (accessed 10 September 2009).

Table 8.3 Population change in 'open' and 'close' villages in the
Bernwood and Claydon areas of north Buckinghamshire

	1524/5	1585	1603	1622	1662/71	1676	1709	1801
Boarstall	158	201	168	153	72	113	100	179
Brill	216	462	333	594	310	500	540	859
Middle Claydon	135		210		217	217	206	103
Steeple Claydon	225	345			361	n/a	j360	646

For the source of these figures see Broad and Hoyle (eds), *Bernwood*, p. 82, table 4.4. and Broad, *Transforming English rural society*, pp. 149, 252.

over long periods, and it would be easy to think of these as dead communities.[32] Yet the Wake returns show both had resident clergy and populations of around 200 and 100 respectively *c.* 1710. Their population centre may have shifted, but they persisted like many other parts of England had always been, as hamlets and dispersed settlements.[33]

New evidence from the Wake visitation

The Wake visitation returns for Lincoln diocese throw light on the survival of village (and parish) life *c.* 1710. This fruitful source covers population, resident gentry, antiquities and church monuments (where applicable), as well as numbers of dissenters, charities, schools and church services. By taking those parishes with twenty houses or fewer *c.* 1710 in Lincolnshire, it might be possible to analyse the characteristics of shrunken parishes and also to match them with identified deserted village sites. Did small parishes share characteristics? Did deserted settlements have a continuing identity? This is ongoing work, but some preliminary pointers are worth pursuing.

For example, let us take the four sites near Leicester visited in 1948 and 2008. Great Stretton in Great Glen parish still had its own chapel in use with services twice a week in 1709. It was still separately enumerated within the parish, and doubtless inhabitants would attend their chapel service rather than Great Glen's. On the other hand, Hamilton had already lost its identity among the townships of the parishes nearby. Old Ingarsby was no more than a hamlet, with four families assigned to it, within the parish of Hungarton. Hungarton contained two other deserted settlements that were treated in the same way, Quenby and Baggrave. Knaptoft still lent its name to a large parish, although most families were in two

32. M. Page, 'Destroyed by the Temples: the deserted medieval village of Stowe', *Records of Buckinghamshire*, 45 (2005), pp. 189–204.
33. J. Broad, *Buckinghamshire dissent and parish life 1669–1712*, Buckinghamshire Record Society, 28 (1993), pp. 85, 91.

Table 8.4 Analysis of continuity and disappearance of deserted villages listed in 1968
in the Lincolnshire Wolds sample area

UK National Grid point of origin of 10km² block	Deserted in 1968 list	Surviving parish identity c. 1710	Evidence of elite park or seat	Surviving place name, house, farm	Completely disappeared by 1710
TF200600	5	4	1	0	1
TF200700	6	3	1	1	2
TF200800	10	7	4	2	1
TF300600	8	2	1	3	3
TF300700	11	7	1	4	0
Total	40	23	8	10	7

other named townships. It was 'Knaptoft an antient enclosure in which lie his Graces Tenants and Shepherd', while the Duke of Rutland's 'Old House' was still recognised as such, although it was apparently no longer used by the family. Six families, including dissenters, were assigned specifically to Knaptoft, and its own chapel held services every Sunday. Cotesbach, the Leicestershire village much implicated in the 1607 Midland Revolt, seems to have survived with a parson, an elite residence used largely as a dower house, and good educational provision for its inhabitants. As it retained seventeen houses, it had clearly escaped the fate it feared in 1607, but more research is needed to see whether it had moved to become the kind of modernised farming community we have seen at Boarstall and Middle Claydon.

Lincolnshire has more identified deserted village sites than any other county – 200 in 1968, in a large county with over 600 parishes, and is thus useful in an attempt to generalise about the evidence for shrunken and deserted parishes. The deserted places do not in practice coincide with those 209 parishes with fewer than 100 inhabitants c. 1710. Over one third of Lincolnshire parishes had fewer than twenty houses but retained their own churches and had a strong continuing sense of identity. The stipends were so poor that in many cases the clergy served two or three parishes simply to gather together a very modest living salary of £50 or £60 a year. Very few had derelict churches and only a handful were defined as sinecures with no parishioners to be served. Skinnard, a parish with only one house – 'one master, one man, two maid servants' – with a decayed church, from which lead and materials were daily stolen and 'two bells expected daily to fall into the rubbish and perish', was very much the exception, with the inhabitants going to the neighbouring parish for services.

Lincolnshire and its settlement patterns reflect its place in the shifting national balance of population and agriculture even before the industrial revolution. The proportion of the population in the counties of eastern England from Suffolk and

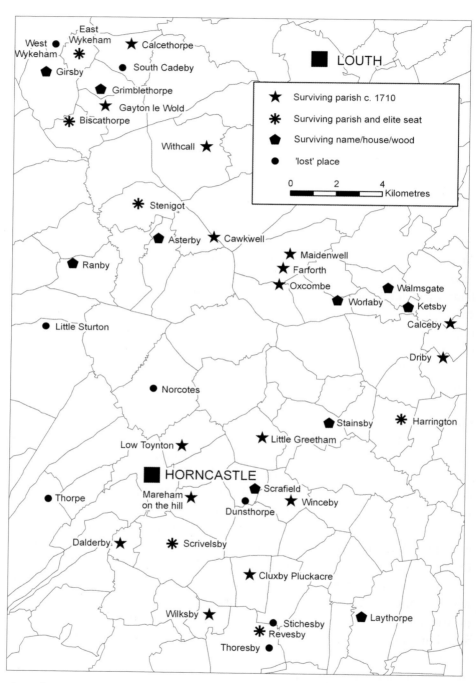

Figure 8.5 The fate of listed settlements in 1968 in the Lincolnshire sample area.

Bedfordshire to the East Riding of Yorkshire was reduced from the 1290s, when they had relatively high population densities, to a lower level by 1756.[34] This reduction was most marked in Lincolnshire. The small acreages of many Lincolnshire parishes may reflect earlier population buoyancy; in Lincolnshire, as elsewhere, small parish populations frequently went with small acreages, but there was no automatic correlation. Almost one-third of those parishes with twenty houses or fewer in *c.* 1710 show evidence of a tradition of elite presence: either a seat, whether inhabited or let out to a tenant, or even in some cases turned into a farmhouse, or monuments to an elite family in the church. Others had links to former monastic property, priory estates and granges, suggesting they had been operated as part of a wider farming system. Among those that remain, there are other remarks in the returns that suggest land consolidation or modern estate administration rather than 'peasant' farming. Some parishes, it was stated in the returns, had only one or two farms, with the rest cottages, although this was not confined to small parishes. East Kirkby, with 700 acres, had fifty families, of which forty-five were cottagers, and in East Keal, most of the forty-six families were cottagers. For one or two parishes it was stated that all the farmers lived outside the parish. In many more the lordship, or complete ownership, was assigned to a single person, often the patron, even if there is no evidence that this individual resided in the parish. In 1706 the parish of Marton had recently been bought up as a piece through a stockjobber.[35]

Some of these parishes with populations below twenty houses or 100 inhabitants have been listed as deserted villages, or had deserted settlements within them. They cluster on the Wolds both east and south of Louth, and around Horncastle, but the phenomenon is widespread across the county. To test the variety of histories associated with communities that have been designated as deserted, that part of Lincolnshire has been analysed here in more detail. The area was divided along the national grid boundaries into five blocks each 10 x 10km. The fate of those places which appeared on the 1968 listing was followed up using both the Wake MSS for their situation *c.* 1710 and the evidence from modern Ordnance Survey maps.

The results of that analysis can be seen in Table 8.4 and Figure 8.5. Some forty deserted villages were found within this area of 500 square kilometres. Of these only seven have completely disappeared in the sense that the name is neither found in the Wake material *c.* 1710, nor observable on modern maps and

34. B. Campbell, 'Benchmarking medieval economic development: England, Wales, Scotland and Ireland, *c.* 1290', *Economic History Review*, 61 (2008), p. 938, suggests that Lincolnshire's population in 1290 was twice that in 1756.

35. Christ Church, Oxford, Wake MS 326, pp. 50, 52 and 117. Estate agents were a new phenomenon in the early eighteenth century; it was not uncommon for them to be described as 'stock-jobbers'.

identifiable as house, farm or place-name. Twenty-three still had identities as parishes *c.* 1710, and in only one of these was the church ́ruinous, although in rather more there was no parsonage. Eight of the places were now the site of an elite house or park, with a notable concentration of such places in the upper Bain valley to the west of Louth. Ten of the deserted villages survive as a house, farm or place-name. Only one of these, Walmsgate, was the site of a ruined church, but there was no functioning parish there in 1710.

This helps us to put into perspective the continuity in the landscape of many settlements where there is evidence of shrunken or deserted settlements. To use Beresford's captivating phrase, only seven of our forty places were truly 'lost villages' and two of these lay in the vicinity of Revesby Abbey, south of Horncastle, where Wake had no responses to his parish questions.

The variety of histories for these Lincolnshire settlements confirms that the process of agrarian modernisation that we have seen in the examples of Boarstall and Middle Claydon was not necessarily combined with the elite presence found there. Outlying parishes in concentrated ownership, where estate management was strong, could also be modernised. The structures of ecclesiastical administration and provision that had been established in the Middle Ages were still working remarkably effectively in *c.* 1710, providing a continuity of parish tradition and loyalty even as settlements shrank.

Conclusion

This chapter has contrasted two perspectives on village desertion in the seventeenth and eighteenth centuries. It has first looked at the evidence for new desertions in that period. The economic and social conditions that had produced settlement clearances in the late medieval period were being replaced by new configurations which altered the nature of village desertion. The first quarter of the seventeenth century saw the last few examples of village clearance for great sheep runs. Later, large-scale village destruction was undertaken by landlords who wished to rebuild their country seats, and extend parks around them, isolating themselves from village communities. But probably more significant was the growth of enclosure by agreement, which often led to profound changes in rural society, including the destruction of small farms and the expansion of ring-fenced tenancies. This process tended to take place over a much longer timescale, and to shrink rather than destroy the villages where it occurred. It was a vital component in village differentiation which in the nineteenth century led to parishes being classified as 'open' or 'close'.

The second perspective has reconsidered whether the deserted settlements from the middle ages had disappeared without a trace by the seventeenth and eighteenth centuries. In Lincolnshire, a county full of deserted settlements, less than 20 per cent of the sample of forty communities noted in 1968 as deserted had completely disappeared by 1700. Elite emparkment and seat-building accounts for an only slightly higher proportion of cases. Equally, when we compare the list of parishes with fewer than twenty houses (around 100 inhabitants) in the county c. 1710 with the list of deserted settlements, there is a substantial mismatch between the two. Lincolnshire's long population decline from a high medieval population density resulted in many small settlements, which were not listed as deserted villages. This chapter has attempted to clarify some of the mechanisms of village desertion in the seventeenth and eighteenth centuries, but has also revealed some of the myths and complexities that remain for future investigation.

9

Abandoning the uplands: depopulation among dispersed settlements in western Britain

ROBERT SILVESTER

At first sight this paper might appear to reside a little uneasily in a volume whose title highlights deserted villages, and whose *raison d'être* celebrates the sixtieth anniversary of a gathering of eminent historians at earthworks in lowland Leicestershire. It is less the lowland/upland dichotomy that provokes that unease, rather the appearance of the term 'village', which, at least to this uplander, still conjures up cosy images of concentrated clusters of dwellings, open greens and, frequently, heavily agriculturalised landscapes.

It is unlikely that those historians sixty years ago gave much thought to the settlements dispersed across the western and northern uplands that were of broadly contemporary date to their newly identified earthworks in Leicestershire. And it is of no surprise that the initial efforts of the Deserted Medieval Village Research Group (DMVRG) from its formation in 1952 focused on the counties of lowland England. In his review of historical research to 1968 Maurice Beresford alluded but briefly to the medieval colonisation of marginal uplands such as Dartmoor and cited examples from the south-west peninsula only because the moorlands there carried the most impressive surface remains of medieval house structures.[1] The uplands, however, attracted their own devotees among archaeologists – Aileen Fox, for instance, had been excavating in the hills of Glamorgan in south Wales in the 1930s, and in the early 1950s followed a similar course on Dartmoor. Dorothy Dudley, E. Marie Minter and others also excavated on the south-western moors, while staff of the Welsh Royal Commission were responsible for progressing the study of rural settlement in several regions of the Principality.[2]

Since 1948 the conceptual distance between upland settlements and lowland villages has diminished. The 1971 volume edited by Beresford and Hurst

---

1. M.W. Beresford, 'A review of historical research (to 1968)', in DMVS, pp. 36, 60.
2. D. Austin, 'The excavation of dispersed settlement in medieval Britain', in M. Aston, D. Austin and C. Dyer (eds), *The rural settlements of medieval England* (Oxford, 1989), p. 236.

incorporated separate overviews of deserted medieval rural settlements in Wales and Scotland.[3] Eighteen years later the volume of essays that honoured those editors appeared under a general title which evoked 'settlement' rather than 'village', and carried several wide-ranging papers touching on issues beyond the regions of village landscapes.[4] The more all-embracing approach was apparent, too, in the transformation of the DMVRG into the Medieval Settlement Research Group in 1986, and has been manifest in some of its more recent statements.[5] The dichotomy is, of course, more than simply a divergence between the varying perceptions of those working in disparate geographical regions. There are fundamental differences, not least in the distinction between nucleated and dispersed settlements, coupled with an appreciation that in many upland areas the former are a rarity. There is, though, a single unifying factor: regardless of type, location and density, settlements are established, they prosper or decline and ultimately many are deserted or, to adopt a slightly more emotive term, abandoned.

This paper focuses primarily on Wales, but also draws on evidence from the south-west of England. I might have looked even further afield, yet settlement histories almost certainly vary across the regions, displaying trends and patterns both of similarity and contrast, and there remains an uncertainty as to whether sufficient research has been completed (or perhaps, it might be argued, published) in some upland regions to permit useful overviews. It was a point made by David Austin twenty years ago and it still appears valid today.[6]

Defining the uplands

What, then, are the uplands? For the south-west of England definition appears reasonably straightforward, with the uplands equating with the moorlands of Dartmoor, Exmoor, Bodmin Moor and arguably the less extensive and lower granite bosses further to the west. Much of Wales could be classed as upland, too, but here individual blocks are less readily definable, and there is a tendency to gauge the uplands in terms of absolute height. By general consent, 244m (800 feet) above sea level has become a marker for the uplands, but both lower (213m,

3. L.A.S. Butler, 'The study of deserted medieval settlements in Wales', in DMVS, pp. 249–69. Nearly forty years later this remains an outstanding and relevant contribution to the study of Welsh rural settlement.
4. M. Aston, D. Austin and C. Dyer (eds), *The rural settlements of medieval England* (Oxford, 1989).
5. See, for instance, M. Gardiner, 'Review of medieval settlement research, 1996–2006', MSRGAR, 21 (2006), pp. 22–8.
6. Austin, 'The excavation of dispersed settlement', p. 238.

700 feet) and higher (305m, 1000 feet) altitudes have been advocated.[7] The word 'upland' may be appropriate, relative to the lowlands of England and the coastal fringes of Wales, but in its precision it can be misleading. Much modern settlement lies above the 244m level in Wales and the majority of land is farmed if not with arable, then certainly with permanent, well-maintained pasture. Many of the abandoned medieval and later settlements that can currently be recognised are found around the fringes of the Welsh moorlands, peripheral to very large tracts of moorland and mountain that are wholly devoid of any trace of human activity from the historic era. So the uplands under consideration here are not co-extensive with the open moors; they are generally areas where there is virtually no sign of human habitation today, but where traces of human activity from the past lie relict in the landscape. It is these settlements and their associated lands that underpin our definition of the uplands.

There is a further issue, that of marginality. The lowland historian may see the uplands and moorlands as environments that were exploited through need. The upland historian, however, would argue that this perspective is distorted by perceptions that are fundamentally centred on agriculture. As Dyer has pointed out, marginality is a relative term and the issue, perhaps, is whether the colonisers were forced into the uplands by external circumstances or whether an element of choice was implicit in their move further into the hills.[8] There is, too, a secondary emphasis in the adoption of the term 'marginality', and that is related to the comparative lack (or perceived lack) of study of dispersed settlement sites compared with their nucleated counterparts. This has been asserted for Wales but is probably applicable to other northern and western regions also.[9]

The myth of the abandonment of agricultural settlements in the fourteenth century?

It is with arable cultivation in the uplands that this assessment opens. Historians have traditionally argued that the impact of the Black Death in the middle of the fourteenth century led to a contraction of land under the plough. Hoskins and

7.   R.J. Silvester, 'The archaeology of the Welsh uplands: an introduction', in D. Browne and S. Hughes (eds), *The archaeology of the Welsh uplands* (Aberystwyth, 2003), p. 9; E.H. Brown, *The relief and drainage of Wales* (Cardiff, 1960), p. 4.

8.   C. Dyer, '"The retreat from marginal land": the growth and decline of medieval rural settlements', in M. Aston, D. Austin and C. Dyer (eds), *The rural settlements of medieval England* (Oxford, 1989), p. 49.

9.   N. Edwards, 'Landscape and settlement in medieval Wales: an introduction', in idem (ed.), *Landscape and settlement in medieval Wales* (Oxford, 1997), p. 5; K. Roberts, 'The deserted rural settlement project: background and methodology", in idem (ed.), *Lost farmsteads. Deserted rural settlements in Wales*, CBA Research Report, 148 (2006), p. 1.

Stamp's view in the early 1960s that 'the heavy mortality of successive epidemics brought about a retreat from marginal lands everywhere in England and Wales ...' was developed by other commentators, as, for instance, in the contributions on Wales and the north of England in *The Agrarian History*.[10]

Landscape archaeology, too, was beginning to make a contribution in the 1960s. Fieldwork on Dartmoor revealed that around the fringes of the moor and along the valleys that penetrated it there were significant numbers of farming settlements, ranging from solitary longhouses to small hamlets, closely associated with arable cultivation. Between 1961 and 1975 Marie Minter excavated the hamlets at Hutholes and Hound Tor I and the solitary farms at Dinna Clerks and Hound Tor II, whose altitudes ranged from 290 to 335m (950 to 1100 feet) above OD.[11] A little earlier limited excavation had also taken place at Garrow Tor, an agriculturally based settlement on the Bodmin Moor granite.[12] Some excavations produced pottery and other finds that could be attributed to no later than the fourteenth century. The archaeological evidence, then, appeared to corroborate the historians' view that the abandonment of the upland agricultural settlements resulted from the passage of the Black Death in the middle of the century coupled with a deteriorating climate induced by reduced temperatures and increased wetness from the later thirteenth century. The conventional view was summed up by Guy Beresford's words: 'By the middle of the fourteenth century the hardships brought about by the deteriorating weather were such that the settlements [on Dartmoor] over the 1000 feet contour were, once again, abandoned to the bracken and the heather.'[13]

In the 1970s, in a different part of Britain – the Lammermuir Hills of southern Scotland bordering Northumberland – Parry recognised traces of relict cultivation associated with settlement to which he attributed a medieval date. Parry argued for the continuing abandonment of the Lammermuir farming settlements established above the 275–300m (900–985 feet) OD contour from around 1300 through to 1530, with further settlements abandoned by 1600, and another eighteen over the next century and a half. But it was for the other examples that he listed – from the North Yorkshire Moors, Dartmoor and elsewhere – that a fourteenth-century

10. W.G. Hoskins and D.L. Stamp, *The common lands of England and Wales* (London, 1963), p. 45; E. Miller (ed.), *The agrarian history of England and Wales*, 3, 1348–1500 (Cambridge, 1991), pp. 38, 104.

11. C.D. Linehan, 'Deserted sites and rabbit-warrens on Dartmoor, Devon', *Med. Arch.*, 10 (1966), pp. 113–44; G. Beresford, 'Three deserted medieval settlements on Dartmoor: a report on the late E. Marie Minter's excavations', *Med. Arch.*, 23 (1979), pp. 98–158.

12. D. Dudley and E.M. Minter, 'The medieval village of Garrow Tor, Bodmin Moor, Cornwall', *Med. Arch.*, 6–7 (1962–3), pp. 272–94.

13. Beresford, 'Three deserted medieval settlements', p. 146.

decline in cultivation and desertion of settlements was explicitly stated.[14] Subsequently, other factors in addition to climate and plague have been added to the mix to explain the abandonment of upland agricultural settlement in the north and elsewhere, including an end to population expansion in the decades around 1300.[15] Additional explanations include unsettled political conditions with regular warfare and raiding, particularly in border regions,[16] and even a decline in the direct farming of demesne lands.[17]

Some of Parry's views on the impact of climate have been challenged, particularly by Tipping, yet his work remains influential and is still cited, although perhaps with less caution than he himself exercised.[18] Winchester, for instance, has claimed relict agricultural traces in the Lake District, the Cheviots and north Pennines as indicative of the abandonment of cultivation as a result of a combination of severe winters and wet summers, a population collapse after the Black Death and border warfare.[19] And when the present writer first assessed the limited evidence for medieval upland cultivation in Wales nearly twenty years ago, he had few reservations in postulating a similar timeframe.[20]

The logic in the argument advocated by both historians and archaeologists is, of course, attractive in its straightforwardness and convenience. Yet there have long been dissenting voices. Austin and his colleagues were already arguing for a longer chronology of abandonment on Dartmoor early in the 1980s. And in the early 1990s Fox was questioning the supposedly rapid decline in arable on Dartmoor after the mid fourteenth century, although comparable figures for Bodmin Moor appeared to confirm conventional beliefs.[21]

On the evidence now available, the Dartmoor settlements apparently came into existence at a late date. None have produced pottery from before 1200, and most

---

14. M.L. Parry, *Climatic change, agriculture and settlement* (Folkestone, 1978), pp. 122–3.
15. Cited in Dyer, '"The retreat from marginal land"', p. 45.
16. Butler, 'The study of deserted medieval settlements in Wales', p. 254.
17. D. Austin, 'Dartmoor and the upland village of the south-west of England', in D. Hooke (ed.), *Medieval villages. A review of current work* (Oxford, 1985), p. 75.
18. R. Tipping, 'Climatic variability and "marginal" settlement in upland British landscapes: a re-evaluation', *Landscapes*, 3.2 (2002), pp. 10–29; A. Caseldine, 'The environment and deserted rural settlements in Wales: potential and possibilities for palaeoenvironmental studies', K. Roberts (ed.), *Lost farmsteads*, pp. 64, 136–40.
19. A.J.L. Winchester, *The harvest of the hills* (Edinburgh, 2000), p. 6.
20. R.J. Silvester, 'Medieval farming on the Berwyn', MSRGAR, 6 (1991), pp. 12–14; R.J. Silvester, 'Medieval upland cultivation on the Berwyns in north Wales', *Landscape History*, 22 (2000), pp. 47–60.
21. D. Austin, R.H. Daggett and M.J.C. Walker, 'Farms and fields in Okehampton Park, Devon: the problems of studying medieval landscape', *Landscape History*, 2 (1980), p. 55; H.S.A. Fox, 'The occupation of the land. Devon and Cornwall', in E. Miller (ed.), *The agrarian history of England and Wales*, 3, 1348–1500 (Cambridge 1991), pp. 154–62.

only after 1250. One site alone – Hutholes – seems to have been abandoned by 1350. The presence of ceramic cisterns at Hound Tor I and II, Sourton, Dean Moor and Dinna Clerks extends the date of their occupation into the late fourteenth or even early fifteenth century, although none have produced pottery post-dating 1450. There may be a conflict in the evidence here, for pollen analysis suggests that at Hound Tor cultivation and settlement retreated in the fourteenth century.[22] A longhouse settlement on Holne Moor appears to have reverted its arable to pasture in the fourteenth century on the basis of detailed analysis of the surface remains; the excavated material shows that the settlement was occupied perhaps into the sixteenth century.[23] Even in Okehampton Park, the one Dartmoor settlement where an argument has been made for a forced abandonment resulting from an agency other than climate or plague, the pottery from the excavations points to continued occupation at a later date.[24] Rare documentary evidence reveals a comparable story. Fox demonstrated from manorial account rolls that the hamlet of Dunnabridge, located in the valley of the West Dart high up on Dartmoor, was established in 1305–6 and retained inhabitants and a field system into at least the seventeenth century. But he was equally able to point to settlements that were abandoned as a result of the Black Death, others where there appeared to be continuity of occupation, and others still that were already exhibiting signs of new growth by 1364.[25]

Bodmin Moor, the other major granite boss in the south-west, displays similarities to Dartmoor, although some of its upland farms may have come into existence earlier than the twelfth century. Nearly forty deserted medieval settlements have been identified, ranging from solitary longhouses to small hamlets, most of them between 225m and 300m (740–985 feet) OD, reflecting the generally lower elevation of the Cornish moorlands. Several have been partially excavated. Both Garrow Tor and Bunnings Park could have seen some abandonment in the fourteenth century, although one house at Garrow was still occupied in the sixteenth century. Settlement continued at Menadue until the mid

22. J. Allan, 'Medieval pottery and the dating of deserted settlements on Dartmoor', *Proceedings of the Devon Archaeological Society*, 52 (1994), pp. 141–7; D. Austin and M.J.C. Walker, 'A new landscape context for Hound Tor, Devon', *Med. Arch.*, 29 (1985), pp. 147–52; Dyer, '"The retreat from marginal land"', p. 47.

23. A. Fleming and N. Ralph, 'Medieval settlement and land-use on Holne Moor, Dartmoor: the landscape evidence', *Med. Arch.*, 26 (1982), pp. 101–37.

24. Abandonment in this case was claimed as a result of emparkment by the lord of Okehampton, Hugh de Courtenay, just before 1300. D. Austin, 'Excavations in Okehampton deer park, Devon, 1976–1978', *Proceedings of the Devon Archaeological Society*, 36 (1978), pp. 191–239; Allan, 'Medieval pottery', p. 145.

25. H.S.A. Fox, 'Medieval Dartmoor as seen through its account rolls', *Proceedings of the Devon Archaeological Society*, 52 (1994), pp. 153–6.

Figure 9.1 Medieval upland cultivation. Medieval strip fields on Ffridd Camen in Llandrillo on the western edge of the Berwyn (Denbighshire). The associated farmstead lies among the surface stone at the top of the photo (Crown Copyright: RCAHMW).

seventeenth century and at Carwether until the early nineteenth.[26] The most intensively studied, but unexcavated, community on the moor is the hamlet of Brown Willy, which offers a variant picture. Until the later thirteenth century a communal group of six longhouses lay at the centre of a field system stretching along the western slopes of the hill. By 1275, on the evidence of a law case, the hamlet had disintegrated and had been replaced by six separate farmsteads strung out at intervals on the western slopes. These thinned out to three during the post-medieval centuries.[27]

Exmoor, the third of the large moorlands in the south-west, has, to date, revealed no more than five major deserted settlements on its sedimentary soils, although desertions of farmsteads rather than hamlets have also been claimed.[28]

26. N. Johnson and P. Rose, *Bodmin Moor. An archaeological survey. Volume 1: the human landscape to c. 1800* (London, 1994), pp. 83–93.

27. P. Herring, 'Medieval fields at Brown Willy, Bodmin Moor', in S. Turner (ed.), *Medieval Devon and Cornwall. Shaping an ancient countryside* (Macclesfield, 2006), pp. 78–103.

28. H. Riley and R. Wilson-North, *The field archaeology of Exmoor* (London, 2001), p. 94.

The settlement of Ley Hill seems to have reached its peak in the thirteenth to fourteenth centuries, yet there was also some fifteenth- to sixteenth-century material found during excavations in 1998/9. Documentary evidence implies that Badgworthy was abandoned by the beginning of the fifteenth century, while the remaining three sites have not been dated. Perhaps significantly, both Badgworthy and Sweetworthy display physical remains whose condition point to a reduction in the size of the hamlet to a single farm.[29]

The paucity of targeted excavations in Wales hampers an assessment comparable to that for the south-west of England. High-altitude farming occurred in the medieval era, but not, it appears, on the scale recognisable in Devon and Cornwall. The topographical context for cultivation linked to settlement varies from the high moorland fringes, as found at Llandrillo (Denbighshire), Llanwddyn (Powys) and Llangynog (Powys), to lower moorland commons such as Penybont (Powys) and coastal plateaux, as on the Great Orme at Llandudno (Conwy).[30] Few newly identified examples have been added to the short list that this writer produced back in 2000: the only convincing examples are on Ffridd Ddu and Cae'r Mynydd in Aber (Gwynedd), where cultivation and long huts spread over upland between 240 and 350m (785 and 1150 feet) OD, and on Mynydd Marchywel, to the north-east of Neath (Neath Port Talbot).[31] Longley has claimed that around 10 per cent of the deserted sites identified during recent survey in north-west Wales (a total number in excess of sixty) have ridge and furrow cultivation in their vicinity.[32] However, medieval settlement sites from other parts of Wales are frequently found in close proximity to traces of post-medieval cultivation, and therefore care is needed in identifying medieval arable.[33]

Most of the authenticated agricultural settlements in Wales are individual farmsteads (Figure 9.1), and associated house platforms point to resident communities only at the remarkable systems of fields above Cwm Pennant in Llandrillo and the less extensive system at Ty Mawr, Llanwddyn.[34] Even these are not nucleated, but, as with Ffridd Ddu, they tend to be spread around the

29. Riley and Wilson-North, *Field archaeology*, p. 95.
30. Silvester, 'Medieval upland cultivation'; M. Aris, *Historic landscapes of the Great Orme* (Llanrwst, 1996).
31. D. Longley, 'Deserted rural settlements in north-west Wales' (p. 64), and M. Locock, 'Deserted rural settlements in south-east Wales' (p. 47), in Roberts (ed.), *Lost farmsteads*.
32. Longley, 'Deserted rural settlements', pp. 64–8.
33. RCAHMW, *Glamorgan volume III: medieval secular monuments part II: non-defensive* (London, 1982), pp. 39–41; Locock, 'Deserted rural settlements', p. 47; R.J. Silvester, 'The commons and the waste: use and misuse in central Wales', in I.D. Whyte and A.J.L. Winchester (eds), *Society, landscape and environment in upland Britain* (Birmingham, 2004), p. 63.
34. Silvester, 'Medieval upland cultivation', figure 2; R.J. Silvester, 'Deserted rural settlements in central and north-east Wales', in Roberts (ed.), *Lost farmsteads*, figure 2.4.

extremities of the field systems, echoing Welsh settlement models advanced by historians.[35] An absence of datable evidence from these places, however, means that the period of their demise can only be the subject of calculated guesswork.

The view, broadly held twenty years ago, that the moorland agricultural settlements in the south-west were finished off within a tight timeframe by a combination of inclement climate and plague now appears too simplistic. The argument has been sustained, it might be suggested, by those with limited first-hand experience of either the documentary record or the archaeology of the south-west moors; others with detailed knowledge of these uplands have been more circumspect. Environmental factors may, indeed, have led to the abandonment of some settlements, and the argument that the survivors moved away from the poor-quality upland grounds to better land that had been depopulated is attractively logical, yet cannot be confirmed in the absence of direct documentary reference.[36] The Dartmoor evidence, however, favours a gradual abandonment through into the mid fifteenth century. Bodmin Moor indicates the reorganisation, and perhaps reduction, of settlement, rather than its abandonment. Here a shift in the agrarian regime with a greater emphasis on livestock and arable fields turned over to pasture seems feasible.[37] Wales remains an unknown, but in the light of the more complex picture of abandonment emerging from the granite moors of the south-west, it would certainly be unwise to assume that the later fourteenth century saw the abandonment of all the Welsh upland agricultural settlements. In all the areas considered here, the number of settlement units were reduced, with hamlets in particular giving way to individual farmsteads. But the cessation of cultivation and the abandonment of settlement are different issues.

The demise of the individual farm

Some solitary upland farms, as we have seen, survived the calamities of the fourteenth century only to succumb over the next couple of hundred years to other agencies. The sequence is common to all of the main upland moors in the south-west. On Exmoor the farmholdings at Badgworthy and Sweetworthy appear to have shrunk to individual farms; the Bodmin Moor settlements at Garrow Tor and Brown Willy continued in modified form; and the hamlet at Hound Tor I may have been succeeded by the single farm of Hound Tor II.

The emergence of the single farm in Wales can also be posited, even though a

---

35. T. Jones Pierce, 'Agrarian aspects of the tribal system in Wales', *Géographie et Histoire Agraires, Annales de l'Est, Memoire no. 21* (Nancy, 1959), reprinted in T. Jones Pierce, *Medieval Welsh society* (Cardiff, 1972), p. 332.

36. J. Barnatt and K. Smith, *The Peak District. Landscapes through time* (Macclesfield, 2004), p. 76.

37. Austin, 'The excavation of dispersed settlement', p. 237.

general lack of excavation on upland settlement sites coupled with a shortage of artefacts severely handicaps interpretation.[38] The latter was an issue with one of the house sites excavated on Gelligaer Common in the early 1930s, and equally so in the much more recent excavations at Cefn Drum, an upland no more than 200m (660 feet) above sea level on the periphery of the Gower Peninsula in south Wales, where three buildings and a structure identified as a sheepcote were completely excavated over three seasons. Apart from a single radiocarbon date of the twelfth to thirteenth centuries, pertaining to a corn-drying kiln, the only small find was a simple whetstone. Kissock, the excavator, had to resort to dating his structures by analogy with better-evidenced sites in Wales and the rest of southern Britain: the platform houses to the medieval era and the sheepcote and an associated dwelling to the late seventeenth or eighteenth century.[39]

The transition from communal settlement to single farm manifests itself at Beili Bedw in that central part of Powys that was formerly western Radnorshire (Figure 9.2). The original settlement at Beili Bedw was, by Welsh standards, rather unusual because, with the exception of one or two outliers, its fifteen house platforms formed a nucleated group. Three of the platforms were excavated and produced a relatively small amount of dating evidence attributable to the fifteenth or sixteenth century. Set among the platforms was a single farmstead: the foundations of a small house accompanied by adjacent, strongly banked enclosures. Unfortunately this was not excavated, but a single glass fragment from the late sixteenth or seventeenth century offers some slender guidance to date.[40] Abandonment of Beili Bedw could have been as late as the eighteenth century, but a seventeenth-century date is as likely, and, by the nineteenth century, farming in the locality was focused on another farm complex, Bailey Bedw, 200m away and 30m lower down the slope.

Beili Bedw, with its contiguous closes and enclosures, provides a yardstick for a series of other single-farm enclosure complexes, most readily recognisable on the upland commons of central Wales, where fieldwork and aerial photography have been fruitfully integrated in recent years. Published examples include

---

38. There are also, of course, other fundamental problems which need to be remarked. Inherent in some of the discussion here is that frequently excavation may not have been sufficiently comprehensive for the period of abandonment to be a certainty, Beili Bedw being a prime example. One farmstead in a settlement may be abandoned but this is no guarantee that the others were.

39. J. Kissock, 'Farmsteads of a presumed medieval date on Cefn Drum, Gower: an interim review', *Studia Celtica*, 34 (2000), pp. 223–48; J. Kissock and R. Johnstone, 'Sheephouses and sheepcotes – a study of the post-medieval landscape of Cefn Drum, Gower', *Studia Celtica*, 41 (2007), pp. 1–23.

40. P. Courtney, 'A native-Welsh mediaeval settlement: excavations at Beili Bedw, St Harmon, Powys', *Bulletin of the Board of Celtic Studies*, 38 (1991), pp. 233–55; Silvester, 'Deserted rural settlements', pp. 28–9.

Figure 9.2 Beili Bedw, Radnorshire. The enclosures of the putative sixteenth-century farmstead stand out in sharp relief, surrounded by the more muted earthworks of the earlier platform settlement (Crown Copyright: RCAHMW).

settlements on Moelfre Hill, Llanbister, where a long hut is enmeshed in a layout of five differently sized enclosures; Fron Top, Llanbister; Upper House I, Glascwm; Garn Fawr, Glascwm; and Carnau Bach and Gardiners Hill East on Mynydd Epynt.[41] But in proposing this rather basic list of individual holdings spread across the uplands of southern Powys, there is a danger of simplifying a more complex picture. Riley and Wilson-North have sensibly voiced concerns about distinguishing medieval from later farm earthworks in the Exmoor uplands on the basis of fieldwork alone. That view is relevant not only to the south-west but perhaps even more so to Wales, where the dating of these abandoned holdings can only be by analogy and intelligent surmise.[42] Historic mapping may provide a

41. Silvester, 'Deserted rural settlements', pp. 28–30, figures 2.10–2.11; *idem*, 'The commons and the waste', plate 5.1.

42. For a comparable view on the Welsh evidence see P. Sambrook, 'Deserted rural settlements in south-west Wales', in Roberts (ed.), *Lost farmsteads*, pp. 92–3. Wales shares with Scotland the fundamental problem of a wealth of evidence which is far from easy to date. For Scotland the umbrella term MOLRS – medieval or later rural settlement – has been coined and this could be equally applicable to Wales.

control that frequently holds only as early as the beginning of the nineteenth century, other than in exceptional circumstances where earlier estate maps of the commons were produced. A case in point is the recently published monastic sheepcote of Troed y Rhiw lying at around 290m (950 feet) above sea level in upland Ceredigion, which is grouped geographically with four farms that are believed to have been established in the late medieval period. With estate maps available it has been possible to show these continuing through into the eighteenth if not the nineteenth century.[43]

Support from historians for a new advance into the hills after the fourteenth century comes more from general syntheses than from detailed case studies, and most would concur with Griffiths in his belief that 'open field was taken into severalty and girdle settlements and bond hamlets shrank to be replaced by dispersed *tyddynnod* standing in their own fields, processes that accelerated after 1500', a process which applied on the higher grounds as much as in the lowlands.[44] If renewed interest in the uplands was becoming apparent in the fifteenth century, it is the Tudor records of various governing bodies such as the Star Chamber and the Council of the Marches that demonstrate the eagerness of farmers to take in new land from the commons and waste, often illicitly, and reflect an era of expansion rather than contraction in farming.[45]

No single factor played a pre-eminent role in the desertion of the single farm. Glyndŵr's rebellion, which led to widespread disruption at the beginning of the fifteenth century, and later conflicts probably played their part, and climatic changes may still have influenced settlement. Undoubtedly settlements were established in the uplands in the two or three centuries after the fourteenth-century catastrophes and many of these in turn were abandoned, some perhaps within a generation or two, others over a rather longer time-span.

43. A. Fleming and L. Barker, 'Monks and local communities: the late-medieval landscape of Troed y Rhiw, Caron Uwch Clawdd, Ceredigion', *Med. Arch.*, 52 (2008), pp. 261–90.
44. M. Griffiths, 'The emergence of the modern settlement pattern, 1450–1700', in D.H. Owen (ed.), *Settlement and society in Wales* (Cardiff, 1989), pp. 225–48, particularly pp. 232–3; C. Thomas, 'Enclosure and the rural landscape of Merionethshire in the sixteenth century', *Transactions of the Institute of British Geographers*, 42 (1967), pp. 153–62.
45. D.H. Owen, 'The occupation of the land. Wales and the Marches', in Miller (ed.), *The agrarian history* p. 106; F. Emery, 'The landscape', in D.H. Owen (ed.), *Settlement and society in Wales* (Cardiff, 1989), p. 62; Silvester, 'The commons and the waste', p. 58.

Summer in the hills

In focusing on permanently occupied upland farmholdings we cannot overlook the less visible, but considerably more numerous, presence of a second, complementary strand to upland settlement. In the hills of northern and western Britain the removal of stock from the home farm to summer grazing grounds at higher altitudes – a long-established form of transhumance – was a standard and necessary practice in the historic era. Prehistorians have occasionally argued, often on the basis of slight evidence, for the seasonal use of the uplands.[46] More certainly, place-names in parallel forms in Wales and the south-west of England imply seasonal use of the uplands in the early medieval (or pre-Conquest) centuries. The term *hendre* for the home farm in Wales is partnered by *hafod* for the summer settlement, first documented in the thirteenth century, and a term that should be recognised as the equivalent of the northern shieling. Markedly similar words – *hendre* and *havos* – found in Old Cornish point to common roots before Wales was separated from the south-west by the westwards expansion of Wessex around the end of the seventh century AD.[47]

While both the south-west and Wales appear to have embraced transhumance in the first millennium AD if not earlier, the two regions subsequently followed divergent paths.[48] Herring has argued that transhumance faded out on Bodmin Moor around the time of the Norman Conquest, because of the relatively small number of sub-rectangular huts that represented the seasonal dwellings.[49] Dartmoor is not likely to have been very different.[50] The picture from Wales offers a fundamental contrast. In north-west Wales there is extensive detail of royal *hafodydd* where the upland pastures were a managed resource during the Middle Ages. In western Wales early travellers, from John Leland in the sixteenth century through to Thomas Pennant and occasional contemporaries at the end of the eighteenth, commented on summer houses in the hills. In southern Montgomeryshire lower-land dwellings that were occupied only during the winter were noted at the end of the eighteenth century; and as late as the early nineteenth

46. F. Lynch (ed.), *Excavations in the Brenig Valley. A Mesolithic and Bronze Age landscape in north Wales* (Cardiff, 1993), p. 161.
47. P. Herring, 'Transhumance in medieval Cornwall', in H.S.A. Fox (ed.), *Seasonal settlement* (Leicester, 1996), p. 35, citing O.J. Padel, *Cornish place-name elements* (Nottingham, 1985), pp. 127, 129.
48. The term 'transhumance' is used here, although there has been discussion in the recent past as to whether it is strictly appropriate to the limited, seasonal movement of stock in some areas of Britain. But as the late Harold Fox noted: 'movement over great distances and altitudes is not a prerequisite for transhumance': H.S.A. Fox, 'Introduction: transhumance and seasonal settlement', in *idem* (ed.), *Seasonal settlement* (Leicester, 1996), p. 3.
49. Herring, 'Transhumance in medieval Cornwall', p. 37.
50. Fox, 'The occupation of the land, in Miller (ed.), *The agrarian history*, p. 159.

century travellers were still noting summer dairy houses in the more remote reaches of Caernarvonshire in north-west Wales.[51] Indeed, the renowned folk-life historian Peate reported that a variant form of transhumance, restricted to a short period of a few weeks, was still operating in western Montgomeryshire in the early part of the twentieth century.[52]

Not that there is any trend towards uniformity across Wales as a whole. Mapping the decline and ultimate demise of transhumance within the Welsh uplands is at an early stage in some areas. Using place-name, archaeological and documentary evidence in combination it can be suggested that, in the uplands of the east such as the hills of Radnorshire and perhaps in Glamorgan too, the role of transhumance was waning as early as the later Middle Ages.[53] In the Brecon Beacons and perhaps the neighbouring upland of Mynydd Epynt the decline came later, while, as already noted, in the most western areas it continued into the nineteenth century. Complications emerge where transhumance segued into an all-year-round, sheep-based economy with the accompanying settlement remains largely indistinguishable from their seasonal predecessors.[54]

A few *hafodydd* have been excavated in Wales. The platforms on Gelligaer Common, believed by their excavator to have been permanently occupied farmsteads, are now generally accepted as seasonal settlements.[55] Of the five buildings in two groups that were examined only one could be dated on the basis of pottery of late-thirteenth- to early-fourteenth-century origin. At the opposite end of the country a group of seven long huts with stone foundations along Nant y Criafolen on the Denbigh Moors appears to have been occupied no earlier than the late fifteenth century and abandoned by the end of the sixteenth.[56] In some putative summer dwellings excavators have had to fall back on radiocarbon dates, analogy and even supposition in the absence of datable material.[57] Those that have

51. D. Longley, 'Deserted rural settlements in north-west Wales', Roberts (ed.), *Lost farmsteads*, pp. 76–81; I.C. Peate, *The Welsh house* (Liverpool, 1946), p. 127.
52. Peate, *The Welsh house*, p. 126.
53. Silvester, 'Deserted rural settlements', p. 37.
54. Sambrook, 'Deserted rural settlements', pp. 100–1.
55. Peate, *The Welsh house*, p. 128; Locock, 'Deserted rural settlements', pp. 52–5.
56. D. Allen, 'Excavations at Hafod y Nant Criafolen, Brenig Valley, Clwyd, 1973–4,' *Post-Med. Arch.*, 13 (1979), pp. 1–59.
57. For example, Penmaenmawr (Caerns.): W.E. Griffiths, 'Excavations on Penmaenmawr, 1950', *Archaeologia Cambrensis*, 103 (1954), pp. 66–84; Bwlch yr Hendre (Cards.), where the assessment of land use pointed to abandonment in the mid-eighteenth century: L.A.S. Butler, 'The excavation of a long hut near Bwlch yr Hendre', *Ceredigion*, 4 (1963), pp. 400–07; Aber (Caerns.), where pottery evidence of the eighteenth century related to the last phase of a multi-phased occupation: L.A.S. Butler, 'A long hut group in the Aber Valley', *Transactions of the Caernarvonshire Historical Society*, 23 (1962), pp. 25–36; and Ynys Ettws (Caerns.): G. Smith and D. Thompson, 'Results of the project excavations', in Roberts (ed.), *Lost farmsteads*, pp. 114–17.

Figure 9.3 The grass-covered foundations of a long hut, without doubt a *hafod* of medieval or early post-medieval date, in the Duhonw valley on Mynydd Epynt in Brecknock (photo: the author).

been dated lasted little more than a century, if that. To Gelligaer Common and Hafod Nant y Criafolen, noted above, could be added Ynys Ettws (Gwynedd), where occupation may have occurred, although only intermittently, from the eleventh through to the seventeenth century.[58]

Excavated sites, though, represent a minute fraction of the total number of *hafodydd* in the Welsh hills (Figure 9.3). A cursory count of platforms and long huts identified to date in the Brecon Beacons of south Wales offers well over 200 examples.[59] Virtually every upland common in Radnorshire – and there are nearly seventy of them, varying in size from less than one hectare to over twenty-seven square kilometres – has several and sometimes many more platforms just inside the common boundary.[60] A few of these might have functioned as permanent farmsteads, but a very much larger majority must have been the sites of seasonally occupied structures, comparable in form to their winter counterparts in the lower

58. Smith and Thompson, 'Results of the project excavations', p. 116.
59. R.J. Silvester, *Deserted medieval and later rural settlements in Powys and Clwyd: the final report* (Welshpool, 2001); Silvester, 'Deserted rural settlements', figure 2.13.
60. Silvester, 'The commons and the waste', p. 56.

valleys but probably smaller in size, and without the trappings of associated enclosures, fields and ancillary structures. The platform, cut into the slope at right angles to the contours, was essentially a component of the medieval period, although there is evidence to suggest that this practice continued into the seventeenth century and perhaps beyond. It seems likely, although this requires confirmation by excavation, that many of the Radnorshire platforms, particularly in the east and centre of the county, were abandoned by the end of the Middle Ages.

Transhumance defined a way of life of extremely long-standing in the Welsh hills, a tradition which must have faded out at different times in different regions, rather than one that was terminated abruptly. The decline in seasonal upland activity and its associated dwellings has been linked directly to the shift in stock keeping from cattle to sheep attributed variously to the sixteenth and seventeenth centuries.[61] While this may have had a strong influence on conventional transhumance, any monocausal explanation for its abandonment is likely to be too simplistic, and would not, for instance, explain why seasonal settlement on the commons of Radnorshire declined so early. The reasons for the decline are of less importance in the context of this paper, however, than the physical manifestations and dates of abandonment which are the legacy of the decline.

The demise of transhumance must certainly have reduced the numbers of people accommodated in the hills, if only during the summer months, but not necessarily drastically. A strong argument has been advanced for the later desertion of the seasonally occupied huts known as *lluestai* or dairy houses on the extensive wastes of western Radnorshire, which were well-evidenced in the Tudor era.[62] Yet while some may have been abandoned, others became permanently occupied, more so when cattle gave way to sheep in the seventeenth century and shepherding as a distinct occupation emerged.[63] Likewise, in the uplands of adjacent Cardiganshire (now Ceredigion) transhumance gave way to round-the-year shepherding and the *lluestai* became permanent dwellings.[64]

61. F. Emery, 'The farming regions of Wales', in J. Thirsk (ed.), *Agrarian history of England and Wales, 4, 1500–1640* (Cambridge, 1967), p. 129.
62. The *lluest* is seen as an alternative term to *hafod*, and the proportions of the two terms vary from region to region. In some uplands, however, both are encountered, and it seems evident that they may disguise subtleties in usage that have yet to be fully elucidated, despite the series of detailed papers by Elwyn Davies, as, for example, E. Davies, 'Hafod, hafoty, and lluest: their distribution, features and purpose', *Ceredigion*, 9.1 (1980), pp. 1–41. See also D.K. Leighton, *Mynydd Du and Fforest Fawr. The evolution of an upland landscape in south Wales* (Aberystwyth, 1997), p. 112, and Sambrook, 'Deserted rural settlements', pp. 95–104, which pushes the link between *lluestai* and sheep, and makes more of a chronological distinction between the *hafod* and the *lluest*.
63. R. Suggett, *Houses and history in the March of Wales. Radnorshire 1400–1800* (Aberystwyth, 2005), pp. 249–54
64. Sambrook, 'Deserted rural settlements', pp. 100–1.

Figure 9.4 The head of a small valley running off Aberedw Common in Radnorshire. In the foreground just beyond the limits of the enclosed land are paired enclosures associated with a *hafod*. In the middle distance a later cottage encroachment, abandoned in the nineteenth century, lies at the centre of its rectangular block of fields (Crown Copyright: RCAHMW).

The last influx

Bowen once described the movement of landless people, otherwise known as squatters or by other, even less salubrious, epithets, on to the commons and wastes of Wales as the final phase in the expansion of the single farm.[65] Attaining a particularly high profile in the later eighteenth century, this movement began in earlier centuries and continued even into Victorian times. That this late wave of encroachment is considered here at all should reinforce the inference, which emerges elsewhere in this paper, that both the occupation and the subsequent desertion of the uplands was governed not by time, but by trends and by factors that were in the main external to the uplands themselves.

Of course, in the post-medieval centuries, new farms and cottages were established on the upland edges of existing holdings by relatives of the landowners or even by their farmworkers. More frequently illicit cottages were built on the commons; the poverty and landlessness of these times gave rise to a remarkably widespread tradition that a family that could put up a dwelling on the common overnight – in Wales the so-called *ty unnos* or *caban unnos* – and have smoke coming out of the chimney by morning would be able to reside there unmolested, claiming land around the dwelling to form a smallholding (Figure 9.4). Having established themselves the family would, in due course, replace the rapidly constructed and poorly built hovel with a more substantial dwelling of stone or timber which could become a solid upland farm. Whether or not the majority of the cottages on the commons originated as *tai unnos* is not as certain as the literature might imply, for there are very few contemporary records of the practice.[66] There are, however, parallels from both Scandinavia and the Basque country for similar traditions underpinning the origin of cottages, and Everitt considered the tradition widespread in early modern England.[67] Notwithstanding the absence of documentation, there can be no doubt at all of the prevalence of cottages on the commons.

The later eighteenth century witnessed a peak in encroachments, or at least that is when the large landowners were made acutely aware of the problem, one which could hamper their own use of the commons but also offered an opportunity to generate revenue from new rents. But by then the move to the moors was of long standing. Suggett, for instance, has recently cited a manorial

---

65. E.G. Bowen, 'The dispersed habitat of Wales', in R.H. Buchanan, E. Jones, and D. McCourt (eds), *Man and his habitat. Essays presented to Emyr Estyn Evans* (London, 1971), p. 192.
66. See, for instance, E. Wiliam, *Home-made homes. Dwellings of the rural poor in Wales* (Cardiff, 1988), p. 12; E. Wiliam, '"Home-made homes": dwellings of the rural poor in Cardiganshire', *Ceredigion*, 12.3 (1995), pp. 24–5.
67. A. Everitt, 'Common land', in J. Thirsk (ed.), *The English rural landscape* (Oxford, 2000), p. 218.

Figure 9.5 Abandoned cottage encroachments along Cwm Twlch in western Montgomeryshire (photo: the author).

court case in Radnorshire in 1594 where Thomas ap Rickard of Cefnllys was prosecuted for 'erecting [a] cottage on [the] commons and keeping Englishmen's cattle', and in 1573, drawing on past custom, the Council in the Marches of Wales directed that without the lord of the manor's permission, the only common where a cottage or hovel could be erected by a freeholder was within his own township, and that such a cottage could be inhabited only between 15 May and 15 August, a clear allusion to the seasonal use of the hills as well as to contemporary developments.[68] A 1734 survey of the commons held by the Crown in northern Radnorshire revealed nearly 800 illicit intrusions on the commons, 421 of them having cottages on them.[69] For virtually every other county in Wales it would be possible to identify comparable examples.

Some encroachment cottages were certainly demolished almost as soon as they were constructed, for few landowners welcomed the invasion of their commons and some actively instructed their bailiffs to tear down new cottages,

68. Suggett, *Houses and history*, p. 255.
69. R.J. Silvester, 'Landscapes of the poor: encroachment in Wales in the post-medieval centuries', in P.S. Barnwell and M. Palmer (eds), *Post-medieval landscapes. Landscape history after Hoskins, 3* (Macclesfield, 2007), pp. 58–9.

seeing them as an urgent problem. It was only after twenty years that the inhabitants of the cottage acquired some protection under the law. Others undoubtedly continued in use for several generations before being abandoned, and some are still occupied today, albeit in forms that would be unrecognisable to those who originally erected them.

Many recently constructed cottages were abandoned when an act of parliament divided up the commons into enclosures, and the injustice of this was a theme of contemporary chroniclers.[70] Late in the nineteenth century the agricultural depression took its toll and, as Bowen put it, 'the upward movement ... carried with it the seeds of its own destruction' because of the difficulties of farming at high altitude.[71] This, though, was probably only the last in a series of factors that determined their survival or desertion (Figure 9.5). For Radnorshire alone, this writer has picked out over 900 encroachment cottages and farms from tithe maps; more than 33 per cent had been abandoned by the time of the first large-scale Ordnance Survey maps in the 1880s, while only a further 15 per cent had been given up by the end of the twentieth century. Elsewhere, in the Black Mountains on the border of south-east Wales, cartographic and oral sources have been used to reveal that in the valleys of those uplands, and particularly in their higher reaches, it was the period between 1840 and 1880 rather than later that witnessed the highest numbers of abandonments.[72] And in the upland parish of Llanwddyn (Powys), now the location of Lake Vyrnwy, the largest reservoir in Wales, the local vicar listed fifty-seven houses that had been abandoned in the parish between the beginning of the nineteenth century and 1872.

Not all of the cottage encroachments were occupied by families whose prime motivation was farming and subsistence. In some districts major industrial activities such as quarrying and mining led to rashes of workers' dwellings being erected on the waste, not least because it was the waste that was rich in the raw materials being exploited. Thus in Snowdonia it was the slate quarrymen who colonised the uplands in the nineteenth century, their settlements going into decline at the end of the century. In upland Cardiganshire the growth period in lead mining from the 1830s to the 1880s, when the value of lead increased and nearly 200 mines were operational, ceased in the early twentieth century and the mining settlements, already in decline, disappeared.[73] On the moorlands of south-

70. Parliamentary enclosure was frequently a nineteenth-century phenomenon in Wales. Hugh Evans (b. 1854) was outspoken about the impact of enclosure on the poor in the vicinity of Mynydd Hiraethog in north Wales in *The Gorse Glen* (Liverpool, 1948).

71. Bowen, 'The dispersed habitat of Wales', p. 192.

72. R. Gant, 'Oral history and settlement change: a case study of abandoned dwellings in the Black Mountains of Wales, 1840–1983', *Cambria*, 12 (1985), pp. 97–112.

73. Wiliam, *Home-made homes*, p. 13; Cambria Archaeology, *Metal mining in upland Ceredigion* (Llandeilo, 2007), p. 20.

west England industrial dwellings may have been in the majority: cottages were abandoned on Dartmoor in the eighteenth and nineteenth centuries as quarries and mines came to an end, and the decline in iron mining on the Brendon Hills in Somerset led to rows of ruinous cottages at the end of the nineteenth century.[74]

Conclusions

Have the uplands ever been completely abandoned? The answer is almost certainly 'no', although during the twentieth century we have come as close to it as we are likely to get: although it is a subjective view, there are probably fewer people occupying the hills now than at any previous time since the beginning of the second millennium AD.

This is to treat the uplands as a single, indivisible entity, which of course they are not. Whichever hill or mountain massif in Wales or the south-west is under consideration, there will be large tracts of it where traces of human activity are completely or almost entirely absent. The settlements discussed above concentrate in certain areas: in the Brecon Beacons along the numerous, deeply cut valleys, but not on the interfluvial ridges that separate them; in the Radnorshire hills around the peripheries of the commons but not in their centres; and on the Denbigh Moors in a few areas seemingly selected from many for reasons that elude us. Even more than in the lowlands, the picture of desertion and abandonment is complex and arguably unpredictable.

Desertion should be seen not as a single phase of sustained activity, nor a result of a single stimulus. Instead, at various times in the historic era there has been a move away from uplands. But to generate desertion and abandonment through an outflow of farmers and cottagers, there has first to be an influx; identifying when and how this occurred is as difficult as identifying when the communities departed. Only in the broadest terms of settlement advance and retreat could this be termed cyclical. Some of the stimuli for upland settlement across the centuries have recurred, and this is particularly the case with land scarcity, just as some of the factors that drove communities off the upland have tended to reassert themselves. Other stimuli have been unique. And while some areas have become a focus for settlement at different times – as with Cadwst in Llandrillo, where agricultural settlement was succeeded by hafodydd and later by an encroachment farm – so other areas witnessed no more than one incursion, with abandonment as the terminal event. Perhaps this enshrines a key difference between upland and lowland. While selected lowland locations supported settlement continuously over

74. Linehan, 'Deserted sites and rabbit-warrens', p. 124; Riley and Wilson-North, Field archaeology, p. 121.

many centuries, upland locations rarely did. Any era of high-altitude farming seems not to have lasted that long, perhaps a couple of hundred years, other than in exceptional cases. Establishing how long some of the individual farms functioned is very much more difficult, however, because so few can be accurately dated. Arguably, it is only the transhumant way of life which has a longer trajectory but, even here, there is little clear evidence of any individual settlement's longevity. The encroachment cottages of the eighteenth century are probably the last in a line of upland occupations that have a limited life span. But this, the most recent phase of expansion and abandonment, fully backed by cartographic depiction and written testimony, amalgamates both the rapid decline of settlement through the collapse of industry and, as its counterpart, the more gradual loss of cottages occupied by those who followed a subsistence way of life. It was not a simple, synchronous retreat from the uplands and this is something we should do well to remember in considering earlier phases of upland settlement.

10

'At Pleasure's Lordly Call': the archaeology of emparked settlements

TOM WILLIAMSON

Ever since geographers, historians and archaeologists first began to pay serious attention to the phenomenon of the 'deserted village', the deliberate destruction of settlements to make way for extensive parks and gardens, mainly but not exclusively in the eighteenth and nineteenth centuries, has – alongside the Black Death and depopulation for sheep farming – loomed large in their discussions.[1] Yet when studying the landscape history of the last few centuries we must always be aware of how the evidence of the landscape can have a mythical, symbolic dimension. Complex patterns of social, economic and agrarian change are most easily summarised in single events with clear physical traces. Parliamentary enclosure is a good example. It is still often cited as a key – if not the key – stage in the destruction of the English 'peasantry,' and in the proletarianisation of the labouring poor.[2] Yet decades of research have shown that enclosure of this kind affected little more than a fifth of the land area of England, and that the engrossment of farms and the deterioration in the living conditions of the rural poor continued as fast in the later eighteenth and nineteenth centuries in places anciently enclosed as in places newly enclosing.[3] To contemporaries, as to some later historians, the sudden and dramatic, as well as highly visual, character of the enclosure experience made it a useful scapegoat for social and economic problems which, in reality, had more complex, longer-term and deeper-seated causes – rampant demographic expansion, rural de-industrialisation and the inexorable rise of agrarian capitalism.

---

1.   See, for example, chapter 9, 'The price of a park', in R. Muir, *The lost villages of Britain* (London, 1985); or chapter 7, 'A journey through parks', in M. Beresford, *History on the ground* (London, 1957).

2.   J. Neeson, *Commoners: common right, enclosure and social change in England 1799–1820* (Cambridge, 1993).

3.   M. Turner, *English Parliamentary enclosure: its historical geography and economic history* (Folkestone, 1980); M. Turner, 'Parliamentary enclosure and landownership change in Buckinghamshire', *Economic History Review*, 2nd series, 28 (1975), pp. 565–81.

The case of villages destroyed for the creation of parks is similar, in the sense that any investigation of the scale, character or chronology of this phenomenon must begin by acknowledging the symbolic power of the earthworks in the parkland, and of the isolated church beside the great house, often rebuilt in modish form. These features represent almost an archaeological shorthand for the post-medieval dominance of great landowners and their withdrawal from the communities around them. Few books on deserted villages fail to quote Goldsmith's poem 'The Deserted Village' of 1761, in which the author describes how he had:

> Seen opulence, her grandeur to maintain,
> Lead stern depopulation in her train,
> And over fields, where scatter'd hamlets rose,
> In barren solitary pomp repose?
> Have we not seen, at pleasure's lordly call,
> The smiling long-frequented village fall;
> Beheld the duteous son, the sire decay'd,
> The modest matron, and the blushing maid,
> Forc'd from their homes, a melancholy train,
> To traverse climes beyond the western main.[4]

On the face of it, the archaeological evidence would appear to confirm that the removal of villages to provide privacy and isolation for major landowners, and to allow space for the creation of extensive designed landscapes, was – if not routine – then at least relatively common in post-medieval England. Settlement earthworks are often encountered in parks, either in the form of complete villages or hamlets or as parts of settlements which still survive immediately beyond the park boundary. M.F. Hughes described in 1982 how, during fieldwork in Hampshire in the previous year, 'approximately seventy country parks and gardens were surveyed, of which nearly fifty per cent contained either village earthworks or an isolated church or both'; while the Royal Commission volumes, especially the Northamptonshire volumes, contain numerous examples of settlement remains within parkland.[5]

Yet the presence of settlement remains within a park does not mean that the two had a direct causal connection; there are other reasons why deserted sites and elite residences should be found in close association. Nor do isolated churches

---

4. O. Goldsmith, The Traveller, lines 401–10; in A. Friedman (ed.), The collected works of Oliver Goldsmith, 4 (Oxford, 1966), pp. 267–8.
5. M.F. Hughes, 'Emparking and the desertion of settlements in Hampshire', MSRGAR, 30 (1982), p. 37. RCHME, West Cambridgeshire (London, 1968); RCHME, Central Northamptonshire (London, 1979); RCHME, North-West Northamptonshire (London, 1981); RCHME, South-West Northamptonshire (London, 1982).

within parks necessarily mark where an associated village was cleared away to create uninterrupted panoramas of parkland turf. Moreover, as I shall argue, there are dangers in defining a discrete phenomenon – the 'emparked village'. Rather, settlement remains in parks need to be viewed as one aspect of the wider relationship between elite residences and settlements in the late medieval and post-medieval periods, and also within the more general context of changing styles of landscape design and their ideological significance.

Parkland and privacy

Deer parks – large enclosures bounded by some combination of earthwork bank, fence and hedge – were a common feature of the medieval countryside, especially in the 'woodland' districts outside the 'champion' Midlands, and in the forest areas within it.[6] They functioned both as venison farms and as hunting grounds, and took a variety of forms. Some were 'compartmentalised', in the sense that they were divided into relatively open areas, known as launds, which were managed as wood-pastures, and areas of coppice, enclosed to prevent damage by browsing stock. Others were 'uncompartmentalised', and consisted entirely of wood-pasture without a coppiced understorey. The substantial fences which were required to prevent the deer from escaping ensured that parks were good places in which to place other demesne assets, such as fish ponds and warrens, and a variety of livestock other than deer were also grazed there. Lodges for the use of the park keeper provided further security and, in some cases, accommodation for hunting parties.

In the twelfth and thirteenth centuries the majority of parks were located on the fringes of agricultural territories: like coppiced woodland, they represented a way of guaranteeing lordly control over diminishing reserves of the common waste,[7] and therefore usually lay at some distance from manor houses. But at the very highest social levels park and mansion were often closer together; even at the time of Domesday some parks were positioned near, although not immediately adjacent to, such major castles as Benington in Hertfordshire, Rayleigh in Essex and Eye in Suffolk, and as the number of parks increased in the following century they became an increasingly important aspect of the seigneurial *capita*, features to be proudly displayed. At Restormel in Cornwall in *c.* 1130 the castle, which also probably served as a lodge, was thus situated within its surrounding park, while at Kenilworth in Warwickshire in the 1120s the attention given to the location of the

---

6.   The best recent examination of the medieval park is R. Liddiard (ed.), *The medieval park: new perspectives* (Macclesfield, 2007).

7.   L.M. Cantor and J.M. Hatherly, 'The medieval parks of England', *Geography*, 64 (1979), pp. 71–85.

park within the overall landscape is clearly indicated in the foundation charter of Kenilworth Priory, in which Geoffrey de Clinton ensured that his endowment to the monks excluded land 'reserved for my castle and my park'.[8]

The vast majority of parks still lay far from the homes of their owners, it is true. But association of residence and park became more common, and spread down the social scale, in late medieval times: increasing numbers of major houses were equipped with adjoining deer parks created at the expense of farmland. This trend intensified, moreover, in the course of the sixteenth and seventeenth centuries, as the park became an expected adjunct for the greatest mansions.[9] Indeed, when the sites for new elite residences were being chosen the potential for laying out a suitably timbered park was a major consideration. In 1670 John Evelyn described how he helped choose the site for a friend's new house at Burrough Green in Cambridgeshire: 'a spot of rising ground, adorned with venerable woods, a dry and swete prospect East and West and fit for a park'.[10]

The extent to which medieval parks were 'designed landscapes' is currently a matter for debate.[11] Areas known as 'little parks' immediately adjacent to the residence, which seem to have functioned as some kind of pleasure ground, may have been deliberately planted or otherwise arranged with aesthetic intent, but manipulation of the wider parkland in this way is less certain, although frequently asserted. It is arguable that aesthetic pleasure was derived principally from the status connotations of possession, and from the use of the park for the elite pursuit of hunting, the form and layout of medieval parks thus being largely determined by their function. Certainly, the cartographic evidence suggests that sixteenth- and even early-seventeenth-century parks were largely uncontrived landscapes, of woodland and wood-pasture, which in aesthetic terms principally served as a contrast to the ordered, geometric regularity of the enclosed gardens laid out around the mansion itself (Figure 10.1). From the late seventeenth century, however, avenues and other formal features were increasingly intruded into the park, breaking down the barrier between park and garden; these tendencies intensified in the early decades of the eighteenth century as gardens were simplified in form and, under the influence of designers like William Kent, became more irregular and serpentine in layout. At the same time, at the highest social levels, the 'ha ha', fosse or sunken fence was employed to obscure the

8.   M.W. Thompson, *The rise of the castle* (Cambridge, 1991), pp. 141–2.
9.   T. Williamson, *Polite landscapes: gardens and society in eighteenth-century England* (Stroud, 1995), pp. 22–4.
10. W. Bray (ed.), *Memoirs illustrative of the life and writings of John Evelyn Esq FRS comprising his diary 1641 to 1705/6* (London, 1870), p. 346.
11. See R. Liddiard and T. Williamson, 'There by design? Some reflections on medieval elite landscapes', *Archaeological Journal* (in press).

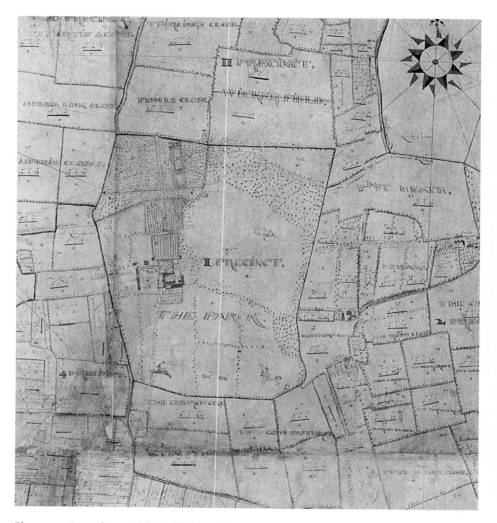

Figure 10.1 Somerleyton Hall (Suffolk), and its park, as shown on an estate map of 1652. The park surrounds the hall on all sides, but has not obviously been 'landscaped' in any way: the lines of trees represent former field boundaries, removed when the park was laid out (Courtesy Lowestoft Record Office).

division between the mowed ground of the garden and the grazed ground of the park, uniting both as a single experience.

From the middle decade of the eighteenth century, under the influence of designers like Lancelot 'Capability' Brown, these developments were taken to their logical conclusion. Walled enclosures and formal gardens were banished from view, formal planting in park and garden fell from favour, and the open, 'naturalistic' landscape park – more manicured and less densely treed than the traditional deer park, but still comprising an area of grazed pasture, scattered with trees and larger blocks of woodland – became the main setting for the house. Two other things, intimately connected, happened at the same time. Parks lost their necessary association with deer, and even at the highest social levels were often grazed mainly, if not solely, by sheep and cattle; and they increased significantly in numbers, becoming the normal possession, if in diminutive form, of even quite minor members of the local gentry, as well as merchants, bankers and industrialists.

Parks continued to be created, on some scale, right through the nineteenth century. Structured geometric gardens generally returned to the immediate vicinity of the house, frequently interposed between it and the park. Geometric planting, in the form of avenues, often returned to the park itself, and the range of species employed in planting tended to become more diverse. But parks continued, in essence, to comprise open panoramas of turf, irregularly scattered with trees, and with clumps and peripheral belts obscuring close views of the working countryside.

There is no space here to discuss the complex social significance of the park as this developed through the post-medieval centuries.[12] Two features are important in the present context, however. First, whereas medieval and sixteenth-century parks had normally been placed to one side of the mansion – statements of power and status, but not the sole setting for the house – from the seventeenth century, and especially in the eighteenth, the park came to encircle the residence and serve as an isolating, insulating space. The eighteenth-century 'landscape park' thus served to separate landowners from local communities, as well as to demonstrate the owner's ability to keep up with the latest fashions at the expense of productive land. Secondly, from the middle decades of the eighteenth century it was not only formal gardens that were removed from around the mansion. A range of other enclosures and facilities, practical and productive in character but also closely associated with and symbolic of lordly status, were likewise destroyed: fish ponds, dovecotes, nutyards, orchards, as well as farmyards and farm buildings. Late-eighteenth-century mansions thus stood within landscapes which ostentatiously shunned any sign of direct involvement with production, and the belts of trees which increasingly defined their margins blocked views out across the productive estate land of fields and farms. Parks, ostensibly at least, were landscapes of leisure and consumption which proclaimed that their owner's lifestyle was very different from that of the wider community, which was kept suitably distanced and hidden by the layout of the park and its plantations.

The creation of extensive private landscapes inevitably involved major

12. But see Williamson, Polite landscapes; and T. Williamson, The archaeology of the landscape park: garden design in Norfolk, England, c. 1680–1840, British Archaeological Reports, British Series, 268 (1998).

disruptions to the existing countryside. Roads and footpaths were closed or diverted, often on some scale, especially after legislative changes in 1773 – the institution of Road Closure Orders – made this cheaper and easier. This was done not merely because public highways interfered with the view; rather, it reflects an almost obsessive desire for isolation and privacy. As the designer Humphry Repton put it in his 'Red Book' for Tewin Water in Hertfordshire:

> Although the possessor of Tewin Water might think a public road no less appropriate than cheerful immediately in front of the house; or a foot path, cutting up the land in another direction, passing close to the windows, leaving the house on a kind of peninsula surrounded by carts, wagons, gypsies, poachers etc etc who feel they have a right of intrusion. Yet when the place with all its defects shall pass under the correcting hand of good taste, the view from the house will be changed with the views of its possessor.[13]

The significance of the park as a landscape of withdrawal and privacy was not lost on contemporaries. One, a blacksmith-poet from Bedale in Yorkshire, described in the late eighteenth century the changes which had occurred within his own lifetime around the local country house, The Rand:

> And now them roads are done away
> And one made in their room
> Quite to the east, of wide display
> Where you may go and come
> Quite unobserved from the Rand
> The trees do them seclude
> If modern times, do call such grand
> Its from a gloomy mood.[14]

At one level, the removal of settlements to make way for parks was simply a consequence of the fact that they were in the way. Where manor house and village lay in close proximity, as was the case in many areas of England, removal of the latter was an inevitable corollary of surrounding the former with the landscape of fashion. But both the specific act of destruction and the more general style of the park itself signalled a widening social gulf within rural communities.

Parks and pasture

One last aspect of parks must be briefly noted: one that is obvious, perhaps, but is of particular relevance to our understanding of the settlement remains so often found within them. Parks were predominantly landscapes of unploughed ground

---

13. Hertfordshire Archives and Local History, D/Z 42Z1P21A, H. Repton, Red Book for Tewin Water.
14. L. Lewis (ed.), *Hird's annals of Bedale* (Northallerton, 1990), stanzas 675–6.

– mainly turf, to a lesser extent woodland. Phases of arable cultivation did occur within the pale or belt, but usually only in the more distant recesses of the park, not close to the hall. Wide expanses of pasture were the essential ingredient of the park, but they also seem to have had an aesthetic appeal as the appropriate setting for a major residence even where a true park was lacking. Certainly, sixteenth- and seventeenth-century maps suggest that the homes of the gentry were usually associated with paddocks and pastures, rather than ploughlands. There were sound practical reasons for this: grassland afforded opportunities for recreation in a way that arable land did not. The fourth Lord North thus asserted that the pleasures of the deer park arose not simply from the deer themselves, but from 'having so much pasture ground lying open for riding, walking or any other pastime'.[15] But there were deeper ideological and aesthetic considerations. Grazing livestock represented a form of effortless and 'natural' production in a way that arable agriculture did not. As Repton put it 1792:

> Labour and hardship attend the operations of agriculture, whether cattle are tearing up the surface of the soil, or man reaping its produce; but a pasture shows us the same animals enjoying rest after fatigue, while others sporting with liberty and ease excite the pleasing idea of happiness and comfort annexed to a pastoral life. Consequently, such a scene must be more in harmony with the residence of elegance and comfort, and marks a degree of affluence, so decidedly that we never see a park ploughed up, but we always attribute it to poverty.[16]

As tracts of unploughed, undisturbed ground, parks form significant islands of archaeological preservation in which earthworks of all kinds generally survive better than in the surrounding farmed landscape. This is particularly true in arable regions like East Anglia. But it is also the case, to a surprising extent, in more pastoral districts, where farm pastures have often been ploughed up and reseeded over the years, or used as arable at times of high grain prices, or farmed in convertible, 'up-and-down' fashion with alternate spells as arable and pasture. Chatsworth Park in the Derbyshire Peak District is particularly instructive in this respect.[17] Today, local farms are entirely devoted to livestock, but in the Middle Ages most of the lower ground in the area was cultivated in arable open fields. The archaeological traces of these, in the form of ridge and furrow, carpet the park: but they are otherwise very rare in the area (Figure 10.2).

---

15. Quoted in K. Thomas, *Man and the natural world* (London, 1983), p. 202.
16. Repton Red Book for Honing Hall, Norfolk: private collection.
17. J. Barnatt and T. Williamson, *Chatsworth: a landscape history* (Macclesfield, 2005), pp. 28–30, 193–222.

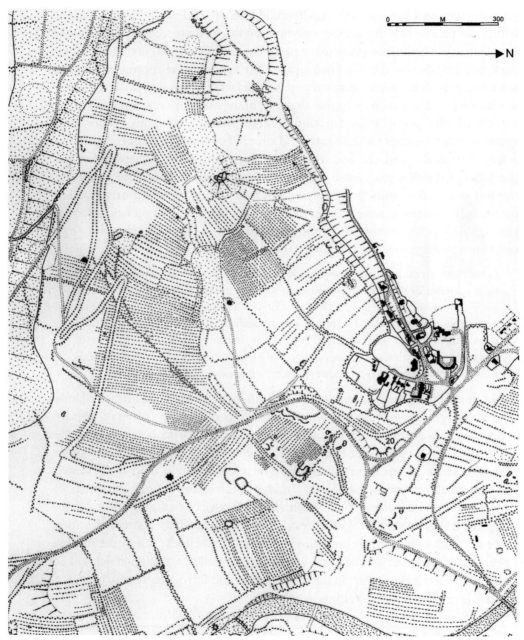

Figure 10.2 Chatsworth Park (Derbyshire). This shows the north-western portion of the park, including Edensor village. The park is carpeted with earthworks, most notably continuous swathes of ridge and furrow. The village of Edensor was partially removed in the eighteenth and early nineteenth century, but systematic levelling has left scant earthwork traces in the parkland turf. The rump of the village was comprehensively rebuilt, in ornamental form, in the 1840s (Courtesy John Barnatt).

Mansion and village

The social significance and archaeological implications of changing styles of landscape design are one context in which we need to consider the 'emparked village'. The other, which overlaps with this to some extent, is the more general relationship between elite residences and the homes of local communities. When parks or extensive gardens were laid out around manor houses, associated settlements had of necessity to be truncated or increasingly, as parks came to surround mansions on all sides, to be removed altogether. What happened to these places – whether and where they were rebuilt, and in what form – changed significantly over time. In the seventeenth century farms and cottages were sometimes rebuilt in view of the mansion, as elements in designed landscapes. At Holdenby in Northamptonshire, for example, part of the village was demolished in the 1580s to make way for extensive terraces and parterres, but it was neatly rebuilt around a green, and could be viewed, through an arcade, from the garden.[18] At Chippenham in Cambridgeshire the village was demolished when the park was laid out around the mansion in the years around 1710 but was rebuilt, as what was probably the first complete 'model' village in England, lining the main approach to the park.[19]

In these and other cases villages were clearly being employed in displays of power and paternalism; but while similar examples can be found in the eighteenth century, it became more usual to hide such replacement settlements from the polite gaze. At Houghton in Norfolk, for example, the village was demolished in the early 1720s to allow the park to be expanded to the south, and was replaced by a settlement described as Houghton 'New Town' (Figures 10.3 and 10.4). Although composed of two neat rows of semi-detached cottages which were built in stripped-down Palladian style, the new village was not originally on display. Estate maps make it clear that it was originally positioned on a side-road, hidden from view of the park by the peripheral belts.[20]

Yet if eighteenth-century villages cleared to make way for parks were usually marginalised within the designed landscape, this was not the case with the parish churches that were left behind in the park. These were often integrated into the design of the landscape, becoming, in effect, garden buildings. At Houghton the church was largely rebuilt in the 1730s in fashionable 'gothick' form, as was that at Hartwell in Buckinghamshire in the 1750s; other examples, such as Nuneham Courtenay, were refashioned as classical temples.

18. RCHME, North-west Northamptonshire, p.105.
19. C. Taylor, The Cambridgeshire landscape (London, 1973), p. 167.
20. Williamson, Archaeology of the landscape park, pp. 47–59.

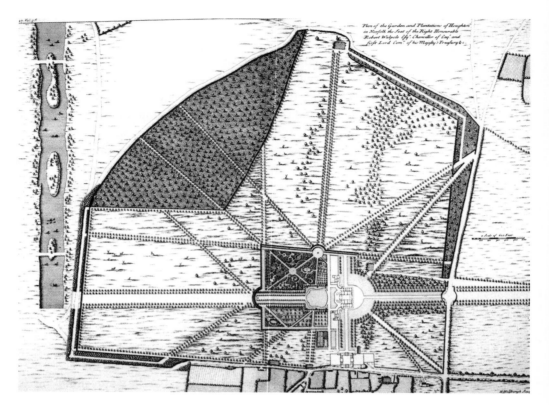

Figure 10.3 Houghton Hall and park, from Colen Campbell's *Vitruvius Britannicus* of 1722. The park is about to be extended, and the village lying immediately to its south demolished.

At the end of the eighteenth century there are clear signs that fashions were beginning to change, coming in a sense full circle: the homes of estate workers were once again integrated into the elite experience of landscape. At Houghton the entrance to the park was thus repositioned so that the park was accessed from the end of the village, which thus appeared to cluster, deferentially, at the park gates. At nearby Holkham the monumental south approach – over a mile (2km) long and ruler-straight, running through estate land and parkland devoid of dwellings – was downgraded in the early decades of the nineteenth century, the drive from the north-east now becoming the normal route taken by visitors. This began in Holkham village, the park gates themselves running between two almshouses: 'the rich man at his castle, the poor man at his gate'.[21]

This reintegration of villages into designed landscapes was part of a wider

21. *Ibid.*, p. 210.

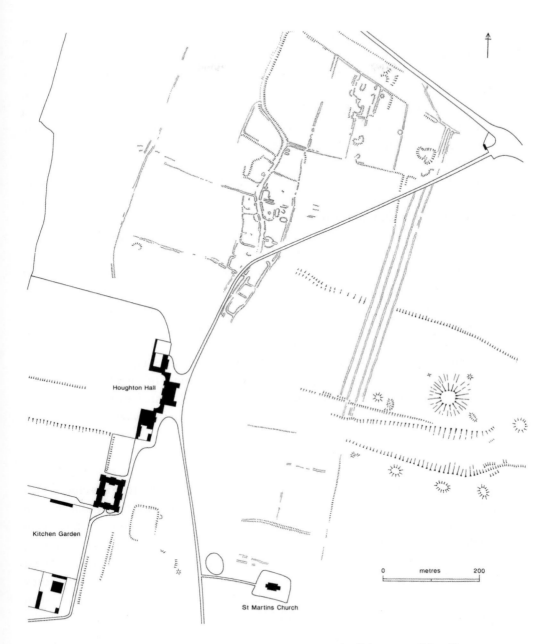

Figure 10.4 Earthworks in Houghton Park (Norfolk). There are only slight traces of the village cleared away in the 1720s, but to the north of the hall extensive settlement remains show that it had once been much larger. Other earthworks relate to lost field boundaries and to the great cutting made to open up the view to the east of the hall.

interest in the provision of cottages for estate workers, and of new farm houses, which increased through the late eighteenth and into the nineteenth century.[22] It was accompanied by major changes in the character of the architectural styles employed, more gothic or picturesque pseudo-vernacular forms becoming popular. Some estate villages were rebuilt in aesthetically pleasing forms even where they were not being relocated. At Somerleyton in Suffolk, for example, the village – which stood on the edge of the park, some way from the hall – was largely refashioned by Sir Morton Peto in the 1850s in flamboyant pseudo-vernacular style. It could be reached via a path, carefully planted, which ran from the pleasure grounds through the woodland belts, and it was clearly a picturesque 'incident' to be enjoyed by family and visitors.

Of perhaps more importance was the more general impact of resident landlords upon the development of neighbouring settlements, and in particular the effect of lordly proximity upon their demography. It has long been recognised that the majority of well-documented examples of villages cleared away when parks were laid out were small in size. Most, as Taylor noted long ago, had once been larger: that is, the destruction of settlements and the incorporation of the area they occupied within parkland often came as the last phase in a long period of decline.[23] Houghton in Norfolk is, once again, a good example. The area of the village removed for emparking in the 1720s was the rump of what had once been a much larger settlement, the earthwork remains of which extend for several hundred metres to the north of the hall. This lost arm of the village had apparently been abandoned before the park was first laid out in the seventeenth century. There are many similar examples of gradual decline followed by termination. Haselbech in Northamptonshire, for instance, was enclosed in 1598 by Thomas Tresham and laid to pasture, with sixty people allegedly evicted. Haselbech Hall was built in 1678. In 1673, thirty-one householders paid hearth tax, but in 1720 there were twenty-four houses in the village. Some time before 1773 these were demolished and the park laid out over their sites.[24] Edgecote, in the same county, contained ninety-five people over the age of fourteen in 1377, but a mere sixteen taxpayers in 1524 and eighteen families in 1720. By 1710 the church was already within the gardens of the hall; but the village was only finally demolished between 1761 and 1788. Two new farms and seven cottages were built elsewhere on the

22. G. Darley, *Villages of vision* (London, 1978); H. Clemenson, *English country houses and landed estates* (London, 1978); H. Fuller, 'Landownership and the Lindsey landscape', *Annals of the Association of American Geographers*, 66 (1976), pp. 45–64; S. Wade Martins, *The English model farm: building the agricultural ideal 1700–1914* (Macclesfield, 2002).
23. C. Taylor, *Village and farmstead: a history of rural settlement in England* (London, 1983).
24. RCHME, *North-west Northamptonshire*, pp. 100–1.

estate as replacements.[25] These were all 'emparked' settlements, but all had already experienced drastic, if gradual, contraction.

'Open' and 'close' parishes

One reason for the decline of such places, and for the fact that elite residences were frequently to be found in parishes with comparatively small populations, is that patterns of landownership had a major influence on the demographic experience of communities. Both modern historians and nineteenth-century commentators have used the terms 'open' and 'close', or closed, to characterise two broad types of parish existing in eighteenth- and nineteenth-century England.[26] In closed parishes there was only one landowner, or a small number of landowners, who strove to control the size of a settlement because, under the terms of the Elizabethan Poor Law, each parish was responsible for supporting its own poor or infirm through a rate levied on the principal landowners and tenants. It therefore made sense to limit the size of the population in order to restrict the number of people who might come, through ill health or ill fortune, to claim relief. Only enough labourers to serve the regular needs of the estate farms and the great house would be housed within the parish. At busy times of the agricultural year extra workers could be imported from neighbouring 'open' settlements. In the latter there were usually several landowners and, in consequence, it was less easy to control the size of the population. But in addition there was less incentive to do so, for owners were often petty rentiers, publicans or shopkeepers who stood to gain from a rising population. Such settlements thus tended to maintain their size, or grew larger. They also usually developed a more diversified economic base than 'close' villages, with numerous shops and pubs, and they often possessed nonconformist chapels and meeting houses. In closed villages the parish church was usually the only place of worship. Established landowners mistrusted religious nonconformity in all its forms, but most especially – in the nineteenth century – the Primitive Methodists, commonly regarded as the Agricultural Workers Union at prayer.

Of course, as a number of scholars have suggested, the reality was more complex than this bald model suggests. It was not simply patterns of ownership which determined the character of rural settlements but also such things as whether the owner was resident in the parish. Simple statistics of ownership are,

25. RCHME, *South-west Northamptonshire*, p. 47.
26. B.A. Holderness, '"Open" and "close" parishes in the eighteenth and nineteenth century', *Agricultural History Review*, 20 (1972), pp. 126–39.

moreover, a poor guide to the degree of 'openness' or 'closeness'.[27] Castle Acre in west Norfolk, a sprawling village with an abundance of shops and chapels, was a notorious open settlement in which numerous individuals owned property. But the wider parish itself was largely in the hands of, albeit forming a distant, outlying portion of, the great Holkham estate. Nevertheless, it is clear that *where the owner was resident* the settlements in closed parishes in general grew slowly, or remained the same size, or even contracted, as cottages considered superfluous to requirements were demolished. Evidently, the character of such settlements was shaped by a range of social and aesthetic factors which, in the last resort, boiled down to this: large landowners did not wish to be associated with large, untidy, busy places.

Such enforced if gradual contraction of settlement probably explains many cases where a village, cleared away when a park was created or expanded, can be shown to have once been larger. But there are other explanations – other reasons why lordly residences and shrunken settlements should be closely associated. In particular, where villages dwindled drastically in size in the later Middle Ages, either through voluntary out-migration or enforced depopulation or both, they often became the centres for extensive landed estates. Again, the explanation lies in part in the fact that major landowners preferred their homes to be associated with smaller settlements, rather than with extensive ones, perhaps because such a situation provided space in which extensive gardens or parks could be laid out. Needless to say, these various kinds of landlord-dominated settlement were not separate or discrete. Shrunken medieval villages often became the closed parishes of the eighteenth and nineteenth centuries.

Settlement remains in parks

It should be apparent from the above brief discussion that the settlement remains so often encountered within parkland do not necessarily represent villages 'swept away' when the park itself was created. They can, in fact, have a range of origins, although these are related in complex ways. First, because parks act as important 'islands of archaeological preservation' it is possible that some such sites are quite unconnected with the presence of mansion, gardens and park. They may represent settlements that had been abandoned long before the park was created, for some organic, voluntary reason quite unrelated to the presence of the great house: they

---

27. S.J. Banks, 'Nineteenth-century scandal or twentieth-century model? A new look at open and close parishes', *Economic History Review*, 2nd series, 41 (1988), pp. 51–73; T. Way, 'Open and close parishes', in T. Kirby and S. Oosthuizen (eds), *An atlas of Cambridgeshire and Huntingdonshire history* (Cambridge, 2000), p. 66.

may indeed have disappeared before the community came to have a resident landowner. This may explain some of the examples of medieval settlement earthworks found in the distant recesses of parks, and which were only incorporated within them – as at Rougham in Norfolk or Great Eversden in Northamptonshire – as they were expanded, at the expense of pasture fields, in the middle or late nineteenth century.

Most settlement remains in parks, however – including possibly even these examples – while not directly related to the creation of a designed landscape, were nevertheless associated with the presence within their parish of a high-status residence. There were two principal connections, as already intimated, which to some extent merged into each other. Some of these remains unquestionably represent places which shrank, or were abandoned, in the fifteenth or sixteenth centuries, leaving only the manor house: the apparent preference for pasture as a setting for late medieval and post-medieval mansions ensured the subsequent survival of the physical traces of contraction. Fawsley in Northamptonshire, where well-preserved settlement remains survive within the park just to the south-east of the hall, is an example. The place had ninety taxpayers in 1377, but only seven in 1524, implying a decline from around forty to around ten households. The village had ceased to exist long before the Knightley family laid out their park across its remains in the middle of the eighteenth century.[28] Where settlements experienced only contraction in the late medieval period, rather than complete desertion, the following centuries usually saw further decline as landlords attempted to reduce their size further in order to lower the poor rates and to secure the full advantages – including, once again, additional privacy – offered by the total control of 'close' settlements. Needless to say, even where places experienced little or no decline in the fifteenth and sixteenth centuries, monopoly ownership and the presence of a resident lord usually led to some reduction in their size during the seventeenth and eighteenth centuries, for these same reasons. There is little doubt that the incidence of such post-medieval contraction has been grossly underestimated, archaeologists assuming too easily that areas of settlement earthworks associated with existing villages represent medieval contraction. Neave's study of the East Riding remains the most detailed demonstration of the fact that, in some areas at least, many such remains are the consequence of deliberate depopulation by post-medieval landowners.[29]

---

28. RCHME, North-west Northamptonshire, pp. 88–90.
29. S. Neave, 'Rural settlement contraction in the East Riding of Yorkshire between the mid-seventeenth and mid-eighteenth centuries', Agricultural History Review, 41 (1993), pp. 124–36.

Figure 10.5 Edensor village, clustering at the gates of Chatsworth Park.

Villages and estate building

Where small or declining settlements were removed to make space for parkland, that act of clearance differed in one important respect from the depopulation of villages to make way for sheep runs in the fifteenth century. The latter places normally ceased to exist, not only as settlements but also as taxable, ecclesiastical or administrative entities. 'Emparked' villages, in contrast, usually continued to have a resident population, a name and a fiscal and administrative existence. The great house itself usually housed a substantial population of servants and workers. But, more importantly, most such settlements were rebuilt, either in one place – as another nucleated village – or at least as more widely dispersed farms and cottages. Emparked villages, in other words, were usually *shifted*, rather than truly *deserted*, settlements.

Indeed, it is arguable that some of these places are better understood as extreme instances of the more general phenomenon of estate 'improvement', which stamped lordly authority over the landscape in the course of the eighteenth and nineteenth centuries.[30] A village like Houghton, moved and rebuilt on a different site, arguably resembles a place like nearby Holkham – comprehensively rebuilt in situ at the park gates – more than a medieval 'deserted village'. Examples like Edensor in Derbyshire complicate the situation further. Here the village was slightly truncated in the 1750s, when Chatsworth Park was expanded, and further reduced in size when more changes were made to the park in the 1810s and 1820s.[31] But the bulk of the settlement survived, and was comprehensively rebuilt in situ around 1840, in a bizarre mixture of styles, to designs by Joseph Paxton and John Robertson (Figure 10.5).[32] It stood just within, and at the main entrance to, the park – an ornamental feature of the landscape and a symbol of the Duke of Devonshire's paternalist interest in his tenants.

The churches rebuilt or remodelled, often in fanciful form, when settlements were cleared to make way for parks are likewise part of a wider phenomenon. Examples well outside parks were sometimes rebuilt to serve as eye-catchers, as at West Wycombe in Buckinghamshire, where in 1764 Sir Arthur Dashwood added a golden globe to the tower so that it could be clearly seen from the hall (the church, which is prominently positioned within an Iron Age hillfort, was modified in other ways – its interior was so ornate that one visitor likened it to a 'very superb Egyptian hall', and a vast hexagonal mausoleum for the Dashwood family was built in the churchyard).[33] Even when we find such churches within parks they are not necessarily there because an associated village has been demolished. In areas of dispersed settlement, church and manor house may always have stood separate from other dwellings; or the church may have become isolated through settlement drift in the early Middle Ages, as probably occurred at Gunton in Norfolk, which was rebuilt in the 1760s (to designs by Robert Adam) as a neat classical temple in the gardens of the hall. In East Anglia, more than other regions, medieval mobility of settlement had littered the landscape with isolated churches like this, and in the nineteenth century especially there is evidence that parks were often expanded specifically to include them, as at Somerleyton in Suffolk. A church within private grounds was a powerful symbol of authority, and the effect could be achieved in a variety of ways. At Ayott St Lawrence in Hertfordshire, for example, the medieval church lay in the village on the edge of the park: Sir Lionel Lyde had it partially

30. H. Clemenson, English country houses and landed estates (London, 1978); J. Gregory, 'Mapping improvement: reshaping rural landscapes in the eighteenth century', Landscapes, 6 (2005), pp. 62–82; C. Rawding, 'Society and place in nineteenth-century north Lincolnshire', Rural History, 3 (1992), pp. 59–85; T. Williamson, 'Archaeological perspectives on estate landscapes', in J. Finch and K. Giles (eds), Estate landscapes: design, improvement and power in the post-medieval landscape (Woodbridge, 2007), pp. 1–18.
31. Barnatt and Williamson, Chatsworth, pp. 157–60.
32. Ibid., pp. 164–9.
33. N. Pevsner, The buildings of England: Buckinghamshire (Harmondsworth, 1960), pp. 287–9.

Figure 10.6 Ayott St Lawrence, Hertfordshire: the parish church, rebuilt within the park in 1764.

demolished in 1778 in order to create a picturesque gothic eye-catcher, and built a replacement in the form of a Neoclassical temple (designed by Nicholas Revett) on a new site in the middle of the park (Figure 10.6).[34]

Conclusion

The growing dominance of large landowners – owning land in the modern sense, untrammelled by local custom – had a profound impact on the development of the landscape in the post-medieval period, and affected the development of settlement, especially in 'home' parishes, in a variety of ways. The parks created as settings for the homes of such people, and the demesne pastures these so often replaced, have moreover served to preserve the archaeological traces of the often complex history of the settlements with which great mansions were associated. As has been shown here, settlement earthworks found within parks do not necessarily represent villages which were cleared away when these were created. There were many and complex connections between elite residences, settlement contraction and patterns of archaeological preservation: and even where places *were* cleared to make way for designed landscapes this was often only the final phase in a long history of decline. Moreover, 'emparking' did not usually involve complete 'desertion'. Most emparked villages continued to exist, if not as nucleated settlements then at least as places with their own ecclesiastical and administrative identity. 'Emparked villages' are perhaps closer in character to other kinds of estate village than to truly deserted settlements of medieval date.

34. L. Munby, *The Hertfordshire landscape* (London, 1977), pp. 161–2.

All this said, it is noteworthy that the incidence of 'emparked villages' appears to display marked regional variations which mirror, to a significant extent, the distribution of other kinds of 'deserted village'. Thus in a midland county like Northamptonshire, where deserted sites of all kinds are notoriously common, around fifteen villages appear to have been cleared or severely truncated by post-medieval emparking. In Norfolk, in contrast, where deserted villages are much rarer, it is unlikely that more than six – Wolterton, Houghton, Holkham, Letton, Merton and Anmer – suffered this fate; while in Hertfordshire, where deserted villages of all kinds are virtually unknown, there is only one certain example, Pendley near Tring, supposedly emparked as early as the 1450s. To a large extent this pattern, like the distribution of village desertion more generally, reflects regional variations in the character of settlement. Northamptonshire is almost entirely a county of villages, Norfolk has a more loosely nucleated settlement pattern, while Hertfordshire has a mixture of villages and a highly dispersed scatter of hamlets and isolated farms. Where compact villages predominate, in other words, sizeable areas of desertion, of all kinds, will be most common. It is possible, however, that to some extent this pattern also reflects regional variations in tenurial organisation, for Northamptonshire was characterised by significant numbers of uni-manorial townships in the Middle Ages, while Norfolk and Hertfordshire had far fewer.

Even the total of fifteen emparked villages suggested for Northamptonshire is not very high: emparking, even as a final act in a long history of decline, was never common, probably because most of these villages were shifted, rather than actually destroyed, and rebuilding farms and cottages on new sites was relatively expensive. Indeed, the most obvious evidence for the rarity of the phenomenon perhaps lies in the character of the archaeological remains themselves: for where villages *were* removed as part of landscaping schemes their sites were usually systematically levelled. To quote the example of Houghton yet again, the portion of the village removed for emparking in the 1720s has left little in the way of earthworks; it is the long arm of the village abandoned (and presumably long forgotten) before the park was laid out which forms a classic area of settlement remains. As a rough guide, if lost settlements survive as well-preserved upstanding earthworks within parkland, then in all probability their demise pre-dates – perhaps by several centuries – the creation of the park itself.

Some villages were destroyed in the course of the post-medieval period to make way for parks. But the settlement remains often found near major houses, and the isolated churches standing beside them, have a more complex and much more interesting story to tell about the relationship between landowners and local communities in the period between the sixteenth and the nineteenth centuries.

11

Deserted villages revisited: in the past, the present and the future

RICHARD JONES AND CHRISTOPHER DYER

The long-lasting academic impact of the seminar held at Cambridge in 1948 could never have been foreseen by those who attended. That sixty years later it should be viewed as the genesis for medieval archaeology in Britain and as a landmark moment in the study of medieval rural settlement in England stems not from what emerged directly out of this meeting, but from the rigour with which the people who took part pursued their research and communicated their findings to a wider audience. Others, of course, were considering the future at this time; as these historians and archaeologists contemplated the earthworks at Hamilton, Ingarsby and Knaptoft, on the Isle of Jura George Orwell was writing *Nineteen Eighty-Four*, to be published almost exactly a year later.

By 1984, deserted village studies had moved on apace. In this year reports were published on the deserted villages of Eaglethorpe (Northants.) and Upton (Glos.), the deserted farmstead of Earlswood (Surrey) and aerial surveys of abandoned sites in west Cheshire and north-west Leicestershire. Contributors to this volume were writing about the Roman countryside of north-west Essex, the industrial landscapes of Shropshire and County Durham, Devon manors and fenland parishes, peasant housing in the north and the towns of Hampshire. One, as he still does, was telling us what to read on town and country in the Middle Ages! Deserted village studies, then, had become part of a broader investigation of the historic landscape with a rich supporting literature.

In 1984 fieldworkers had at their disposal an array of technologies that in 1948 could not have been envisaged. Even a cursory glance at the archaeological publications of this year reveals the widespread use of remote prospecting and aerial reconnaissance for site identification and the availability of such things as chemical signalling, geophysical survey, geomagnetic and thermoluminescence dating, computer mapping and metal-detecting for their exploration. Many more techniques have since been added: ground-penetrating radar, LIDAR and GIS analysis to name but three. The study of deserted villages has benefited from them all. But methodological advancement offers only a partial explanation for the modifications in approach taken to these places over the last sixty years. The very frameworks within which they have been studied have also changed. In archaeology, the culture-historical paradigm, closely associated with Clark, one of the 1948 group, was replaced by processual archaeology in the 1960s, which was later to be superseded by post-processualism. In historical writing the original interpretations of Hoskins and Beresford were adapted by those who saw deserted villages as one of the symptoms of the crisis of feudal society, and they are compatible with those who have developed a conception of a strongly commercialised medieval countryside.

What the sixty-year history of deserted village studies shows is that it always has been, and continues to be, a dynamic area of research. Those who have sought to explain the phenomenon of settlement desertion or abandonment have been readily willing to try out new techniques or to re-examine the evidence in the light of prevailing schools of historical thought. There is no reason to believe that we have reached the point where we can claim to have exhausted all the possibilities of these sites or to say that they are now fully understood. The papers in this volume demonstrate the subject's life and vigour. They show that the research has become more inclusive, as our vision must be wide enough to include settlements that were not villages, both the scattered farms, in isolation or in groups, located in uplands and woodlands, and the hamlets interspersed among the larger nucleations in the central belt of open-field England. The approaches must include different disciplines which can tell the whole story of a settlement's life and decline: documents can reveal property holding and social relationships, place-names give insights into settlements before written records, excavation informs us about houses and their contents, field survey contributes not just to an understanding of the planning behind the settlement, but also of its growth, shrinkage and replacement. These essays emphasise the long period during which desertion took place, and the often long-drawn-out process for individual settlements that removes some of the distinctions between the 'deserted' and the 'shrunken' village. If abandonment occurred in every century between the twelfth and the eighteenth, then a whole range of causes has to be brought into the analysis, and no single agent can be assigned responsibility for a settlement's decay or removal.

In the twenty-first century it is still the case that this subject is a portal through which we can explore fundamental questions about landscape, material culture and society before, during and after desertion. We can predict with confidence that these places will continue to hold a fascination for academics and the informed public, and that future research will take us into new dimensions.

Bibliography

Adams, W.H., *The French garden 1500–1800* (London, 1979)

Airs, M. and Broad, J., 'The management of rural building in seventeenth-century Buckinghamshire', *Vernacular Architecture*, 29 (1998)

Allan, J., 'Medieval pottery and the dating of deserted settlements on Dartmoor', *Proceedings of the Devon Archaeological Society*, 52 (1994)

Allcroft, H., *Earthwork of England* (London, 1908)

Allen, D., 'Excavations at Hafod Y Nant Criafolen, Brenig Valley, Clwyd, 1973–74', *Post-Med. Arch.*, 13 (1979)

Allerston, P., 'English village development: findings from the Pickering district of North Yorkshire', *Transactions of the Institute of British Geographers*, 51 (1970)

Anon., 'Archaeology in Leicestershire and Rutland 1963–1966', *Transactions of the Leicestershire Archaeological and Historical Society*, 41 (1965–6)

Aris, M., *Historic landscapes of the Great Orme* (Llanrwst, 1996)

Aston, M., *Interpreting the landscape: landscape archaeology in local studies* (London, 1985)

Aston, M., Austin, D. and Dyer, C. (eds), *The rural settlements of medieval England* (Oxford, 1989)

Aston, T.H. and Philpin, C.H. (eds), *The Brenner debate. Agrarian class structure and economic development in pre-industrial Europe* (Cambridge, 1985)

Austin, D., 'Excavations in Okehampton deer park, Devon, 1976–1978', *Proceedings of the Devon Archaeological Society*, 36 (1978)

Austin, D., 'Dartmoor and the upland village of the south-west of England', in D. Hooke (ed.), *Medieval villages. A review of current work* (Oxford, 1985)

Austin, D., 'The excavation of dispersed settlement in medieval Britain', in M. Aston, D. Austin and C. Dyer (eds), *The rural settlements of medieval England* (Oxford, 1989)

Austin, D., 'The future', in K. Roberts (ed.), *Lost farmsteads. Deserted rural settlements in Wales*, CBA Research Report, 148 (2006)

Austin, D. and Walker, M.J.C., 'A new landscape context for Hound Tor, Devon', *Med. Arch.*, 29 (1985)

Austin, D., Daggett, R.H. and Walker, M.J.C., 'Farms and fields in Okehampton Park, Devon: the problems of studying medieval landscape', *Landscape History*, 2 (1980)

Babb, L., 'A thirteenth-century brooch hoard from Hambleden, Buckinghamshire', *Med. Arch.*, 41 (1997)

Bailey, M., 'The concept of the margin in the medieval English economy', *Economic History Review*, 2nd series, 42 (1989)

Baker, D., Baker, E., Hassall, J. and Simco, A., 'Excavations in Bedford 1967–1977', *Bedfordshire Archaeological Journal*, 13 (1979)

Baker, J., *Cultural transition in the Chilterns and Essex region, 350 AD to 650 AD*, Studies in Regional and Local History, 4 (Hatfield, 2006)

Banks, S.J., 'Nineteenth-century scandal or twentieth-century model? A new look at open and close parishes', *Economic History Review*, 2nd series, 41 (1988)

Barley, M., 'Cistercian land clearances in Nottinghamshire: three deserted villages and their moated successor', *Nottingham Medieval Studies*, 1 (1957)

Barnatt, J. and Smith, K., *The Peak District. Landscapes through time* (Macclesfield, 2004)

Barnatt, J. and Williamson, T., *Chatsworth: a landscape history* (Macclesfield, 2005)

Barnet, P. and Dandridge, P., *Lions, dragons and other beasts: aquamanilia of the Middle Ages, vessels for church and table* (New Haven/London, 2006)

Barrett, J.C., 'Agency, the duality of structure and the problem of the archaeological record', in I. Hodder (ed.), *Archaeological theory today* (Cambridge, 2001)

Batey, M., 'Nuneham Courtenay: an Oxfordshire eighteenth-century deserted village', *Oxoniensia*, 33 (1968)

Bedell, J., 'Memory and proof of age in England 1272–1327', *Past and Present*, 162 (1999)

Beresford, G., 'Three deserted medieval settlements on Dartmoor: a report on the late E. Marie Minter's excavations', *Med. Arch.*, 23 (1979)

Beresford, M.W., 'The deserted villages of Warwickshire', *Transactions of the Birmingham and Midland Archaeological Society*, 66 (1950)

Beresford, M.W., *The lost villages of England* (London, 1954)

Beresford, M., *History on the ground* (London, 1957; rev. edn, 1971)

Beresford, M.W., 'A review of historical research (to 1968)', in M.W. Beresford and J.G. Hurst (eds), *Deserted medieval villages: studies* (London, 1971).

Beresford, M.W., 'Documentary evidence for the history of Wharram Percy', in D.D. Andrews and G. Milne (eds), *Wharram. A study of settlement on the Yorkshire Wolds, I, domestic settlement, 1: areas 10 and 6*, SMAMS, 8 (1979)

Beresford, M.W., 'Professor Sir Michael Postan', *Medieval Village Research Group Annual Report*, 29 (1981)

Beresford, M.W., 'The earliest pre-desertion plan of an English village', *Medieval Village Research Group Annual Report*, 33 (1985)

Beresford, M.W., 'The documentary evidence', in R.D. Bell, M.W. Beresford et al., *Wharram. A study of settlement on the Yorkshire Wolds, III, Wharram Percy: the church of St Martin*, SMAMS, 11 (1987)

Beresford, M.W. and Hurst, J.G. (eds), *Deserted medieval villages: studies* (London, 1971)

Beresford, M. and Hurst, J., *Wharram Percy deserted medieval village* (London, 1990)

Berstan, R., Stott, A.W., Minnitt, P., Bront Ramsey, C., Hodges, R.E.M. and Evershed, R.P., 'Direct dating of pottery from its organic residues', *Antiquity*, 82 (2008)

Biddle, M., 'Towns', in D. Wilson (ed.), *The archaeology of Anglo-Saxon England* (London, 1976)

Bindoff, S.T., *History of Parliament: the Commons 1509–1558*, 1 (London, 1982)

Blinkhorn, P., 'The trials of being a pot: pottery functions at the medieval hamlet of West Cotton, Northamptonshire', *Medieval Ceramics*, 22/3 (1998–9)

Bond, C.J., 'Deserted medieval villages in Warwickshire and Worcestershire', in T.R. Slater and P.J. Jarvis (eds), *Field and forest: an historical geography of Warwickshire and Worcestershire* (Norwich, 1982)

Bourin, M. and Durand, R., *Vivre au village au moyen age. Les solidarités paysannes du Xe au XIIIe siècles* (Rennes, 2000)

Bowden, M. (ed.), *Unravelling the landscape: an inquisitive approach to archaeology* (Stroud, 1999)

Bowden, P., 'Agricultural prices, profits and rents', in J. Thirsk (ed.), *The agrarian history of England and Wales*, 4, 1500–1640 (Cambridge, 1967)

Bowen, E.G., 'The dispersed habitat of Wales', in R.H. Buchanan, E. Jones, and D. McCourt (eds), *Man and his habitat. Essays presented to Emyr Estyn Evans* (London, 1971)

Bray, W. (ed.), *Memoirs illustrative of the life and writings of John Evelyn Esq FRS comprising his diary 1641 to 1705/6* (London, 1870)

Brears, P., *Cooking and dining in medieval England* (Totnes, 2008)

Bridges, J., *History and antiquities of Northamptonshire* (London, 1791)

Britton, E., *The community of the vill: a study in the history of the family and village life in fourteenth-century England* (Toronto, 1977)

Broad, J., *Buckinghamshire dissent and parish life 1669–1712*, Buckinghamshire Record Society, 28 (1993)

Broad, J., 'Housing the rural poor in southern England, 1650–1850', *Agricultural History Review*, 48 (2000)

Broad, J., *Transforming English rural society: the Verneys and the Claydons 1600–1820* (Cambridge, 2004)

Broad, J. (ed.), *Bishop Wake's visitation returns 1706–15* (forthcoming)

Broad, J. and Hoyle, R. (eds), *Bernwood: life and death of a royal forest* (Preston, 1997)

Brown, A.E. and Taylor, C.C., 'The origins of dispersed settlement; some results from fieldwork in Bedfordshire', *Landscape History*, 11 (1989)

Brown, D.H., 'Pottery and manors', in M. Carroll, D.M. Hadley and H. Willmott (eds), *Consuming passions. Dining from antiquity to the eighteenth century* (Stroud, 2005)

Brown, D.H., 'Pots from houses', *Medieval Ceramics*, 21 (1997)

Brown, E.H., *The relief and drainage of Wales* (Cardiff, 1960)

Bruce-Mitford, R.L.S., 'The excavations at Seacourt, Berkshire. An interim report', *Oxoniensia*, 5 (1940)

Brück, J., 'The architecture of routine life', in J. Pollard (ed.), *Prehistoric Britain* (Oxford, 2008)

Brunskill, R.W., *Traditional buildings of Britain: an introduction to vernacular architecture* (London, 1981)

Bryant, V., 'Death and desire', *Medieval Ceramics*, 28 (2004)

Butler, L. and Wade-Martins, P., *The deserted medieval village of Thuxton, Norfolk*, East Anglian Archaeology, 46 (1989)

Butler, L.A.S., 'A long hut group in the Aber Valley', *Transactions of the Caernarvonshire Historical Society*, 23 (1962)

Butler, L.A.S., 'The excavation of a long hut near Bwlch yr Hendre', *Ceredigion*, 4 (1963)

Butler, L.A.S., 'The study of deserted medieval settlements in Wales', in M.W. Beresford and J.G. Hurst (eds), *Deserted medieval villages: studies* (London, 1971)

Cambria Archaeology, *Metal mining in upland Ceredigion* (Llandeilo, 2007)

Cameron, A. and O'Brien, C., 'The deserted mediaeval village of Thorpe-in-the-Glebe, Nottinghamshire', *Transactions of the Thoroton Society*, 20 (1981)

Campbell, B., 'Benchmarking medieval economic development: England, Wales, Scotland and Ireland, c. 1290', *Economic History Review*, 61 (2008)

Cantor, L.M. and Hatherly, J.M., 'The medieval parks of England', *Geography*, 64 (1979)

Carpenter, C., *Locality and polity. A study of Warwickshire landed society, 1401–1499* (Cambridge, 1992)

Carpenter, C., '"Town and country": the Stratford guild and political networks of fifteenth-century Warwickshire', in R. Bearman (ed.), *The history of an English borough. Stratford-upon-Avon, 1196–1996* (Stratford, 1997)

Carter, W.F. (ed.), *The subsidy roll for Warwickshire of 6 Edward III (1332)*, Dugdale Society, 6 (1926)

Caseldine, A., 'The environment and deserted rural settlements in Wales: potential and possibilities for palaeoenvironmental studies', in K. Roberts (ed.), *Lost farmsteads. Deserted rural settlements in Wales*, CBA Research Report, 148 (2006)

Clapham, J.H., *The concise economic history of Great Britain* (Cambridge, 1949)

Clarke, D.T.-D., 'Archaeology in Leicestershire 1939–1951', *Transactions of the Leicestershire Archaeological Society*, 28 (1952)

Clemenson, H., *English country houses and landed estates* (London, 1978)

Cooke, J.G., *The lost village of Knaptoft* (Leicester, c. 1958)

Courtney, P., 'A native-Welsh mediaeval settlement: excavations at Beili Bedw, St Harmon, Powys', *Bulletin of the Board of Celtic Studies*, 38 (1991)

Courtney, P., 'The tyranny of constructs: some thoughts on periodisation and culture change', in D. Gaimster and P. Stamper (eds), *The age of transition. The archaeology of English culture 1400–1600*, SMAMS, 15 (1997)

Cox, B., *The place-names of Rutland*, English Place-Name Society, 67–9 (Nottingham, 1994)

Crawford, O.G.S., 'Air photograph of Gainsthorpe, Lincolnshire', *Antiquaries Journal*, 5 (1925)

Cullen, P., Jones, R. and Parsons, D., *Thorps in a changing landscape* (Hatfield, forthcoming)

Darley, G., *Villages of vision* (London, 1978)

Department for Culture, Media and Sport, *Treasure Annual Report 2005/6* (London, 2008)

Donkin, R.A., *The Cistercians: studies in the geography of medieval England and Wales* (Toronto, 1978)

Draper, J., *Dorset country pottery. The kilns of the Verwood district* (Ramsbury, 2002)

Dudley, D. and Minter, E.M., 'The medieval village of Garrow Tor, Bodmin Moor, Cornwall', *Med. Arch.*, 6–7 (1962–3)

Dugdale, W., *Antiquities of Warwickshire* (London, 1656)

Dyer, C., 'Population and agriculture on a Warwickshire manor in the later Middle Ages', *University of Birmingham Historical Journal*, 11 (1968)

Dyer, C., 'Deserted medieval villages in the west Midlands', *Economic History Review*, 2nd series, 35 (1982)

Dyer, C., 'Power and conflict in the medieval English village', in D. Hooke (ed.), *Medieval villages: a review of current work* (Oxford, 1985)

Dyer, C., 'English peasant buildings in the later Middle Ages 1200–1500', *Med. Arch.*, 30 (1986)

Dyer, C., '"The retreat from marginal land": the growth and decline of medieval rural settlements', in M. Aston, D. Austin and C. Dyer (eds), *The rural settlements of medieval England* (Oxford, 1989)

Dyer, C., 'Dispersed settlements in medieval England: a case study of Pendock, Worcestershire', *Med. Arch.*, 34 (1990), reprinted in *Everyday life in Medieval England* (London, 1994)

Dyer, C., *Hanbury: settlement and society in a woodland landscape* (Leicester, 1991)

Dyer, C., 'Peasants and coins: the uses of money in the Middle Ages', *British Numismatic Journal*, 67 (1997)

Dyer, C., 'Compton Verney: landscape and people in the Middle Ages', in R. Bearman (ed.), *Compton Verney. A history of the house and its owners* (Stratford, 2000)

Dyer, C., *Making a living in the Middle Ages. The people of Britain 850–1520* (London, 2002)

Dyer, C., 'Villages and non-villages in the medieval Cotswolds', *Transactions of the Bristol and Gloucestershire Archaeological Society*, 120 (2002)

Dyer, C., *An age of transition? Economy and society in England in the later middle ages* (Oxford, 2005)

Dyer, C., 'Were late medieval English villages "self-contained"?', in idem (ed.), *The self-contained village?* (Hatfield, 2007)

Edwards, N., 'Landscape and settlement in medieval Wales: an introduction', in idem (ed.), *Landscape and settlement in medieval Wales* (Oxford, 1997)

Egan, G., 'Urban and rural finds: material culture of country and town, c. 1050–1200', in K. Giles and C. Dyer (eds), *Town and country in the Middle Ages*, SMAMS, 22 (2005)

Emery, F., 'The farming regions of Wales', in J. Thirsk (ed.), *Agrarian history of England and Wales, 4, 1500–1640* (Cambridge, 1967)

Emery, F., 'The landscape', in D.H. Owen (ed.), *Settlement and society in Wales* (Cardiff, 1989)

English Heritage, *Post-medieval formal gardens*, single monument class description for the Monuments Protection Programme of English Heritage (1997)

Evans, D.H. and Jarrett, M.G., 'The deserted village of West Whelpington, Northumberland: third report, part one', *Archaeologia Aeliana*, 15 (1987)

Evans, D.H., Jarrett, M.G. and Wrathmell, S., 'The deserted village of West Whelpington, Northumberland: third interim report, part two', *Archaeologia Aeliana*, 16 (1988)

Evans, H., *The Gorse Glen* (Liverpool, 1948)

Everett, J. (ed.), *An historical atlas of Norfolk* (Norwich, 1993)

Everitt, A., 'Common land', in J. Thirsk (ed.), *The English rural landscape* (Oxford, 2000)

Everson, P.L., Taylor, C.C. and Dunn, C.J., *Change and continuity. Rural settlement in north-west Lincolnshire* (London, 1991)

Fasham, P.J. and Keevil, G., *Brighton Hill South (Hatch Warren): an Iron Age farmstead and deserted medieval village in Hampshire*, Wessex Archaeology Report, 7 (1995)

Fentress, J. and Wickham, C., *Social memory* (Oxford, 1992)

Fleming, A. and Barker, L., 'Monks and local communities: the late-medieval landscape of Troed y Rhiw, Caron Uwch Clawdd, Ceredigion', *Med. Arch.*, 52 (2008)

Fleming, A. and Ralph, N., 'Medieval settlement and land-use on Holne Moor, Dartmoor: the landscape evidence', *Med. Arch.*, 26 (1982)

Foard, G., 'Systematic fieldwalking and the investigation of Saxon settlement in Northamptonshire', *World Archaeology*, 9 (1978)

Foster, C.W. and Longley, T., *Lincolnshire Domesday*, Lincolnshire Record Society, 19 (1924)

Fox, A., 'Early Welsh homesteads on Gelligaer Common', *Archaeologica Cambrensis*, 94 (1939)

Fox, H., 'Servants, cottagers and tied cottages during the later Middle Ages: towards a regional dimension', *Rural History*, 6 (1995)

Fox, H., 'The Wolds before *c.* 1500', in J. Thirsk (ed.), *Rural England* (Oxford, 2000)

Fox, H.S.A., 'The occupation of the land. Devon and Cornwall', in E. Miller (ed.), *The agrarian history of England and Wales, 3, 1348–1500* (Cambridge, 1991)

Fox, H.S.A., 'Medieval Dartmoor as seen through its account rolls', *Proceedings of the Devon Archaeological Society*, 52 (1994)

Fox, H.S.A., 'Introduction: transhumance and seasonal settlement', in idem (ed.), *Seasonal settlement* (Leicester, 1996)

Friedman, A. (ed.), *The collected works of Oliver Goldsmith*, 4 (Oxford, 1966)

Fuller, E.H., 'The tallage of 6 Edward II (Dec. 16, 1312) and the Bristol rebellion', *Transactions of the Bristol and Gloucestershire Archaeological Society*, 19 (1894–5)

Fuller, H., 'Landownership and the Lindsey landscape', *Annals of the Association of American Geographers*, 66 (1976)

Gant, R., 'Oral history and settlement change: a case study of abandoned dwellings in the Black Mountains of Wales, 1840–1983', *Cambria*, 12 (1985)

Gardiner, M., 'Vernacular buildings and the development of the later medieval domestic plan in England', *Med. Arch.*, 44 (2000)

Gardiner, M., 'Review of medieval settlement research, 1996–2006', MSRGAR, 21 (2006)

Gay, E., 'The midland revolt and the inquisitions of depopulation of 1607', *Transactions of the Royal Historical Society*, new series, 18 (1904)

Gelling, M., 'Towards a chronology for English place-names', in D. Hooke (ed.), *Anglo-Saxon settlements* (Oxford, 1988)

Gelling, M., *Place-names in the landscape* (London, 1993)

Gerrard, C., *Medieval archaeology. Understanding traditions and contemporary approaches* (London, 2003)

Gerrard, C., 'Not all archaeology is rubbish; the elusive life histories of three artefacts from Shapwick, Somerset', in M. Costen (ed.), *People and places. Essays in honour of Mick Aston* (Oxford, 2007)

Gerrard, C., 'The study of the deserted medieval village: Caldecote in context', in G. Beresford (ed.), *Caldecote. The development and desertion of a Hertfordshire village*, SMAMS, 28 (2009)

Gerrard, C.M. and Youngs, S.M., 'A bronze socketed mount and blade from Shapwick House, Somerset', *Med. Arch.*, 41 (1997)

Gerrard, C. with Aston, M., *The Shapwick project, Somerset. A rural landscape explored*, SMAMS, 25 (2007)

Gilchrist, R., 'Magic for the dead? The archaeology of magic in later medieval burials', *Med. Arch.*, 52 (2008)

Gilchrist, R. and Sloane, B., *Requiem: the medieval monastic cemetery in Britain* (London, 2005)

Goldberg, P.J.P., 'Masters and men in later medieval England', in D. Hadley (ed.), *Masculinity in medieval England* (London, 1999)

Gover, J.E.B., Mawer, A. and Stenton, F.M., *The place-names of Devon*, English Place-Name Society, 8–9 (Cambridge, 1931–2)

Graves, C.P., 'Social space in the English medieval parish church', *Economy and Society*, 18 (1989)

Gray, I., 'A Gloucestershire postscript to the "Domesday of Inclosures"', *Transactions of the Bristol and Gloucestershire Archaeological Society*, 94 (1976)

Gregory, J., 'Mapping improvement: reshaping rural landscapes in the eighteenth century', *Landscapes*, 6 (2005)

Grenville, J., *Medieval housing* (London, 1997)

Griffiths, M., 'The emergence of the modern settlement pattern, 1450–1700', in D.H. Owen (ed.), *Settlement and society in Wales* (Cardiff, 1989)

Griffiths, N., 'An unusual medieval strap-end from Market Lavington', *Wiltshire Archaeological and Natural History Magazine*, 91 (1998)

Griffiths, W.E., 'Excavations on Penmaenmawr, 1950', *Archaeologia Cambrensis*, 103 (1954)

Gutiérrez, A., 'The pottery', in C. Gerrard with M. Aston, *The Shapwick project, Somerset. A rural landscape explored*, SMAMS, 25 (2007)

Hadley, D.M., 'Dining in disharmony in the later Middle Ages', in M. Carroll, D.M. Hadley and H. Willmott (eds), *Consuming passions. Dining from antiquity to the eighteenth century* (Stroud, 2005)

Hall, D. and Martin, P., 'Brixworth, Northamptonshire: an intensive field survey', *Journal of the British Archaeological Association*, 132 (1979)

Hall, M.A., 'Burgh mentalities; a town-in-the-country case study of Perth, Scotland', in K. Giles and C. Dyer (eds), *Town and country in the Middle Ages*, SMAMS, 22 (2005)

Hallam, H., *Settlement and society. A study of the early agrarian history of South Lincolnshire* (Cambridge, 1965)

Hamerow, H., '"Special deposits" in Anglo-Saxon settlements', *Med. Arch.*, 50 (2006)

Harden, D.B., 'Objects of glass', in M. Biddle, 'The deserted medieval village of Seacourt, Berkshire', *Oxoniensia*, 26/27 (1961–2)

Harley, J.B., *Ordnance Survey maps: a descriptive manual* (Southampton, 1975)

Harley, J.B. and Oliver, R.R., *The Old Series Ordnance Survey maps of England and Wales*, 7 (Lympne Castle, 1989)

Harris, A., *The rural landscape of the East Riding of Yorkshire, 1700–1850* (Oxford, 1961)

Harrison, B. and Hutton, B., *Vernacular houses in North Yorkshire and Cleveland* (Edinburgh, 1984)

Hartley, D. and Elliot, M.M., *Life and work of the people of England. Volume one: the Middle Ages*,

A.D. 1000–1490 (London; n.d. c. 1931)

Hartley, R.F., *The medieval earthworks of Rutland*, Leicestershire Museums Publications, 47 (1983)

Hartley, R.F., *The medieval earthworks of north-west Leicestershire*, Leicestershire Museums Publications, 56 (1984)

Hartley, R.F., *The medieval earthworks of north-east Leicestershire*, Leicestershire Museums Publications, 88 (1987)

Hartley, R.F., *The medieval earthworks of central Leicestershire*, Leicestershire Museums Publications, 103 (1989)

Harvey, P.D.A., 'Initiative and authority in settlement change', in M. Aston, D. Austin and C. Dyer (eds), *The rural settlements of medieval England* (Oxford, 1989)

Harvey, P.D.A. and McGuinness, A., *A guide to British medieval seals* (London, 1996)

Hasler, P.W., *History of Parliament: the Commons 1558–1603*, 1 (London, 1981)

Hayfield, C., 'The pottery', in G. Coppack, 'St Lawrence Church, Burnham, South Humberside', *Lincolnshire Archaeology and History*, 21 (1986)

Hearne, T. (ed.), *J. Rous: Historia regum Angliae* (Oxford, 1745)

Herring, P., 'Transhumance in medieval Cornwall', in H.S.A. Fox (ed.), *Seasonal settlement* (Leicester, 1996)

Herring, P., 'Medieval fields at Brown Willy, Bodmin Moor', in S. Turner (ed.), *Medieval Devon and Cornwall. Shaping an ancient countryside* (Macclesfield, 2006)

Hillier, B. and Hanson, J., *The social logic of space* (Cambridge, 1984)

Hilton, R.H., *The English peasantry in the later Middle Ages* (Oxford, 1975)

Hilton, R.H. (ed.), *The transition from feudalism to capitalism* (London, 1976)

Hindle, S., *On the parish?* (Oxford, 2004)

Hindle, S., 'Dearth and the English Revolution: the harvest crisis of 1647–50', *Economic History Review*, 61, supplement 1 (2008)

Hinton, D.A., 'A cruck house at Lower Radley, Berkshire' *Oxoniensia*, 32 (1967)

Hinton, D.A., 'A medieval cistern from Churchill', *Oxoniensia*, 33 (1968)

Hinton, D.A., 'Excavations at Otterbourne old church, Hampshire', *Proceedings of the Hampshire Field Club and Archaeological Society*, 46 (1981)

Hinton, D.A., *Archaeology, economy and society: England from the fifth to the fifteenth century* (London, 1990)

Hinton, D.A., *Gold and gilt, pots and pins. Possessions and people in medieval Britain* (Oxford, 2005)

Hoeniger, F.D. (ed.), *Pericles* (Arden edition, London, 1963)

Holderness, B.A., '"Open" and "close" parishes in the eighteenth and nineteenth century', *Agricultural History Review*, 20 (1972)

Holt, R., *The mills of medieval England* (Oxford, 1988)

Holton, R.J., *The transition from feudalism to capitalism* (London, 1985)

Hoskins, W.G., 'The deserted villages of Leicestershire', *Transactions of the Leicestershire Archaeological Society*, 22 (1946)

Hoskins, W.G., 'The deserted villages of Leicestershire', in idem., *Essays in Leicestershire history* (Liverpool, 1950)

Hoskins, W.G., *The making of the English landscape* (London, 1955)

Hoskins, W.G., 'Seven deserted village sites in Leicestershire', *Transactions of the Leicestershire Archaeological and Historical Society*, 32 (1956). Reprinted in idem, *Provincial England* (London, 1963)

Hoskins, W.G. and Stamp, D.L., *The common lands of England and Wales* (London, 1963)

Hughes, M.F., 'Emparking and the desertion of settlements in Hampshire', MSRGAR, 30 (1982)

Hurst, J., 'Medieval period discussion', in A.B. Powell, P. Booth, A.P. Fitzpatrick and A.D. Crockett, *The archaeology of the M6 Toll 2000–2003*, Oxford Wessex Archaeology Monograph, 2 (2008)

Hurst, J.G., 'A review of archaeological research (to 1968)', in M.W. Beresford and J.G. Hurst (eds), *Deserted medieval villages: studies* (London, 1971)

Hurst, J., 'The medieval countryside', in I. Longworth and J. Cherry (eds), *Archaeology in Britain since 1945* (London, 1986)

Hurst, J.G. and Hurst, D.G., 'Excavations at Hangleton', *Sussex Archaeological Collections*, 102 (1964)

Ingold, T., 'The temporality of the landscape', reprinted in J. Thomas (ed.), *Interpretive archaeology: a reader* (London, 2000 [1994])

Ivens, R., Busby, P. and Shepherd, N., *Tattenhoe and Westbury. Two deserted medieval settlements in Milton Keynes*, Buckinghamshire Archaeological Society Monograph Series, 8 (1995)

John, T. (ed.), *The Warwickshire hundred rolls of 1279–80* (Oxford, 1992)

Johnson, M., *Housing culture: traditional architecture in an English landscape* (London, 1993)

Johnson, M., *An archaeology of capitalism* (Oxford, 1996)

Johnson, M., 'Houses, power and everyday life in early modern England', in J. Maran, C. Juwig, H. Schwengel and U. Thaler (eds), *Constructing power: architecture, ideology and social practice* (Hamburg, 2006)

Johnson, N. and Rose, P., *Bodmin Moor. An archaeological survey. Volume 1: the human landscape to c. 1800* (London, 1994)

Johnson South, T. (ed.), *Historia de Sancto Cuthberto: a history of St Cuthbert and a record of his patrimony*, Anglo-Saxon Texts, 3 (2002)

Jones, G., 'Multiple estates and early settlement', in P. Sawyer (ed.), *Medieval settlement. Continuity and change* (London, 1976)

Jones, H.C., 'Wawne, East Yorkshire', *Med. Arch.*, 6–7 (1963)

Jones, M., *The secret world of the Middle Ages. Discovering the real medieval world* (Stroud, 2002)

Jones, R., 'Signatures in the soil: the use of pottery in manure scatters in the identification of medieval arable farming regimes', *Archaeological Journal*, 161 (2004)

Jones, R. and Page, M., *Medieval villages in an English landscape: beginnings and ends* (Macclesfield, 2006)

Jones, R., Dyer, C. and Page, M., 'Changing settlements and landscapes: medieval Whittlewood, its predecessors and successors', *Internet Archaeology*, 19 (2006) at http://intarch.ac.uk/journal/issue19/jones_index.html

Jones Pierce, T., 'Agrarian aspects of the tribal system in Wales', *Géographie et Histoire Agraires, Annales de l'Est, Memoire no. 21* (Nancy, 1959), reprinted in T. Jones Pierce, *Medieval Welsh society* (Cardiff, 1972)

Jope, E.M. and Threlfall, R.I., 'Excavation of a medieval settlement at Beere, North Tawton, Devon', Med. Arch., 2 (1958)

Jope, E.M., 'The regional cultures of medieval Britain', in I.L.L. Foster and L. Alcock (eds), Culture and environment. Essays in honour of Cyril Fox (London, 1963)

'JW' [The Rev. John Wilson], 'Antiquities found at Woodperry, Oxon', Archaeological Journal, 3 (1846)

Kerridge, E., The agricultural revolution (London, 1967)

King, D.J., Castellarium Anglicanum (London/New York, 1983)

Kissock, J., 'Farmsteads of a presumed medieval date on Cefn Drum, Gower: an interim review', Studia Celtica, 34 (2000)

Kissock, J. and Johnstone, R., 'Sheephouses and sheepcotes – a study of the post-medieval landscape of Cefn Drum, Gower', Studia Celtica, 41 (2007)

Langdon, J., 'Agricultural equipment', in G. Astill and A. Grant (eds), The countryside of medieval England (Oxford, 1988)

Leadam, I.S., 'The Inquisition of 1517. Inclosures and evictions, part II', Transactions of the Royal Historical Society, new series, 7 (1893)

Leadam, I.S., The Domesday of Inclosures 1517–1518, 2 (Oxford, 1897)

Lefebvre, H., The production of space, trans. D. Nicholson-Smith (Oxford, 1991)

Leighton, D.K., Mynydd Du and Fforest Fawr. The evolution of an upland landscape in south Wales (Aberystwyth, 1997)

Le Patourel, H.E.J., 'Medieval pottery', in R.D. Bell, M.W. Beresford et al. (eds), Wharram. A study of settlement on the Yorkshire Wolds, III, Wharram Percy: the church of St Martin, SMAMS, 11 (1987)

Lethbridge, T.C. and Tebbutt, C.F., 'Huts of the Anglo-Saxon period', Proceedings of the Cambridge Antiquarian Society, 33 (1933)

Lewis, C., 'New avenues for the investigation of currently occupied medieval rural settlements: preliminary observations from the Higher Education Field Academy', Med. Arch., 51 (2007)

Lewis, C., Mitchell-Fox, P. and Dyer, C., Village, hamlet and field. Changing medieval settlements in central England (1997, Macclesfield, repr. 2001)

Lewis, L. (ed.), Hird's annals of Bedale (Northallerton, 1990)

Liddiard, R. (ed.), The medieval park: new perspectives (Macclesfield, 2007)

Liddiard, R. and Williamson, T., 'There by design? Some reflections on medieval elite landscapes', Archaeological Journal (in press)

Lindley, K., Fenland riots and the English Revolution (London, 1982)

Linehan, C.D., 'Deserted sites and rabbit-warrens on Dartmoor, Devon', Med. Arch., 10 (1966)

Lipson, E., The economic history of England, 1 (London, 1947)

Lloyd, T., 'Some documentary sidelights on the deserted Oxfordshire village of Brookend', Oxoniensia, 29/30 (1964/5)

Locock, M., 'Deserted rural settlements in south-east Wales', in K. Roberts (ed.), Lost farmsteads. Deserted rural settlements in Wales, CBA Research Report, 148 (2006)

Longley, D., 'Deserted rural settlements in north-west Wales', in K. Roberts (ed.), Lost *farmsteads. Deserted rural settlements in Wales*, CBA Research Report, 148 (2006)

Lynch, F. (ed.), *Excavations in the Brenig Valley. A Mesolithic and Bronze Age landscape in north Wales* (Cardiff, 1993)

Macdonald, M. (ed.), *The Register of the Guild of the Holy Cross, Stratford-upon-Avon*, Dugdale Society, 42 (2007)

McDonnell, J., 'Upland Pennine hamlets', *Northern History*, 26 (1990)

Maitland, F.W., *Domesday Book and beyond* (1897, London, repr. 1960)

Martin, J., 'Enclosure and the Inquisitions of 1607: an examination of Dr Kerridge's article "The returns of the Inquisitions of Depopulation"', *Agricultural History Review*, 30 (1982)

Mellor, M., 'Early Saxon, medieval and post-medieval pottery', in T. Allen, 'A medieval grange of Abingdon Abbey at Dean Court Farm, Cumnor, Oxon.', *Oxoniensia*, 59 (1994)

Mepham, L., 'Medieval pottery from West Mead', in C.M. Hearne and V. Birbeck, *A35 Tolpuddle to Puddletown Bypass DBFO, Dorset, 1996–8*, Wessex Archaeology Report, 15 (1999)

Mercer, E., *English vernacular houses: a study of traditional farmhouses and cottages* (London, 1975)

Merrifield, R., *The archaeology of magic and ritual* (London, 1987)

Mew, K., 'The dynamics of lordship and landscape as revealed in a Domesday study of the Nova Foresta', *Anglo-Norman Studies*, 23 (2000)

Miles, D. and Rowley, T., 'Tusmore deserted village', *Oxoniensia*, 41 (1976)

Miller, D. and Tilley, C., 'Ideology, power and prehistory: an introduction', in D. Miller and C. Tilley (eds), *Ideology, power and prehistory* (Cambridge, 1984)

Miller, E. (ed.), *The agrarian history of England and Wales, 3, 1348–1500* (Cambridge, 1991)

Mills, J.M., 'The finds catalogue', in Ivens *et al.*, *Tattenhoe and Westbury*

Moore, H., 'Bodies on the move: gender, power and material culture: gender, difference and the material world', reprinted in J. Thomas (ed.), *Interpretive archaeology: a reader* (London, 2000)

Moorhouse, S., 'The ceramic contents of a thirteenth-century timber building destroyed by fire', *Medieval and later pottery in Wales*, 8 (1985)

Moorhouse, S., 'The non-dating uses of medieval pottery', *Medieval Ceramics*, 10 (1986)

Morton, J., *The natural history of Northamptonshire: with some account of the antiquities* (1712)

Muir, R., *The lost villages of Britain* (London, 1985)

Müller, M., 'A divided class? Peasants and peasant communities in later medieval England', in C. Dyer, P. Coss and C. Wickham (eds), *Rodney Hilton's Middle Ages*, Past and Present Supplement no. 2 (2007)

Munby, L., *The Hertfordshire landscape* (London, 1977)

Murray, J., 'Individualism and consensual marriage: some evidence from medieval England', in C.M. Rousseau and J.T. Rosenthal (eds), *Women, marriage and family in medieval Christendom: essays in memory of Michael M. Sheehan C.S.B.* (Kalamazoo, 1998)

Musty, J. and Algar, D.J., 'Excavations at the deserted medieval village of Gomeldon, near Salisbury', *Wiltshire Archaeological and Natural History Magazine*, 80 (1986)

Mynard, D.C., Zeepvat, R.J. and Williams, R.J., *Excavations at Great Linford, 1974–80*, Buckinghamshire Archaeological Society Monograph, 3 (1991)

Naylor, J. and Richards, J.D., 'Detecting the past', MSRGAR, 20 (2005)

Neave, S., 'Rural settlement contraction in the East Riding of Yorkshire, c. 1660–1760' (PhD thesis, Hull, 1990)

Neave, S., 'Rural settlement contraction in the East Riding of Yorkshire between the mid-seventeenth and mid-eighteenth centuries', Agricultural History Review, 41 (1993)

Neave, S. and Ellis, S. (eds), An historical atlas of East Yorkshire (Hull, 1996)

Neeson, J., Commoners: common right, enclosure and social change in England 1799–1820 (Cambridge, 1993)

Nichols, J., The history and antiquities of the county of Leicester, 4, part 1 (London, 1807)

Norton, A. and Cockin, G., 'Excavations at the Classics Centre, 65–7 St Giles, Oxford', Oxoniensia, 73 (2008)

Oliver, T., Howard-Davis, C. and Newman, R., Transect through time: the archaeological landscape of the Shell north-western ethylene pipe-line (English section) (Lancaster, 1996)

Oswald, A., Wharram Percy deserted medieval village, North Yorkshire: archaeological investigation and survey, English Heritage Archaeological Investigation Report Series, A1/19/2004 (2004)

Owen, D.H., 'The occupation of the land. Wales and the Marches', in E. Miller (ed.), The agrarian history of England and Wales, 3, 1348–1500 (Cambridge, 1991)

Padel, O.J., Cornish place-name elements (Nottingham, 1985)

Page, M., 'Destroyed by the Temples: the deserted medieval village of Stowe', Records of Buckinghamshire, 45 (2005)

Page, M. and Jones, R., 'Stable and unstable village plans: case-studies from Whittlewood', in Gardiner, M. and Rippon, S. (eds), Medieval landscapes in Britain (Macclesfield, 2007)

Palmer, W.M., 'A history of Clopton', Proceedings of the Cambridge Antiquarian Society, 33 (1933)

Parker, L., 'The agrarian revolution at Cotesbach, 1501–1612', Transactions of the Leicestershire Archaeological Society, 24 (1948)

Parker Pearson, M. and Richards, C., Architecture and order: approaches to social space (London, 1994)

Parker Pearson, M., Smith, H., Mulville, J. and Brennand, M., 'Cille Pheadair: the life and times of a Norse-period farmstead c. 1000–1300', in J. Hines, A. Lane and M. Redknap (eds), Land, sea and home, SMAMS, 20 (2003)

Parry, M.L., Climatic change, agriculture and settlement (Folkestone, 1978)

Parry, S., Raunds area survey: an archaeological study of the landscape of Raunds, Northamptonshire (Oxford, 2006)

Peate, I.C., The Welsh house (Liverpool, 1946)

Pevsner, N., The buildings of England: Buckinghamshire (Harmondsworth, 1960)

Pevsner, N. with Williamson, E., The buildings of England: Leicestershire and Rutland (Harmondsworth, 2nd rev. edn, 1984)

Pimsler, M., 'Solidarity in the medieval village? The evidence of personal pledging at Elton, Huntingdonshire', Journal of British Studies, 17 (1977)

Pope, R., 'Ritual and the roundhouse: a critique of recent ideas on the use of domestic space in later British prehistory', in C. Haselgrove and R. Pope (eds), The earlier Iron Age *in Britain and the near Continent* (Oxford, 2007)

Porter, S., 'The Civil War destruction of Boarstall', *Records of Buckinghamshire*, 26 (1984)

Postan, M.M., 'Some agrarian evidence of declining population in the late Middle Ages', *Economic History Review*, 2nd series, 2 (1950)

Rahtz, P.A., 'Holworth medieval village', *Proceedings of the Dorset Natural History and Archaeological Society*, 81 (1959)

Rawding, C., 'Society and place in nineteenth-century north Lincolnshire', *Rural History*, 3 (1992)

RCAHMW, *Glamorgan volume III: medieval secular monuments part II: non-defensive* (London, 1982)

RCHME, *West Cambridgeshire* (London, 1968)

RCHME, *Central Northamptonshire* (London, 1979)

RCHME, *South-west Northamptonshire* (London, 1982)

RCHME, *North-west Northamptonshire* (London, 1981)

RCHME, *Dorset* (London, 1970)

RCHME, *Buckinghamshire* (London, 1913)

RCHME, *Huntingdonshire* (London, 1926)

Rigold, S.E., 'Appendix', in E.M. Jope, 'The regional cultures of medieval Britain', in I.L.L. Foster and L. Alcock (eds), *Culture and environment. Essays in honour of Cyril Fox* (London, 1963)

Riley, H. and Wilson-North, R., *The field archaeology of Exmoor* (London, 2001)

Rimington, F.C., *The deserted medieval village of Hatterboard, near Scarborough*, Scarborough and District Archaeological Society Research Report, 2 (1961)

Rippon, S., *Beyond the medieval village. The diversification of landscape character in Southern Britain* (Oxford, 2008)

Rippon, S., Fyfe, R. and Brown, A., 'Beyond villages and open fields: the origins and development of a historical landscape characterised by dispersed settlement in south-west England', *Med. Arch.*, 50 (2006)

Roberts, B.K., *Rural settlement in Britain* (London, 1977)

Roberts, B.K., 'Nucleation and dispersion: towards an explanation', *Medieval Village Research Group Annual Report*, 31 (1983)

Roberts, B.K., *Landscape, documents and maps: villages in northern England and beyond AD 900–1250* (Oxford, 2008)

Roberts, B.K. and Wrathmell, S., *An atlas of rural settlement in England* (London, 2000)

Roberts, B.K. and Wrathmell, S., *Region and place: a study of English rural settlement* (London, 2002)

Roberts, K., 'The deserted rural settlement project: background and methodology", in idem (ed.), *Lost farmsteads. Deserted rural settlements in Wales*, CBA Research Report, 148 (2006)

Roberts, K. (ed.), *Lost farmsteads. Deserted rural settlements in Wales*, CBA Research Report, 148 (2006)

Salter, H.E. (ed.), *Eynsham cartulary*, Oxford Historical Society, 2 (1908)

Sambrook, P., 'Deserted rural settlements in south-west Wales', in K. Roberts (ed.), *Lost farmsteads. Deserted rural settlements in Wales*, CBA Research Report, 148 (2006)

Saunders, M.J., 'The excavation of a medieval site at Walsingham School, St Paul's Cray, Bromley, 1995', *Archaeologia Cantiana*, 117 (1997)

Schofield, P.R., *Peasant and community in medieval England* (Basingstoke, 2003)

Sharpe, K., *The personal rule of Charles I* (Newhaven/London, 1992)

Silvester, R.J., 'Medieval farming on the Berwyn', MSRGAR, 6 (1991)

Silvester, R.J., 'Medieval upland cultivation on the Berwyns in north Wales', *Landscape History*, 22 (2000)

Silvester, R.J., *Deserted medieval and later rural settlements in Powys and Clwyd: the final report* (Welshpool, 2001)

Silvester, R.J., 'The archaeology of the Welsh uplands: an introduction', in D. Browne and S. Hughes (eds), *The archaeology of the Welsh uplands* (Aberystwyth, 2003)

Silvester, R.J., 'The commons and the waste: use and misuse in central Wales', in I.D. Whyte and A.J.L. Winchester (eds), *Society, landscape and environment in upland Britain* (Birmingham, 2004)

Silvester, R.J., 'Deserted rural settlements in central and north-east Wales', in K. Roberts (ed.), *Lost farmsteads. Deserted rural settlements in Wales*, CBA Research Report, 148 (2006)

Silvester, R.J., 'Landscapes of the poor: encroachment in Wales in the post-medieval centuries', in P.S. Barnwell and M. Palmer (eds), *Post-medieval landscapes. Landscape history after Hoskins*, 3 (Macclesfield, 2007)

Skelton, R. and Harvey, P. (eds), *Local maps and plans from medieval England* (Oxford, 1986)

Smith, G. and Thompson, D., 'Results of the project excavations', in K. Roberts (ed.), *Lost farmsteads. Deserted rural settlements in Wales*, CBA Research Report, 148 (2006)

Smith, M.W., 'Snap, a modern example of depopulation', *Wiltshire Archaeological Magazine*, 57 (1960)

Smith, R.M., 'Human resources', in G. Astill and A. Grant (eds), *The countryside of medieval England* (Oxford, 1988)

Smith, S.V., 'Towards a social archaeology of the medieval English peasantry: power and resistance at Wharram Percy', *Journal of Social Archaeology*, 9 (2009)

Soja, E.W., 'The spatiality of social life: towards a transformative retheorisation', in D. Gregory and J. Urry (eds), *Social relations and spatial structures* (Basingstoke, 1985)

Sørensen, M.L.S., *Gender archaeology* (Cambridge, 2000)

Spoerry, P., *Ely wares*, East Anglian Archaeology, 122 (2008)

Stacey, N.E. (ed.), *Charters and custumals of Shaftesbury Abbey 1089–1216* (Oxford, 2006)

Stern, W.B., Gerber, Y. and Helmig, G., 'Residues in medieval pottery from Basel', in G. Helmig, B. Scholkmann and M. Untermann (eds), *Centre, region, periphery: medieval Europe: Basel 2002*, Volume 3, Third International Conference of Medieval and Later Archaeology (Hertingen, 2002)

Stone, S., 'Antiquities discovered at Standlake', *Proceedings of the Society of Antiquaries*, 1st series, 4 (1857)

Suggett, R., *Houses and history in the March of Wales. Radnorshire 1400–1800* (Aberystwyth, 2005)

Surtz, E. and Hexter, J.H. (eds), *The complete works of St Thomas More* (New Haven, 1965)

Sweely, T.L., 'Introduction', in idem (ed.), *Manifesting power: gender and the interpretation of* power in archaeology (London, 1999)

Tawney, R.H., The agrarian problem in the sixteenth century (London, 1912)

Taylor, C., The Cambridgeshire landscape (London, 1973)

Taylor, C., Fieldwork in medieval archaeology (London, 1974)

Taylor, C., 'Aspects of village mobility in medieval and later times', in S. Limbrey and J.G. Evans (eds), The effects of man on the landscape: the lowland zone, CBA Research Report, 21 (1978)

Taylor, C., The archaeology of gardens (Princes Risborough, 1983)

Taylor, C., Village and farmstead: a history of rural settlement in England (London, 1983)

Taylor, C., 'Dispersed settlement in nucleated areas', Landscape History, 17 (1995)

Taylor, C., 'Nucleated settlement: a view from the frontier', Landscape History, 24 (2002)

Taylor, C., 'W.G. Hoskins and The making of the English landscape', The Local Historian, 35.2 (2005)

Tebbutt, C.F., 'Excavations at Winteringham', Transactions of the Cambridgeshire and Huntingdonshire Archaeological Society, 5 (1937)

Thirsk, J., 'Agrarian history, 1540–1950', in VCH, Leicestershire, 2

Thomas, C., 'Enclosure and the rural landscape of Merionethshire in the sixteenth century', Transactions of the Institute of British Geographers, 42 (1967)

Thomas, K., Man and the natural world (London, 1983)

Thompson, F.H., 'The deserted village of Riseholme', Med. Arch., 4 (1960)

Thompson, M.W., The rise of the castle (Cambridge, 1991)

Thompson, S., 'Parliamentary enclosure, property, population, and the decline of classical republicanism in eighteenth-century Britain', The Historical Journal, 51 (2008)

Thorpe, H., 'The lord and the landscape', Transactions of the Birmingham Archaeological Society, 80 (1962)

Tilley, C., A phenomenology of landscape: places, paths and monuments (Oxford, 1994)

Tipping, R., 'Climatic variability and 'marginal' settlement in upland British landscapes: a re-evaluation', Landscapes, 3.2 (2002)

Toulmin Smith, L. (ed.), The itinerary of John Leland in or about the years 1535–1543, 2, part 5 (London, 1964)

Tringham, R., 'Archaeological houses, households, housework and the home', in D.N. Benjamin, D. Stea and D. Saile (eds), The home: words, interpretations, meanings and environment (Aldershot, 1995)

Turner, M., 'Parliamentary enclosure and landownership change in Buckinghamshire', Economic History Review, 2nd series, 28 (1975)

Turner, M., English Parliamentary enclosure: its historical geography and economic history (Folkestone, 1980)

Tylecote, R.F., 'Metallurgical report', in G. Beresford, The medieval clay-land village: excavations at Goltho and Barton Blount, SMAMS, 6 (1975)

Tyson, R., Medieval glass vessels found in England c. AD 1200–1500, CBA Research Report, 121 (2000)

Upton, P., 'The lost parish church of All Saints, Bishops Itchington', Warwickshire History, 13 (2007/8)

Upton, P., 'Thomas Fisher and the depopulation of Nether Itchington in the sixteenth century', *Local Historian*, 39 (2009)

VCH, *Northamptonshire*, 5 (Woodbridge, 2002)

VCH, *Warwickshire*, 3 (London, 1945)

Wade Martins, S., *The English model farm: building the agricultural ideal 1700–1914* (Macclesfield, 2002)

Wadge, R., 'Medieval arrowheads from Oxfordshire', *Oxoniensia*, 73 (2008)

Watts, V., *A dictionary of County Durham place-names* (Nottingham, 2002)

Way, T., 'Open and close parishes', in T. Kirby and S. Oosthuizen (eds), *An atlas of Cambridgeshire and Huntingdonshire history* (Cambridge, 2000)

Webster, C.J., 'Excavations within the village of Shapwick', *Proceedings of the Somerset Archaeological and Natural History Society*, 136 (1992)

Welding, J.D. (ed.), *Leicestershire in 1777. An edition of John Prior's map of Leicestershire with an introduction and commentary by members of the Leicestershire industrial historical society*, Leicestershire Libraries and Information Service (1984)

Widgren, M., 'Is landscape history possible? Or, how can we study the desertion of farms?', in P. Ucko and R. Layton (eds), *The archaeology and anthropology of landscape. Shaping your landscape* (London, 1998)

Wiliam, E., *Home-made homes. Dwellings of the rural poor in Wales* (Cardiff, 1988)

Wiliam, E., '"Home-made homes": dwellings of the rural poor in Cardiganshire', *Ceredigion*, 12.3 (1995)

Williams, R.J., *Pennyland and Hartigans. Two Iron Age and Saxon sites in Milton Keynes*, Buckinghamshire Archaeological Society Monograph Series, 4 (1993)

Williamson, T., *Polite landscapes: gardens and society in eighteenth-century England* (Stroud, 1995)

Williamson, T., *The archaeology of the landscape park: garden design in Norfolk, England, c. 1680–1840*, British Archaeological Reports, British Series, 268 (Oxford, 1998)

Williamson, T., *Shaping medieval landscapes: settlement, society, environment* (Macclesfield, 2003)

Williamson, T., *Rabbits, warrens and archaeology* (Stroud, 2007)

Williamson, T., 'Archaeological perspectives on estate landscapes', in J. Finch and K. Giles (eds), *Estate landscapes: design, improvement and power in the post-medieval landscape* (Woodbridge, 2007)

Wilson, J., 'Antiquities found at Woodperry', *Archaeological Journal*, 3 (1846)

Winchester, A.J.L., *The harvest of the hills* (Edinburgh, 2000)

Wood, R., 'What did medieval people eat from?', *Medieval Ceramics*, 29 (2005)

Woodward, A. and Blinkhorn, P., 'Size matters: Iron Age vessel capacities in central and southern England', in C.G. Cumberpatch and P.W. Blinkhorn (eds), *Not so much a pot, more a way of life*, Oxbow Monograph, 83 (1997)

Woodward, D., *The farming and memorandum books of Henry Best of Elmswell*, Records of Social and Economic History, new series, 8 (Oxford, 1984)

Wordie, J.R., 'The chronology of English enclosure, 1500–1914', *Economic History Review*, 2nd series, 36 (1983)

Wrathmell, S., 'Deserted and shrunken villages in southern Northumberland' (PhD thesis, University of Wales, 1975)

Wrathmell, S., 'Village depopulation in the 17th and 18th centuries: examples from
    Northumberland', *Post-Med. Arch.*, 14 (1980)

Wrathmell, S., 'The vernacular threshold of northern peasant households', *Vernacular
    Architecture*, 15 (1984)

Wrathmell, S., *Wharram. A study of settlement on the Yorkshire Wolds, VI. Domestic settlements 2:
    Medieval peasant farmsteads*, York University Publications, 8 (1989)

Wrathmell, S., 'Rural settlements in medieval England: perspectives and perceptions', in
    B. Vyner (ed.), *Building on the past*, Royal Archaeological Institute (1994)

Wrathmell, S., 'The documentary evidence', in C. Treen and M. Atkin (eds), *Wharram: a
    study of settlement on the Yorkshire Wolds, X, water resources and their management*, York
    University Archaeological Publications, 12 (2005)

Wrathmell, S., 'The rectory, chantry house and vicarage from the 14th to 19th centuries', in
    C. Harding and S. Wrathmell (eds), *Wharram: a study of settlement on the Yorkshire Wolds,
    XII, The post-medieval farm and vicarage*, York University Archaeological Publications, 14
    (2009)

Wrathmell, S., 'Farming, farmers and farmsteads from the 16th to 19th centuries', in
    C. Harding and S. Wrathmell (eds), *Wharram: a study of settlement on the Yorkshire Wolds,
    XII, The post-medieval farm and vicarage*, York University Archaeological Publications, 14
    (2009)

Index